HUMAN RIGHTS IN THICK AND THIN SOCIETIES

Sociocentric societies have vibrant – albeit different – concepts of human flourishing than is typical in the individualistic West. These concepts influence the promotion of human rights, both in domestic contexts with religious minorities and in international contexts where Western ideals may clash with local norms. *Human Rights in Thick and Thin Societies* uncovers the original intentions of the drafters of the Universal Declaration of Human Rights, finds inspiration from early leaders in the field such as Eleanor Roosevelt, and examines the implications of recent advances in cultural psychology for understanding difference. The case studies that are included illustrate the need to vary the application of human rights in differing cultural environments, and the book suggests a new framework: a flexible universalism that returns to basics – focusing on the great evils of the human condition. This approach will help the human rights movement succeed in a multipolar era.

Seth D. Kaplan is Professorial Lecturer in the Paul H. Nitze School of Advanced International Studies (SAIS) at Johns Hopkins University. He is Senior Adviser for the Institute for Integrated Transitions and consultant to organizations such as the World Bank, United Nations, and Organisation for Economic Co-operation and Development (OECD). He is author of two books and over 100 articles, and is coauthor of the landmark United Nations–World Bank flagship report, *Pathways for Peace*: *Inclusive Approaches to Preventing Violent Conflict* (2018).

T0382145

"In this timely and eminently readable book, Seth Kaplan charts a path for the survival of the universal human rights idea in an increasingly inter-dependent and conflict-ridden world. His 'flexible pluralist' approach is a fitting tribute to the Universal Declaration of Human Rights on its 70th anniversary."

Mary Ann Glendon, Learned Hand Professor of Law,
Harvard University

"Universal claims to human rights appeal to our common humanity, but they can provoke resistance – both at home and abroad – when they fail to acknowledge varied cultural and religious contexts. Seth Kaplan's book is at once a guide to this resistance, an analysis of cultural diversity, and a program for dealing with disagreement and protecting those rights most critical to human flourishing."

Michael Walzer, Professor Emeritus, Institute for Advanced Study

"This book explores the tension between universal human rights and cultural particularity with theoretical sophistication and empirical depth. It is the best effort I know to give each of these claims its due – and to chart a course that combines strengths of both into practical guidance for reformers. Even readers who disagree with some of Kaplan's recommendations will profit from his path-breaking analysis."

Bill Galston, Ezra K. Zilkha Chair and Senior Fellow,
Brookings Institution

"This brilliant book both honors and advances the Universal Declaration on Human Rights. As he traces the fate of moral universals in culture and history, Seth Kaplan shows us how to be a moral pluralist and uphold principal rights at the same time – how to be a social justice advocate without being parochial and ethnocentric. It is a great accomplishment."

Richard Shweder, Harold H. Swift Distinguished Service Professor,
University of Chicago

Human Rights in Thick and Thin Societies

UNIVERSALITY WITHOUT UNIFORMITY

SETH D. KAPLAN

Johns Hopkins University

CAMBRIDGE
UNIVERSITY PRESS

University Printing House, Cambridge CB2 8BS, United Kingdom

One Liberty Plaza, 20th Floor, New York, NY 10006, USA

477 Williamstown Road, Port Melbourne, VIC 3207, Australia

314-321, 3rd Floor, Plot 3, Splendor Forum, Jasola District Centre, New Delhi - 110025, India

79 Anson Road, #06-04/06, Singapore 079906

Cambridge University Press is part of the University of Cambridge.

It furthers the University's mission by disseminating knowledge in the pursuit of education, learning and research at the highest international levels of excellence.

www.cambridge.org
Information on this title: www.cambridge.org/9781108457323
DOI: 10.1017/9781108557887

First published 2018
First paperback edition 2019

A catalogue record for this publication is available from the British Library

Library of Congress Cataloging in Publication data
NAMES: Kaplan, Seth D., 1966–, author.
TITLE: Human rights in thick and thin societies : universality without uniformity / Seth D. Kaplan.
DESCRIPTION: New York : Cambridge University Press, 2018.
IDENTIFIERS: LCCN 2018013797 | ISBN 9781108471213 (hardback) | ISBN 9781108457323 (paperback)
SUBJECTS: LCSH: Human rights. | Civil rights. | BISAC: POLITICAL SCIENCE / Political Freedom & Security / Human Rights.
CLASSIFICATION: LCC K3240 .K367 2018 | DDC 323–dc23
LC record available at https://lccn.loc.gov/2018013797

ISBN 978-1-108-47121-3 Hardback
ISBN 978-1-108-45732-3 Paperback

The world that we encounter in ordinary experience is one in which we are faced with choices between ends equally ultimate, and claims equally absolute, the realisation of some of which must inevitably involve the sacrifice of others.
– Isaiah Berlin[1]

[1]   Isaiah Berlin, "Two Concepts of Liberty," *Four Essays on Liberty* (Oxford: Oxford University Press, 1969), 29–30.

Contents

Figures

Tables

xiii

Foreword

Human rights are by definition universal; they are the rights of all human beings. But the list of human rights is disputed across humanity, and so is the relative importance of the different rights. These disputes derive from the simple fact that there are many ways to live a human life. Human beings have created very different cultures and religions that shape the lives of their adherents and give them meaning. Universal claims appeal to what is, no doubt, their common humanity, but at the same time, they engender cultural resistance. Seth Kaplan's book is at once a guide to this resistance, an analysis of cultural diversity, and a program for dealing with disagreement and protecting those rights most critical to human flourishing.

Imagine that you are a human rights activist, born somewhere in the West, a child of the Enlightenment. You live in what Kaplan calls a "thin" society. "Thin" describes a society that is highly individualistic, one where the conception of human rights that its activists promote is organized around the ideas of individual freedom and equality. But most of the rest of the world is made up of "thick" societies, which pull the individual into a tight web of obligations and responsibilities in a hierarchical society. The West is also hierarchical, of course, as anyone studying inequality in the United States would know, but its doctrines, and especially its human rights doctrines, are hostile to all hierarchical arrangements. So how do Western rights activists deal with societies based on thick relationships and responsibilities?

Even in the West they have some difficulty. They commonly insist on the full set of human rights as these have been understood since the American and French revolutions. They disagree about the relative urgency of social/economic rights and political rights, but that's an old disagreement, and the arguments are well known and readily rehearsed. But these activists also have to address minorities in the West who have formed enclaves of "thick" culture – the Amish, say, or ultra-orthodox Jews, or Muslims in Europe. Here are men and women with different, sometimes radically different, ideas about their rights, who aren't much concerned with the relative value of social/economic and political rights. So the argument about cultural difference begins at home. What form should it take?

Kaplan's own argument is developed with careful attention to both theory and practice; he provides examples of conflicts both at home and abroad. He opposes any absolutist affirmation of all the rights that we (Westerners) believe in – or, better, he wants our affirmations to be modified by a politically prudent engagement with human difference and a respect for other cultures. Neither of these precludes sharp criticism of oppression and discrimination wherever they occur. But they require a willingness to compromise some of the time, in some places, with regard to some rights.

Women's rights make for the hardest test of an argument of this sort. But there are now women activists working in all the major religious communities against gender discrimination; they search for texts and precedents within their own traditions that support their claim to equal rights, and they make political decisions about which rights to emphasize, how best to do that, when to compromise, and when not. Kaplan acknowledges the difficult decisions activists such as these must make and maps the factors that influence those decisions.

Readers may disagree with Kaplan about some of the compromises he recommends. But his argument for political engagement and cultural respect is very strong. Activists who act without any commitment to these two are not likely to advance the cause of human rights.

Michael Walzer
Professor Emeritus, Institute for Advanced Study

Preface

This book is a product of a long journey. Its lessons are distilled from decades working and living alongside people from all over the world. During my years advising on fragile states for organizations such as the World Bank and listening to students at the Paul H. Nitze School of Advanced International Studies (SAIS) at Johns Hopkins University, I have encountered firsthand the huge disconnect between abstract, inflexible policies formulated in the West and local realities in the East and South.

Despite the complicated interaction between culture and rights in pluralistic settings, I still believe human rights is the ultimate framework for bettering the human condition. It is because of differences across and within societies – not despite them – that a more flexible approach can succeed. Exploring the delicate negotiations behind the drafting and passage of the Universal Declaration of Human Rights (UDHR) – the field's most important document – provides a platform to explore this approach more deeply. As we mark the seventieth anniversary of the UDHR, it is crucial that we ask whether we should continue along the current – and increasingly controversial – path of uniformity or return to the document's pluriform basics.

Too often, arguments or promises that fit a particular ideology or that fulfill a particular institutional mandate are divorced from local needs and ignorant of local knowledge and values. The challenges of simply getting from point A to point B, whether physically – as I experienced in Nigeria and around West Africa right after college – or figuratively (turning ideas that seemed good on paper to the policy makers into something concrete that actually improved lives on the ground) have always been much larger when seen up close.

My career and research have required listening, learning, and empathizing across cultural differences; this has informed my thinking on fragile states, human rights, and the development of societies. The simple concept that progress must build on what people know and believe and can do on their own has always seemed obvious to me, but it plays only a cameo role in how most international organizations think and operate. Instead, these assume that Western approaches are the only way forward and that secular culture is universal or at least an ideal that all cultures should pursue. People, as a rule, have an extremely difficult time "escaping" from their own culture or perspective and seeing "reality" from another culture or perspective. Those advancing human rights do not appreciate that Western culture, especially Western cosmopolitan elite culture, is but one culture among many.

More recently, like many people, I have grown alarmed by the growing polarization within the West. But informed by my myriad experiences working in different cultures, well versed in the opinions of both left and right, and maybe more willing than most to recognize my own fallibility, I can see the role that culture plays in these debates. Culture – and the values and ideas and norms that it brings – is essential to the survival of any group or society; it can, however, easily blind those on the inside from identifying or even empathizing with those on the outside, those in other groups or societies. It is hard for anyone to escape their culture and see another, quite different, perspective unless they literally live within it (and ideally speak its language) for an extended period of time. I have had the opportunity to do this in Japan, China, Nigeria, Turkey, Israel, France, and the United States.

My interest has always been in uncovering the ingredients of a healthy, robust society. The capacity of people to cooperate and build common institutions to manage their affairs – and disagreements – is key. In working mostly from the inside to overcome the challenges fragile states face and in trying to understand growing polarization, I repeatedly see the need to develop frameworks that build a common, highly legitimate base that everyone can build on while simultaneously accepting that different societies and groups may have stark differences of opinion on crucial issues, priorities, and even some aspects of morality. Identifying the core values and morals that are truly universal and accepting not only that these differences exist, but that they are innate to human nature – something to be treasured, not supplanted – is crucial to ensuring we can all live together more peacefully and productively. I hope that this book will not only better inform human rights discourse and policy but also that it will equip leaders worldwide with confidence and a new vocabulary as they champion human rights in their own various contexts.

Acknowledgments

Many more people have contributed to this book than I can name here. After all, it emerged from decades of wandering and working throughout the world, talking to innumerable people, and thinking deeply about human nature and culture and what people from different places and with different beliefs share in common and what they do not.

Let me therefore focus my thanks on the few who directly contributed to the manuscript itself. This whole project came about due to my relationship with Tom Zwart. He found me after a talk I gave many years ago in Amsterdam, and he gradually helped me observe the parallels between his work on human rights and culture and my work on fragile states. Many of the ideas are either products of discussions we have had or the result of him cajoling me to refine the manuscript more. Rick Shweder, who enthusiastically joined my small advisory group before he had ever met me, helped refine many aspects of the book, pushing me to sharpen many of my core arguments. His immense work across related fields was essential to the development of the manuscript from the start; he is easily the most cited author. Both Michael Walzer and Bill Galston improved the manuscript in many ways, forcing me to address contemporary issues and preparing me for the opponents this book will inevitably provoke. Each of these four people have written about some aspect of this book's argument in various fora. Although I have taken the discussion in many directions that they have not, I am surely building on the work of kings. The two anonymous referees from Cambridge also contributed to improving the manuscript through their healthy critique.

I also owe a great debt to my editor, Anna Carrington, who not only ensured the book read well but also that it was coherent and comprehensive. She more than a few times corrected faulty thinking and ideas that did not sufficiently take into account the perspective of some of the people I was writing about.

In addition, I want to thank the small group of students and former students working on culture and human rights centered around the University of Utrecht in the Netherlands, most notably Mimi Zou, Stacey Links, Julie Fraser, Ingrid Roestenburg-Morgan, and Qiao Cong-ru. Your friendship and support have helped immeasurably at various points along the way to keep the engine of this undertaking humming. Esther Heldenbergh, who helped with numerous trips and scheduling complications, also deserves special thanks.

Last, my wife Esther, a real "woman of valor," deserves special thanks for all of her patience and support over the years as I have pursued the most unorthodox of careers. The book would surely have never been completed without her help in many areas.

Obviously, any flaws in the manuscript are my responsibility alone.

1

Introduction

The role of culture has long been a point of contention in the international human rights field.[1] "Western universalists" see those who appeal to cultural difference as withholding rights from individuals.[2] Defenders of this difference, "flexible universalists," feel Western universalists are imposing a view of rights that improperly emphasizes individual autonomy over one's communal and religious commitments.[3] Debates are fruitless: using different reference points, the two sides seem to be speaking completely different languages – with little hope that they will find a translator anytime soon.

This disagreement is increasingly impacting both domestic politics and international relations. In European countries such as Norway, Denmark, Switzerland, Germany, and France, there is a growing divide between a secular state (backed by a secularized majority population) that promotes, among others, animal rights, children's rights, and nondiscrimination, and

---

[1] See, for instance, Jack Donnelly, *Universal Human Rights in Theory and Practice* (Ithaca, NY: Cornell University Press, 2003); Rhoda Howard, "Cultural Absolutism and the Nostalgia for Community," *Human Rights Quarterly* 15, no. 2 (May 1993): 315–338; Michael Perry, *The Idea of Human Rights: Four Inquiries* (Oxford: Oxford University Press, 1998), 57–86; John Tilley, "Cultural Relativism," *Human Rights Quarterly* 22, no. 2 (May 2000): 501–547; Makau Mutua, *Human Rights: A Political and Cultural Critique* (Philadelphia, PA: University of Pennsylvania Press, 2002); Daniel Bell, *East Meets West: Human Rights and Democracy in East Asia* (Princeton, NJ: Princeton University Press, 2000).

[2] See, for instance, Elizabeth Zechenter, "In the Name of Culture: Cultural Relativism and the Abuse of the Individual," *Journal of Anthropological Research* 53, no. 3 (Autumn 1997): 319–347; Jack Donnelly, "Cultural Relativism and Universal Human Rights," *Human Rights Quarterly* 6, no. 4 (November 1984): 400–419.

[3] See, for instance, Daniel Bell, "East Asian Challenge to Human Rights: Reflections on an East West Dialogue," *Human Rights Quarterly* 18, no. 3 (August 1996): 641–667; Eva Brems, "Reconciling Universality and Diversity in International Human Rights: A Theoretical and Methodological Framework and Its Application in the Context of Islam," *Human Rights Review* 5, no. 3 (2004): 5–21.

minority religious groups defending their right to faithful practice. In the United States, which is more devout and generally upholds a broader concept of freedom,[4] similar dynamics exist in debates over healthcare and gay marriage.

International disputes over human rights are also increasing due to the growing disconnect between Western-dominated human rights actors and Asian, African, Middle Eastern, and Latin American societies. Although the late twentieth and early twenty-first centuries were characterized by Western ideological ascendancy, in which the human rights field broadened its scope and pursued an ambitious agenda,[5] the rising power of Southern countries (a category defined later) is leading to greater pushback.[6] Disagreements over democracy in places such as Cambodia, Egypt, and Ethiopia; the use of the International Criminal Court in Kenya, South Africa, and elsewhere in Africa; minority rights in many parts of the Middle East and Asia; international intervention in Syria; women's rights in the Middle East; labor rights in the Persian Gulf; and the use of force in Israel are increasingly common. Although the language of rights has spread far and wide, interpretations and priorities vary widely – and fights over these differences risk undermining the legitimacy of advocates and even the overall human rights agenda.[7]

The contentious climate in which these human rights debates take place reflects different visions of how societies flourish, how human beings achieve their potential, and how human rights are conceived and realized.[8] These differing positions have been shaped by social, historical, and political forces, which sometimes go back millennia.[9] "Thin societies" are based on

---

[4] See, for instance, Peter Berger, Grace Davie, and Effie Fokas, *Religious America, Secular Europe? A Theme and Variation* (Burlington, VT: Ashgate Publishing, 2008).

[5] Stephen Hopgood, *The Endtimes of Human Rights* (Ithaca, NY: Cornell University Press, 2013).

[6] See, for instance, Thomas Carothers and Saskia Brechenmacher, "Closing Space: Democracy and Human Rights Support under Fire," *Carnegie Endowment for International Peace*, February 2014, http://carnegieendowment.org/2014/02/20/closing-space-democracy-and-human-rights-support-under-fire/h1by.

[7] See, for instance, R. R. Reno, "Against Human Rights," *First Things* (May 2016), www.firstthings.com/article/2016/05/against-human-rights.

[8] For an excellent overview of many of the debates relating to human rights concepts and definitions, see Amartya Sen, "Elements of a Theory of Human Rights," *Philosophy and Public Affairs* 32, no. 4 (Autumn 2004): 315–356.

[9] Tom Zwart, "Balancing Yin and Yang in the International Human Rights Debate," Collected Papers of the Sixth Beijing Forum on Human Rights, China Society for Human Rights Studies, Beijing, 2013, 410–421; Alison Dundes Renteln, "Relativism and the Search for Human Rights," *American Anthropologist* 90, no. 1 (March 1988): 56–72.

maximizing individual freedom, while "thick societies" are based on maximizing the robustness of relationships and institutions.[10]

A changing context has broad implications for the human rights field. The secularization and individualization of Western populations – combined with an increase in religious minorities due to migration into Europe – is leading to clashes in Western countries.[11] The rise of populism and a growing backlash against parts of the rights agenda indicate an emerging crisis. The emergence of a new set of powerful actors – non-Western, postcolonial, and wary of Western motives – threatens to make Western-leaning international institutions and Western-inspired global norms untenable unless they can encompass the needs of non-Western countries in a way that is seen as inclusive.[12] This has contributed to the "democratic recession" and pushback against Western non-governmental organizations (NGOs).[13]

Human rights organizations, staffed by Western universalists, often take positions rooted in thin society worldviews that contrast with positions held by religious minorities in the West and non-Western societies outside it, who seek to live as their thick society worldviews dictate.[14] Western universalists hold that international human rights treaties prescribe the adoption of values like autonomy, individualism, equality, choice, secularity, and rationality[15] and that there is a particular ordering of these values vis-à-vis family, work, justice, politics, reproduction, and sexuality. When commentators describe human rights as universal, they are often implying that a certain way of life rooted in the Western, thin society concept of liberalism, individualism, and modernity ought to hold sway. States ought to uphold and enforce these values; all institutions (political, associational, and family) ought to be ruled by them; and international organizations such as the United Nations ought to

---

[10] Chapter 4 includes a full discussion of these terms.

[11] See, for instance, Yolande Jansen, *Secularism, Assimilation and the Crisis of Multiculturalism* (Chicago, IL: University of Chicago Press, 2014).

[12] See, for instance, Dries Lesage and Thijs Van de Graaf (eds.), *Rising Powers and Multilateral Institutions* (New York, NY: Palgrave Macmillan, 2015); and Council on Foreign Relations, Emerging Powers and International Institutions Meeting Series, 2009–2013, www.cfr.org/projects/world/emerging-powers-and-international-institutions-meeting-series/pr1447.

[13] Larry Diamond, "Facing Up to the Democratic Recession," *Journal of Democracy* 26, no. 1 (January 2015): 141–155; Carothers and Brechenmacher, "Closing Space."

[14] See, for instance, Abdullahi Ahmed An-Na'im (ed.), *Human Rights in Cross-Cultural Perspectives: A Quest for Consensus* (Philadelphia, PA: University of Pennsylvania Press, 1992); and Abdullahi An-Na'im (ed.), *Cultural Transformation and Human Rights in Africa* (London: Zed Books, 2002).

[15] See, for instance, Donnelly, *Universal Human Rights*, 7–53; Perry, *The Idea of Human Rights*, 11; Mark Goodale, *Surrendering to Utopia: An Anthropology of Human Rights* (Stanford, CA: Stanford University Press, 2009), 18.

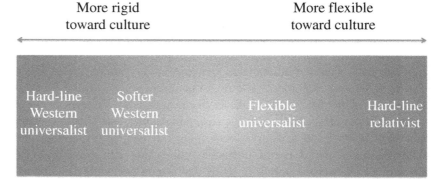

FIGURE 1.1 Human rights promotion: the universalist to relativist spectrum

promote them where they do not exist.[16] Religious groups and Southern societies are urged to give up or at least de-emphasize traditional social institutions and values if they stand in the way.[17] This is a dramatic change from an earlier era, when there was an "overlapping consensus" on human rights.[18]

Opinions on the role of culture in human rights can be plotted along a spectrum. On one side, there is a relatively inflexible, secular human rights viewpoint, and on the other side there are those who claim no universal rights (see Figure 1.1).[19] Each end of the spectrum hosts a hard-line approach that sees no room for compromise, and there are various softer approaches

---

[16] Richard Shweder, "'What about Female Genital Mutilation?' And Why Understanding Culture Matters in the First Place," in Richard Shweder, Martha Minow, and Hazel Rose Markus (eds.), *Engaging Cultural Differences: The Multicultural Challenge in Liberal Democracies* (New York, NY: Russell Sage Foundation, 2002), 234.

[17] See, for instance, Makau Mutua, "The Ideology of Human Rights," *Virginia Journal of International Law* 36 (1996): 592–593; and Tom Zwart, "Using Local Culture to Further the Implementation of International Human Rights: The Receptor Approach," *Human Rights Quarterly* 34, no. 2 (May 2012): 546–569. Ross Douthat makes a similar point with regard to religious groups: Douthat, "The Terms of Our Surrender," *The New York Times*, March 2, 2014, www.nytimes.com/2014/03/02/opinion/sunday/the-terms-of-our-surrender.html.

[18] This phrase originally comes from John Rawls. See, for instance, Rawls, *Political Liberalism* (New York, NY: Columbia University Press, 2005). The usage in relationship to human rights is more akin to Charles Taylor's "unforced consensus." See Taylor, "Conditions of an Unforced Consensus on Human Rights," in Joanne Bauer and Daniel Bell (eds.), *The East Asian Challenge for Human Rights* (Cambridge: Cambridge University Press, 1999), 124–144.

[19] Donnelly, for instance, discusses a spectrum of different interpretations both at the more rigid Western universalist end of the spectrum as well as among those who adopt a more flexible interpretation. Donnelly, "The Relative Universality of Human Rights," *Human Rights Quarterly* 29, no. 2 (May 2007): 298–299.

toward the middle of the spectrum that attempt to provide more room for cultural difference and heterodoxy.[20]

Flexible universalism[21] exists toward the middle and holds that although human rights are universal, they need to be implemented in a way that takes the local social and political context into account, especially in thick societies and communities.[22] Underlying these positions is the idea that human rights will be respected and supported only if they are culturally embedded, and that there are many different ways for a society to flourish besides that espoused by Western universalists. Different groups of people may have legitimate differences, especially when it comes to ordering certain values. Social institutions, religious traditions, and collective interests all matter much more in thick than thin societies. These should receive priority over individual rights at times, and responsibilities and duties may sometimes be as or even more important than rights. In developed countries, the state should not impose a one-size-fits-all interpretation of rights on all regions and groups. In developing countries, economic and social needs may need to be balanced alongside civil and political rights.

Part of the problem is that some of the boldest defenders of cultural difference use it to defend authoritarian social arrangements or despotic governments, which means that their critiques of universalism are, not coincidentally, rather self-serving. Many Middle Eastern and African tyrants, for instance, have long excused their corrupt, self-serving, unaccountable governments in this way.[23] Russia under Putin has used this tactic to defend

---

[20] At the more rigid end of the spectrum, there is, among others, Fred Halliday, "Relativism and Universalism in Human Rights: The Case of the Islamic Middle East," *Political Studies* 43, S1 (August 1995): 152–167; Michael Perry, "Are Human Rights Universal? The Relativist Challenge and Related Matters," *Human Rights Quarterly* 19, no. 3 (August 1997): 461–509; and Charles Beitz, "Human Rights as a Common Concern," *American Political Science Review* 95, no. 2 (June 2001): 269–282. Softer approaches include Andrew Nathan, "Universalism: A Particularistic Account," in Lynda Bell, Andrew Nathan, and Ilan Peleg (eds.), *Negotiating Culture and Human Rights* (New York, NY: Columbia University Press, 2001).

[21] Richard Shweder has used the term "universalism without uniformity" in various contexts to mean something very similar. See, for instance, Shweder, "Moral Maps, 'First World' Conceits, and the New Evangelists," in Lawrence Harrison and Samuel Huntington (eds.), *Culture Matters: How Values Shape Human Progress* (New York, NY: Basic Books, 2000), 164.

[22] See, for instance, An-Na'im (ed.), *Human Rights in Cross-Cultural Perspectives*; An-Na'im (ed.), *Cultural Transformation and Human Rights in Africa*; Bell, "East Asian Challenge to Human Rights"; and Brems, "Reconciling Universality and Diversity in International Human Rights.".

[23] Abdullahi Ahmed An-Na'im, "The Cultural Mediation of Human Rights: The Al-Arqam Case in Malaysia," in Joanne Bauer and Daniel Bell (eds.), *The East Asian Challenge for Human Rights* (Cambridge: Cambridge University Press, 1999), 154–155. For example, associates of

autocratic, militaristic policies.[24] Religious and traditional leaders who deny women or minorities an education and other opportunities similarly use culture as an excuse to deny the rights of many.[25] But the fact that the unease about some elements of the human rights agenda extends across most of the non-Western world and encompasses many religious groups within Western countries should perhaps give human rights proponents greater pause than it does now.

Though various cultural elements are sometimes used to further the overall human rights agenda, they could be more prominently used if they were better understood. When Western universalists ignore the concerns of Southern and, within the West, religious actors, they may be weakening their ability to achieve broader human rights goals. This is especially true when those expressing concern genuinely support human rights but have specific qualms about how narrowly they are often construed.

A number of prominent Western human rights actors, such as Mary Ann Glendon, have argued that the existing foundation for human rights allows for a flexible universalism – that is, for different societies to prioritize different rights, create their own balances between the individual and community, and make a greater effort to embed individual rights within a social context. According to these voices, the Universal Declaration of Human Rights (UDHR), by far the most important human rights agreement, established a "common standard of achievement" that could be interpreted and implemented in a variety of legitimate ways,[26] and many prominent documents that followed pursued a similar approach. This perspective argues that the understanding of rights has evolved since the postwar period, however, becoming more

---

Zimbabwe's Robert Mugabe, who was in power from 1980 until 2017, argued that in the country's culture, kings are only replaced when they die "and Mugabe is our king." Joseph Winter, "Zimbabwe's Robert Mugabe," *BBC*, August 16, 2013, www.bbc.com/news/world-africa-23431534.

[24] Russia has, for instance, used humanitarian assistance as a pretext to invade parts of Ukraine. See, for instance, Mark Kersten, "Does Russia Have a 'Responsibility to Protect' Ukraine? Don't Buy It," *The Globe and Mail*, March 4, 2014, www.theglobeandmail.com/opinion/does-russia-have-a-responsibility-to-protect-ukraine-dont-buy-it/article17271450/.

[25] See, for instance, Patience Akumu, "'African Culture' Is the Biggest Threat to the Women's Rights Movement," *African Arguments*, March 9, 2015, http://africanarguments.org/2015/03/09/african-culture-is-the-biggest-threat-to-the-womens-rights-movement-by-patience-akumu/. Even rape has sometimes been defended as protected by culture. Sally Engle Merry, *Human Rights and Gender Violence: Translating International Law into Local Justice* (Chicago, IL: University of Chicago Press Books, 2006), 7.

[26] Mary Ann Glendon, *A World Made New: Eleanor Roosevelt and the Universal Declaration of Human Rights* (New York, NY: Random House, 2001), 191.

focused on the individual and valuing less institutions and the social fabric.[27] The change in how rights are interpreted has sparked greater disagreement among stakeholders than existed before.[28]

This book examines how the overlapping consensus evident in the Universal Declaration can help bridge the gap between thick and thin societies with regard to human rights. The drafters of the UDHR overcame significant differences to garner the wide support necessary for the United Nations to adopt the Declaration in 1948. This book argues that a return to its fundamental ideas – the building blocks of the whole human rights field – can create a broad consensus on human rights again. To better understand the issues underlying today's challenges, the book surveys the latest research on the role of culture in determining behavior and values, reviews what human rights documents say about how societies can be organized, and explores two case studies – a domestic dispute involving a thick community living in a thin society (male circumcision in Europe) and an international dispute between thick and thin societies (Rwanda's *gacaca* courts). It then considers how a commitment to the liberal pluralism of the drafters of the UDHR is essential to overcoming the differences in how diverse actors worldwide promote human flourishing.

Originally articulated by political philosophers such as Isaiah Berlin, who argues "there are a plurality of values which men can and do seek, and that these values differ," liberal pluralism is a well-developed intellectual framework that can help implement the kind of flexible universalism human rights needs to succeed across the globe. According to Berlin, one-size-fits-all formulations about how to organize societies reduce positive freedom.[29] If the goal of the human rights field is to help human beings and societies achieve their maximum potential, then a greater appreciation for the diversity of human experience is essential.

The field of cultural psychology provides a tool for reframing the debate.[30] It highlights the finding that humans are born with the ability to function in any culture, but as they grow up their psyches develop according to the

---

[27] Daniel Elazar, "How Present Conceptions of Human Rights Shape the Protection of Rights in the United States," in Robert Licht (ed.), *Old Rights and New* (Washington, DC: The AEI Press, 1993), 38–50.

[28] The largest clashes were originally between Western capitalist countries that favored political rights and the communist bloc that favored economic and social rights.

[29] Isaiah Berlin, "My Intellectual Path," in Henry Hardy (ed.), *The Power of Ideas* (Princeton, NJ: Princeton University Press, 2002), 12 and 15–16.

[30] See below for full list of references.

specific culture in which they are raised.[31] According to *The Handbook of Social Psychology*, research shows that "the capacity to form culturally prescribed social relationships is essential for human survival, reproduction, and well-being ... People must think, feel, and act with reference to local practices, relationships, institutions, and artifacts. To do this, people must use the local cultural models, which consequently become an integral part of their psychology."[32]

Different ecologies, social structures, and histories have yielded different cultures with different moral matrices, and although these share fundamental principles, they can diverge substantially in their emphases, especially when it comes to prioritizing the needs of the individual versus the group and determining whether people ought to be independent agents free to act as they wish or interdependent members of a larger society and institutional framework. According to Richard Shweder, a leading thinker in the field, societies order the role of the individual, community, and divinity differently. As Jonathan Haidt writes, people "become righteous" about different concepts and emphases depending on their environments, especially during childhood.[33] From parents, schools, community, media, and so on, they are exposed to a particular culture made up of the "ideas, institutions, and interactions that tell a group of people how to think, feel, and act."[34]

A certain segment of Western populations – which have been shown by cultural psychology researchers to be outliers on a global level in their individualistic orientation – set the agenda for the whole human rights field.[35] This group plays an outsized role in major human rights organizations, which may explain the widespread belief in the field that the particular moral matrix of people from thin societies is universal. As the same group dominates Western universities, academic literature, the social sciences, and

---

[31] Alan Page Fiske, Shinobu Kitayama, Hazel Rose Markus, and Richard Nisbett, "The Cultural Matrix of Social Psychology," in Susan Fiske, Daniel Gilbert, and Gardner Lindzey (eds.), *The Handbook of Social Psychology*, Volume 2, 4th ed. (San Francisco, CA: McGraw-Hill, 1998), 915–916.

[32] Fiske, Kitayama, et al., "The Cultural Matrix of Social Psychology," 916–917.

[33] Jonathan Haidt, *Righteous Mind: Why Good People Are Divided by Politics and Religion* (New York, NY: Pantheon Books, 2012), 109.

[34] Hazel Rose Markus and Alana Conner, *Clash! 8 Cultural Conflicts That Make Us Who We Are* (New York, NY: Hudson Street Press, 2013), xix.

[35] An-Na'im has often discussed this issue. For instance, see An-Na'im (ed.), *Human Rights in Cross-Cultural Perspectives*, 428. The cultural psychology research will be discussed in detail in Chapter 3. Also, Alex de Waal, *Advocacy in Conflict: Critical Perspectives on Transnational Activism* (London: Zed Books, 2015). Joseph Henrich, Steven Heine, and Ara Norenzayan, "The Weirdest People in the World?" *Behavioral and Brain Sciences* 33, no. 2–3 (June 2010): 61–83.

the media[36]; has access to more resources to participate in debates and negotiations; and plays the leading role in funding NGOs in poor countries,[37] there is a receptive ideological climate for its ideas, which are widely disseminated and rarely challenged. The one-sided discourse makes it difficult for flexible universalists who wish to constructively seek alternative approaches, and it increases the "bunker mentality" of thick society groups and countries that feel that their core values are constantly under attack.

Cultural psychology can help shift the unsatisfying dynamics that characterize human rights debates because it helps explain why differences are so embedded. It can help construct a framework, based on empirical research, for understanding those differences and how they impact the interpretation, prioritization, and even acceptance of various rights. In doing so, it provides what thick societies in the East and South and thick religious groups in the West and North have lacked: a construct for understanding and articulating their unease about the contemporary human rights agenda and how they might legitimately adjust that agenda for different contexts. Cultural psychology reveals how the social order (community) and human morality (divinity) have been undervalued, even though these have always been an integral part of human experience. It also shows the importance of integrating duties and responsibilities into any framework for how a society functions.

It is helpful to note that the disagreements between Western and flexible universalists have some overlap with but differ from debates about the desirability or implementation of multiculturalism.[38] The latter, which has been an important government policy in many (mostly Western) countries since the 1970s, emphasizes the coexistence and acceptance of diverse ethnic or religious groups living within the same political jurisdiction. Instead of aiming to develop a "melting pot" through social integration or cultural assimilation, multiculturalism aims to develop a "cultural mosaic" by allowing

---

[36] Zwart, "Balancing Yin and Yang in the International Human Rights Debate"; David Booth and Frederick Golooba-Mutebi, "Developmental Regimes and the International System," Developmental Regimes in Africa, Policy Brief 5, January 2014.

[37] Merry, *Human Rights and Gender Violence*, 224–225.

[38] For more on multiculturalism, see, among others, Charles Taylor and Amy Gutmann (ed.), *Multiculturalism* (Princeton, NJ: Princeton University Press, 1994); David Bennett (ed.), *Multicultural States: Rethinking Difference and Identity* (New York, NY: Psychology Press, 1998); Gad Barzilai, *Communities and Law: Politics and Cultures of Legal Identities* (Ann Arbor, MI: University of Michigan Press, 2005); Gerd Baumann, *The Multicultural Riddle: Rethinking National, Ethnic, and Religious Identities* (New York, NY: Psychology Press, 1999); Bhikhu Parekh, *Rethinking Multiculturalism: Cultural Diversity and Political Theory* (Cambridge, MA: Harvard University Press, 2002).

each cultural group to maintain its distinctiveness.[39] In many cases, it has led
to an emphasis on tolerance while avoiding the promotion of any specific set
of values as being central to society.[40] Proponents of multiculturalism argue
that it is a fairer system that allows people to truly express who they are and that
culture and values must naturally adjust to outsiders.[41] Opponents, in contrast,
worry about the desirability or sustainability of such an ideal and fear there
may be cultural and practical losses if the host nations' distinct cultures
weaken.[42]

Disputes about culture and human rights operate along different dimensions with different foci than those about multiculturalism. First, the center of
many arguments is multinational, between countries on different continents
and between people not sharing a common political jurisdiction.[43] Multiculturalism has rarely had a cross-country element. Second, disagreements within
Western countries are usually about the role of religion in increasingly secular
societies, and not, as in the case with multiculturalism, about the role of
immigrants in what were previously relatively homogenous societies.[44] In both
cases, there is the question of how much a minimal standard of norms need
to be applied, with some of the issues (such as women's rights) being similar.
But whereas in debates over multiculturalism, liberals are typically supportive
and thus tolerant of differences in behavior and values while conservatives are
typically opposed and thus in favor of strong minimal standards, in debates
over culture and human rights, the sides are reversed.[45] Liberals are in favor of

---

[39] Ann Carroll Burgess and Tom Burgess, *Guide to Western Canada* (Guilford, CT: Globe
Pequot Press, 2005), 31.
[40] Anne-Marie Mooney Cotter, *Culture Clash: An International Legal Perspective on Ethnic
Discrimination* (Burlington, VT: Ashgate Publishing, 2011).
[41] Antony Lerman, "In Defence of Multiculturalism," *The Guardian*, March 22, 2010, www
.theguardian.com/commentisfree/2010/mar/22/multiculturalism-blame-culture-segregation.
[42] John Nagle, Multiculturalism's Double Bind: Creating Inclusivity, Cosmopolitanism, and
Difference (Burlington, VT: Ashgate Publishing, 2009), 129; "Report Attacks
Multiculturalism," *BBC News*, September 30, 2005, http://news.bbc.co.uk/2/hi/uk_news/
4295318.stm; Steve Sailer, "Fragmented Future," *American Conservative*, January 15, 2007,
www.theamericanconservative.com/articles/fragmented-future/; Frank Salter, *On Genetic
Interests: Family, Ethnicity, and Humanity in an Age of Mass Migration* (Piscataway, NJ:
Transaction Publishers, 2006), 146.
[43] See, for instance, Donnelly, *Universal Human Rights in Theory and Practice*; Mutua, *Human
Rights*; and Bell, *East Meets West*.
[44] See, for instance, Will Kymlicka, *Multicultural Citizenship* (New York, NY: Oxford University
Press, 1995).
[45] Yuval Levin, *The Fractured Republic: Renewing America's Social Contract in the Age of
Individualism* (New York, NY: Basic Books, 2016), 179–180. A resurgence of strong nationalistic
feeling, partly a product of what some Europeans perceive as a "Muslim invasion," has moved
politics in many countries toward the right. The backlash against multiculturalism that

imposing strong standards and intolerant of differences (at home as well as abroad), while conservatives are often in favor of accepting differences in some important areas (such as with regard to religious freedom).[46]

This book focuses on the UDHR both because it has maintained wide acceptance in a way no other subsequent document has and because it provides an example of pluralism for those seeking to advance human rights across thick and thin societies. As a 1990s survey by Hurst Hannum shows, the UDHR "has been the foundation of much of the post-1945 codification of human rights, and the international legal system is replete with global and regional treaties based, in large measure, on the Declaration."[47] Over eighty national constitutions reference it, at least sixty give some degree of authority to it, and twenty-six explicitly acknowledge the UDHR as having priority over domestic legal systems.[48] The framers achieved a distinctive synthesis of previous thinking from all over the world and represented a widespread consensus that "no nation would wish openly to disavow."[49] It passed in the United Nations in 1948 with no dissenting votes (and but a few abstentions).

The two case studies presented here – one an intrasociety disagreement within Western countries, and the other an intersociety disagreement that divides Western actors and Southern countries – highlight differences in how societies are organized, balance competing needs, think about morality, and prioritize competing values. Both display starkly different interpretations of human rights. Circumcision – an ancient ritual practiced by Jews and Muslims – has increasingly come under fire by human rights proponents in Europe in recent years as the definition of human rights has expanded to

accompanied this has shifted the focus (and even definition) of human rights from one based on groups' rights back toward one focused on individual rights. Whereas conservatives played defense when liberals were pushing multiculturalism, liberals now play defense when conservatives push ideas related to traditional values and religion. For an analysis of the contradictions within human rights that allow different interpretations to flourish at different times, see Dov Maimon and Nadia Ellis, "The Circumcision Crisis: Challenges for European and World Jewry," The Jewish People Policy Institute, Jerusalem, Israel, 2012, 6–10, http://jppi.org.il/news/117/58/The-Circumcision-Crisis/.

[46] See, for instance, Levin, *The Fractured Republic*. For how ideas on human rights have changed to make this possible, see Suzanne Last Stone, "Religion and Human Rights: Babel or Translation, Conflict or Convergence," paper presented at *Role of Religion in Human Rights Discourse* conference, Israel Democracy Institute, May 16–17, 2012.

[47] Hurst Hannum, "The Status of the Universal Declaration of Human Rights in National and International Law," *Georgia Journal of International and Comparative Law* 25, no. 1–2 (1995/1996): 289.

[48] Hannum, "The Status of the Universal Declaration of Human Rights in National and International Law," Annex 1, 355 ff.

[49] Glendon, *A World Made New*, xviii.

include children's bodily integrity and the space for religious freedom has narrowed. It exemplifies a broader set of disagreements occurring in Europe and the United States between religious groups and an increasingly secular state. Rwanda's *gacaca* community-based courts proved remarkably successful at prosecuting hundreds of thousands of suspected perpetrators of the 1994 genocide while yielding significant benefits in terms of truth and healing, but they have been heavily criticized by Western human rights actors.[50] The latter have argued that *gacaca* does not uphold proper legal due process and encourages corruption and government interference. The case study highlights Western versus Southern approaches to the process and substance of human rights as well as the gap that often exists between human rights organizations working in abstract "ideals" and developing countries that must address many practical constraints and make trade-offs to advance.

A few notes on terms will aid the discussion. This book draws two distinctions: first, between "the West" and "the South" and, second, between *religious groups* and *secular actors* within the West. The West consists of the rich, developed, democratic, thin society countries of North America, Europe, Australia, and New Zealand (all occasionally called "the North"). The South consists of less-developed, thick society countries in Asia, the Middle East, Latin America, and Africa (parts of which have been called "the East"). Although divisions among actors within the West and the South on human rights are not black and white – some Southern individuals and governments take Western positions on certain issues, and vice versa, and degrees of thickness and thinness can differ substantially across and even within borders – the differences highlighted are generally true; for the sake of clarity and argument, the shades of gray have been de-emphasized.[51]

Within the West, religious thick community groups consist of the Christian, Muslim, and Jewish communities that place scripture and tradition at the center of how they live and that share a similar perspective on human rights. Secular actors, which now often include the administrative and judicial organs of the state, consist of those who hold secular rational values; believe that institutions, communities, religion, and traditions should give way to the needs of the individual; and share a common view on human rights. Here too there are not always distinct divisions among groups – some secular actors may

---

[50] Phil Clark, *The Gacaca Courts, Post-Genocide Justice and Reconciliation in Rwanda: Justice without Lawyers* (Cambridge: Cambridge University Press, 2010); Phil Clark and Zachary D. Kaufman (eds.), *After Genocide: Transitional Justice, Post-Conflict Reconstruction and Reconciliation in Rwanda and Beyond* (New York, NY: Columbia University Press, 2009).

[51] This definition borrows from Zwart, "Balancing Yin and Yang in the International Human Rights Debate," 1–2.

hold traditional views on human rights on certain issues and vice versa.[52] Even though cultures are ever changing and contested, and more a mosaic of different values that differ across groups and issues than a monolithic, static entity, there are substantial and consistent differences between Western and Southern countries and between religious groups and secular actors within the West.

When the book discusses *culture*, it is referring to what Clifford Geertz calls "an historically transmitted pattern of meanings embodied in symbols, a system of inherited conceptions expressed in symbolic forms by means of which men communicate, perpetuate, and develop their knowledge about and their attitudes toward life."[53] The widely accepted, community-specific, inherited ideas reflect what is valuable, true, good, and beautiful. The common institutions shape how individuals and groups relate and interact with each other; they are concerned with the practices, coordination mechanisms, symbols, rituals, norms, meanings, identities, aspirations, and beliefs that serve relational ends.[54]

Institutions are relatively stable sets of rules and structures that shape human activity, especially with regard to resolving fundamental problems related to sustaining communities and important resources. They encompass both formal institutions, such as laws issued by the government, and informal institutions, such as traditional rules and values that come from society, community, family, or religion. The latter, often known as *social institutions*, are essential to the development of complex social organization and cooperation because of how they efficiently guide behavior and frame choice. They exercise authority in two ways: by providing meaning and

---

[52] For instance, there are a number of progressive Christian churches in the United States, such as the Alliance of Baptists, Christian Church (Disciples of Christ), the Episcopal Church, and Presbyterian Church (USA). On the other hand, some atheists and agnostics support traditional values, such as some conservative groups in Europe (e.g., Christian Democrat parties that have long lost their religious ties).

[53] Clifford Geertz, "Religion as a Cultural System," in *The Interpretation of Cultures: Selected Essays* (New York, NY: Basic Books, 1973), 89. Michael Walzer says of culture, "A community's culture is the story its members tell so as to make sense of all the different pieces of their social life – and justice is the doctrine that distinguishes the pieces." Walzer, *Spheres of Justice: A Defense of Pluralism and Equality* (New York, NY: Basic Books, 1983), 319.

[54] Markus and Conner, *Clash!*, xix–xx; Vijayendra Rao and Michael Walton, "Culture and Public Action: Relationality, Equality of Agency, and Development," in Vijayendra Rao and Michael Walton (eds.), *Culture and Public Action* (Stanford, CA: Stanford University Press, 2004), 4; and Shweder, "Moral Maps, 'First World' Conceits, and the New Evangelists," 163.

ambition that individuals see as desirable and by pressuring and coercing individuals to comply.[55]

Liberal modernity refers to a set of sociocultural norms, attitudes, and practices that arose in the West after the Enlightenment. It is marked by a questioning or rejection of tradition; the prioritization of values such as autonomy, individualism, equality, choice, secularity, and rationality; and a belief in inevitable social, scientific, and technological progress, human perfectibility, secularization, market capitalism, and democratization.[56] Although some have argued that there is more than one possible modernity, Western universalists act as if there just one;[57] this understanding of modernity is used here for the sake of clarity.

A number of important books examine the role of culture in interpreting human rights. Most touch on the subject as part of a larger analysis; only a few focus exclusively or predominantly on the issue. Among the more well-known of the former are Jack Donnelly's *Universal Human Rights in Theory and Practice*; Michael Freeman's *Human Rights: An Interdisciplinary Approach*; Philip Alston and Ryan Goodman's *International Human Rights*; William Twining's *General Jurisprudence*; and Mary Ann Glendon's *A World Made New: Eleanor Roosevelt and the Universal Declaration of Human Rights*. The latter include Alison Dundes Renteln's *International Human Rights: Universalism versus Relativism*; Abdullahi Ahmed An-Na'im's edited volumes *Human Rights in Cross-Cultural Perspectives: A Quest for Consensus* and *Human Rights in Africa: Cross-Cultural Perspectives*; Daniel Bell and Joanne Bauer's edited *The East Asian Challenge for Human Rights*; and Mark Goodale and Sally Engle Merry's edited *The Practice of Human Rights: Tracking Law between the Global and the Local*.

The remainder of the book is organized as follows. Chapter 2 looks at the UDHR, which has achieved a unique cross-cultural legitimacy. A product of extensive negotiations, it depended on a wide range of very different

[55] See also the definitions in Chapter 4. I used a number of sources for this definition: Jonathan Turner, *The Institutional Order: Economy, Kinship, Religion, Polity, Law, and Education in Evolutionary and Comparative Perspective* (New York, NY: Longman Publishing, 1997), 6; Talcott Parsons, *The Social System* (New York, NY: Free Press, 1951), 39–40; David Popenoe, *Sociology* (Englewood Cliffs, NJ: Prentice Hall, 1995), 83; David Blackenhorn, *The Future of Marriage* (New York, NY: Encounter Books, 2007), 60–61 and 168.

[56] Michel Foucault, *Discipline and Punish: The Birth of the Prison*, translated by Alan Sheridan (New York, NY: Vintage Books, 1995), 170–177; Marshall Berman, *All That Is Solid Melts into Air: The Experience of Modernity* (London: Verso, 2010).

[57] Shmuel Noah Eisenstadt, *Comparative Civilizations and Multiple Modernities*, 2 vols. (Boston, MA: Brill, 2003); Gerard Delanty, "Modernity," in George Ritzer (ed.), *Blackwell Encyclopedia of Sociology*, 11 vols. (Malden, MA: Blackwell Publishing, 2007).

philosophical foundations. The Declaration's drafters understood that it was to be articulated differently in dissimilar parts of the world. Many of its key elements show an appreciation for the fact that most societies around the world are thick. Chapter 3 introduces the field of cultural psychology, which suggests that there are substantial differences in how people from different cultures think. Different cultures – as well as different groups within societies – develop different moral matrices, concepts of the self, and ideas related to their relationships with others.

Chapter 4 examines the characteristics of thick and thin societies. Whereas "thin societies" are highly individualistic and value choice, fairness, justice, and rights, "thick societies" are highly sociocentric and value order, tradition, duty, sanctity, and purity. Each has starkly dissimilar perceptions vis-à-vis social institutions, the state, and human rights. Liberal pluralism, with its focus on eliminating a narrower set of evils, can bridge these differences. But, as Chapter 5 explains, Western normative assumptions frequently dominate the human rights discourse today, creating an unnecessarily divisive environment. Most human rights campaigners are Western universalists and believe that human rights treaties commit countries around the world to the Western view on human rights – a view that sometimes conflates Western cultural norms with universal rights and ends up promoting liberal monism.

Chapters 6 and 7 look at the two case studies mentioned earlier. Chapter 6 covers the intrasociety debate in Europe on male circumcision. Chapter 7 examines the intersociety debate on *gacaca* between Rwanda and Western human rights organizations. In both cases, there is a clash between thick and thin communities and differences in how Western universalists and flexible universalists interpret human rights.

Chapter 8 looks at why broader trends will require the human rights movement to garner wider support by adapting to the perspectives of thick societies. This calls for a flexible universalist approach and a return to basics. It proposes a fourfold approach to moving forward and outlines in detail how this would work.

2

The UDHR: Flexible Universalism

There was once a much broader consensus on human rights and the need for a flexible yet universal approach. The Universal Declaration of Human Rights (UDHR), a product of extensive negotiations, passed the United Nations with no dissensions in 1948, and it has legitimacy worldwide because it embodied such an approach. A number of major international treaties signed in the years since have also achieved broad support for similar reasons. The UDHR is by far the single most important human rights document, a "constitution" for the movement, an "international bill of rights for governments,"[1] and an independent moral beacon for world affairs.[2] It is the foundation for much of the post-1945 codification of human rights, many international treaties are based on the Declaration, and many state constitutions make use of it in some form.[3] Yet, the human rights field is today often mired in controversy, and advocates risk losing support in many parts of the world. What happened?

For many, "the gross inflation in the number of human rights treaties and nonbinding international instruments adopted by international organizations"[4] over the last several decades "cheapens the purpose" and "makes it far more

---

[1] Mary Ann Glendon and Elliott Abrams, "Reflections on the UDHR," *First Things* 82 (April 1998), www.firstthings.com/article/1998/04/002-reflections-on-the-udhr.

[2] Johannes Morsink, *The Universal Declaration of Human Rights: Origins, Drafting, and Intent* (Philadelphia, PA: University of Pennsylvania Press, 1999), 20.

[3] Hurst Hannum, "The Status of the Universal Declaration of Human Rights in National and International Law," *Georgia Journal of International and Comparative Law* 25, no. 1–2 (1995/1996): 289.

[4] Jacob Mchangama and Guglielmo Verdirame, "The Danger of Human Rights Proliferation: When Defending Liberty, Less Is More," *Foreign Affairs*, July 24, 2013, www.foreignaffairs.com/articles/139598/jacob-mchangama-and-guglielmo-verdirame/the-danger-of-human-rights-proliferation.

difficult to achieve the broad intercultural assent to rights that an international human rights regime requires to be effective."[5] According to the Freedom Rights Project, there are 64 human rights agreements under the auspices of either the United Nations or the Council of Europe, including 1,377 provisions (some of which may be technical rather than substantive).[6] In contrast, the drafters of the UDHR felt compelled to keep it short and punchy. There are but thirty provisions in it.[7] The two international covenants and many follow-on treaties are not nearly as important to the cause of human rights as were the principles embedded in the Declaration.[8]

In this chapter, we will look in detail at the flexible universalism of the Universal Declaration, showing how it was formulated to comfortably operate across societies even if they had significantly different value systems. The drafters believed both that it was the right approach and that it was necessary in order to attain broad support. In Chapter 5, we will contrast their approach with the predominant discourse in the human rights field in the twenty-first century.

THE UDHR: A "COMPOSITE SYNTHESIS"

The UDHR's framers achieved a distinctive synthesis, developing the document over two years with remarkably little disagreement regarding the basic substance despite wrangling about specifics. The final product combined many elements, connected to and interdependent with each other, greater as a whole than a simple sum of the individual components.[9] Some elements focus on the individual, others on community and society. Some focus on freedom, others on solidarity and duty. The vision of liberty is inseparable from the call for social responsibility.[10] Influenced by a combination of sociocentric (mostly from Latin America and Europe) and individualistic concepts (from the Anglo-American tradition), and gaining support from a wide assortment of European, Middle Eastern, Latin American, Asian,

---

[5]   Amy Gutmann, "Introduction," in Gutmann (ed.), *Human Rights as Politics and Idolatry* (Princeton, NJ: Princeton University Press, 2003), x.

[6]   Mchangama and Verdirame, "The Danger of Human Rights Proliferation."

[7]   Pedro Pizano, "The Human Rights That Dictators Love," *Foreign Policy*, February 26, 2014, www.foreignpolicy.com/articles/2014/02/26/the_human_rights_that_dictators_love.

[8]   The two international human rights covenants are the International Covenant on Civil and Political Rights (ICCPR) and International Covenant on Economic, Social and Cultural Rights (ICESCR). Mary Ann Glendon, *A World Made New: Eleanor Roosevelt and the Universal Declaration of Human Rights* (New York, NY: Random House, 2001), 216.

[9]   Glendon, *A World Made New*, xx.

[10]   Ibid., xviii.

communist, capitalist, developed, and developing countries, the framers
believed, as Mary Ann Glendon argues in her popular study of the UDHR,
that the Declaration

> achieved a distinctive synthesis of previous thinking about rights and duties.
> After canvassing sources from North and South, East and West, they believed
> they had found a core of principles so basic that no nation would wish openly
> to disavow them. They wove those principles into a unified document.[11]

The Communist bloc and Saudi Arabia voted in favor of most of the clauses
even though they abstained in the final vote.[12] The General Assembly, then
consisting of fifty-eight member states, eventually approved 23 of the 30 articles
unanimously.[13]

Although far from a perfect integration of views from every part of the
world – especially given that large sections of the globe were still colonized
at the time – the United Nations' Commission on Human Rights, which drew
up the initial draft, did include people from a broad range of different cultural,
religious, economic, and political systems. Although some scholars, most
notably Abdullahi Ahmed An-Na'im, argue that a certain Western perspective
and set of norms were overemphasized at the beginning[14] – at the expense of
non-Western and religious perspectives – others, such as Mary Ann Glendon,
disagree. Individuals from a diverse set of countries, including France, Chile,

---

[11] Ibid., xviii.
[12] Ibid., 226.
[13] Ibid., 143 and 161.
[14] See, for instance, Abdullahi Ahmed An-Na'im's many publications on the subject. "Given the
historical context within which the present standards have been formulated, it was unavoidable
that they were initially based on Western cultural and philosophical assumptions . . . formative
Western impact continues to influence the conception and implementation of human rights
throughout the world." An-Na'im (ed.), *Human Rights in Cross-Cultural Perspectives: A Quest
for Consensus* (Philadelphia, PA: University of Pennsylvania, 1992), 428. Elsewhere, he argues
that because of the fifty-one original members of the United Nations, only three were African
(Egypt, Ethiopia, Liberia), and eight were Asian, and that these were mainly authoritarian,
while the vast majority of states were still colonized by the West, few non-Western states
actually participated in drafting the UDHR and the formative early stages of the two covenants.
The only two non-Western representatives on the drafting committee were both educated in
the US. Moreover the "representatives" were more reflective of Western cultural perspectives,
and the laws related to the UDHR were not adopted by the public in most countries but by a
small clique of Westernized lawyers, bureaucrats, and intellectuals. An-Na'im, "Problems of
Universal Cultural Legitimacy for Human Rights," in An-Na'im and Francis Deng (eds.),
Human Rights in Africa: Cross-Cultural Perspectives (Washington, DC: Brookings Institution
Press, 1990), 346–350. Makau Mutua is even more critical of how Western the UDHR is in
Mutua, *Human Rights: A Political and Cultural Critique* (Philadelphia, PA: University of
Pennsylvania Press, 2002).

Lebanon, precommunist China, the USSR, Canada, and the United States played prominent roles in the debates. The result was a more sociocentric document than would have been possible if only Europeans and Americans were present. The document itself was influenced more by the dignitarian rights tradition of Latin America and continental Europe than by the more individualistic Anglo-American rights tradition, at least partly because this was necessary to gain acceptance in Asia and Africa.[15] The former emphasizes social institutions such as the family and community and sees rights both as having clear limits and as being accompanied by responsibilities to other citizens and the state.[16]

Concern that it would be hard to produce a document flexible enough to encompass all of the world's diversity prompted the UN Educational, Scientific and Cultural Organization (UNESCO) to recruit some of the world's greatest thinkers to join a Committee on the Theoretical Bases of Human Rights to facilitate the work being undertaken by the Commission on Human Rights. It also motivated the executive board of the American Anthropological Association to write the Commission in 1947 to warn against adopting any statement "conceived only in terms of the values prevalent in the countries of Western Europe and America."[17]

The major players shaping the original document – including Peng-chun Chang (張彭春), Charles Malik, René Cassin, and Eleanor Roosevelt – were universalists but not homogenizers. They were thus much more akin to flexible universalists than Western universalists.[18] They believed they had adopted a pluralistic document that was flexible enough to respond to different needs in terms of emphasis and implementation, but was not malleable enough such that none of the basic rights would become eclipsed or subordinated for the sake of others.[19] Chang, the Chinese delegate, argued in his

---

[15] Glendon, *A World Made New*, 227.

[16] Ibid., 227.

[17] It argued that the Commission would need to "formulate a statement of human rights that will do more than just phrase respect for the individual as an individual. It must also take into full account the individual as member of the social group of which he is part, whose sanctioned modes of life shape his behavior, and with whose fate his own is thus inextricably bound." Executive Board, American Anthropological Association, "Statement on Human Rights," *American Anthropologist* 49, no. 4, part 1 (October–December 1947): 539–543; Karen Engle, "From Skepticism to Embrace: Human Rights and the American Anthropological Association from 1947–1999," *Human Rights Quarterly* 23, no. 3 (August 2001): 536–559.

[18] Glendon, *A World Made New*, 230.

[19] Ibid., 232. "One of the most common and unfortunate misunderstandings today involves the notion that the Declaration was meant to impose a single model of right conduct rather than to provide a common standard that can be brought to life in different cultures in a legitimate variety of ways. This confusion has fostered suspicion of the Universal Declaration in many

speech to the General Assembly urging adoption that there was no single way of thinking or living, and that such a uniformity could only be achieved by force or at the expense of truth and would be unsustainable. He condemned the colonial powers – which still controlled much of the world in 1948 – for trying to do just this.[20]

Lebanon's representative at the United Nations, Charles Malik, who served as Rapporteur for the Commission on Human Rights in 1947 and 1948 and played a critical role in shepherding the document through the General Assembly afterward (when he was president of the Economic and Social Council), encapsulated the diverse influences on the Declaration in his speech urging acceptance. Directing his arguments to the public and posterity as much as to his fellow delegates, Malik said that the UDHR was "a composite synthesis of all these outlooks and movements and of much Oriental and Latin American wisdom. Such a synthesis has never occurred before in history." He pointed to different parts of the document as examples to show where Latin America, India, the United Kingdom, the United States, the Soviet Union, China, France, and other countries had contributed.[21]

The diverse origin of the Declaration's values is perhaps best represented by the presence of the Chinese concept of "two-man mindedness" – a rather unwieldy literal translation – or, in its Westernized translation, "consciousness of one's fellow man." Proposed by Chang, and based on the core Confucian ethic *rén* (仁),[22] this way of thinking – embodied in the ability to see things from another's perspective as well as one's own – permeates the document.[23]

quarters, and lends credibility to the charge of Western cultural imperialism so often leveled against the entire human rights movement." Glendon, *A World Made New*, xviii.
[20] Summary Records, UN General Assembly, 182nd Plenary Session, 895.
[21] Glendon, "Knowing the Universal Declaration of Human Rights," *Notre Dame Law Review* 73, no. 5 (1999): 1161–1162.
[22] *Rén* (仁) is the foundational virtue of Confucianism, characterizing the ideal behavior and bearing that a human should exhibit in order for a community to flourish. This means being able to see things from another people's perspective and doing what is best for them with that perspective in mind. In *Analects* 6.30, Confucius explains this by saying that "benevolence is a matter of going on to establish other people because one seeks to establish oneself, and of bringing other people to perfection because one desires perfection for oneself." It can be roughly translated as "humaneness," "benevolence," "human connectedness," or "comprehensive virtue." *Encyclopædia Britannica*, "ren," *Encyclopædia Britannica Online*, 2015, www.britannica.com/topic/ren; Kurtis Hagen, "Confucian Key Terms: Ren 仁," SUNY Plattsburgh website, August 2007, http://faculty.plattsburgh.edu/kurtis.hagen/keyterms_ren .html.
[23] Glendon, *A World Made New*, 142 and 228; Tore Lindholm, "Article 1," in Guðmundur Alfreðsson and Asbjørn Eide (eds.), *The Universal Declaration of Human Rights: A Common Standard of Achievement* (The Hague: Martinus Nijhoff Publishers, 1999), 43; 鞠成伟 (Ju Chengwei), "儒家思想对世界新人权理论的贡献: 从张彭春对《世界人权宣言》订立的贡

It appears, at Chang's insistence, in Article 1, as "conscience" and "the spirit of brotherhood."[24] It appears elsewhere in various attempts to prevent the document from becoming a source of selfishness or self-centeredness.[25] In the Chinese version of the UDHR, which has equal status with the English and French versions, the emphasis is even greater because the original Confucian concepts are better articulated.[26] The term *conscience* in Article 1, for instance, is replaced by *liangxin* (良心)[27], which has a close historical association with *rén* and means the "innate goodness" (first character) of the "mind/heart" (second character); it thus conveys a much stronger sense of what makes a person moral than the original.[28] As Chang argued during one of the General Assembly debates, "The aim of the United Nations was not to ensure the selfish gains of the individual but to try and increase man's moral stature. It was necessary to proclaim the duties of the individual, for it was a consciousness of his duties which enabled man to reach a high moral standard."[29]

Chang's emphasis on Confucian ideas about the moral capacity of human beings, the importance of community, and the need to be conscious of others prevented the UDHR from becoming an overly Western document.[30] For those pursuing flexible universalism today, it also shows an alternative way, in addition to the liberal modern way, that human rights could be developed under the UDHR. Such a framework would emphasize interrelatedness and humanism more than autonomy and individualism, seeking to contribute to every person's moral growth and maturation rather than only protecting

---

献出发 (The Contribution of Confucianism on the World's New Human Rights Thinking: Zhang Pengchun's Contribution to the 'Universal Declaration')," 环球法律评论 (*Global Law Review*) 33, no. 1 (2011): 141–149.

[24] Sumner Twiss, "Confucian Contributions to the Universal Declaration of Human Rights: A Historical and Philosophical Perspective," in Arvind Sharma (ed.), *The World's Religions: A Contemporary Reader* (Minneapolis, MN: Fortress Press, 2010), 111.

[25] Ibid., 111–112.

[26] UN General Assembly, *Universal Declaration of Human Rights*, December 10, 1948, 217 A (III), Chinese version available at www.un.org/zh/documents/udhr/.

[27] The other two usages of conscience in the English version (in the preamble and in Article 18) are translated differently because the meaning is different.

[28] Lydia H. Liu, "Shadows of Universalism: The Untold Story of Human Rights around 1948," *Critical Inquiry* 40 (2014): 413.

[29] Third Social and Humanitarian Committee of the UN General Assembly, "Draft International Declaration of Human Rights (E/800) (continued)," October 6, 1948, 95th meeting, summary records, Official Records of the Third Session of the General Assembly, 87.

[30] Pierre-Étienne Will provides a balanced assessment of the overall Chinese contribution to the UDHR. Will, ""La contribution chinoise à la Déclaration universelle des droits de l'homme/ The Chinese Contribution to the Universal Declaration of Human Rights, 1947–48: A Re-examination," in Will and Mireille Delmas-Marty (eds.), *La Chine et la Démocratie: Tradition, Droit, Institutions* (Paris: Fayard, 2007), 297–366.

their rights. Such an approach would emphasize the "human" in human rights more than the "rights." The best parts of Confucian family relationship ethics and private morality could be expanded for use with strangers – and thus society as a whole – and public morality. Roles, and the responsibilities and duties they entail, would matter more than rights.[31]

Though the UDHR's drafters agreed on foundational ideals, there were clearly divergent cultural conceptions of human rights that remained unreconciled at the time of drafting. Some of the fault lines and debates have continued down to the present. Arab states challenged the right to change one's religion. Communist countries were opposed to the prevalence of civil liberties.[32] These two sets of disagreements played a large role in seven of the eight abstentions at the time of passage.[33] Outside the United Nations, there was opposition from some religious conservatives, who disliked a number of clauses and the lack of a religious basis; economic conservatives, who disliked the document's myriad employment and social rights; anthropologists, who did not think any set of rights could truly be universal; and non-Westerners, who believed that the document was too steeped in Western values and norms.[34]

The drafters went out of their way to balance civil, cultural, economic, political, and social rights, and in Articles 28–30 they expressly referenced duties and an international order for realization of the rights. Their nuanced approach produced a special document that "continues to be a classical instrument and a possible bridge, currently and in the future, between different points of view."[35] They expected the Declaration's fertile principles to be interpreted in a variety of legitimate ways, and they anticipated that each country would provide experiences and ideas for others to learn from.

---

[31] Twiss, "Confucian Contributions to the Universal Declaration of Human Rights," 110–114; Henry Rosemont, Jr., "Rights-bearing Individuals and Role-bearing Persons," in Mary I. Bockover (ed.), *Rules, Rituals, and Responsibilities: Essays Dedicated to Herbert Fingarette* (LaSalle, IL: Open Court, 1991), 71–102; Tom Zwart, "Re-Rooting International Human Rights by Revisiting the Universal Declaration of Human Rights," unpublished draft, 5–7; Liu, "Shadows of Universalism," 404–417.

[32] Alison Dundes Renteln, *International Human Rights: Universalism versus Relativism* (Newbury Park, CA: Sage Publications, 1990), 30.

[33] South Africa was the other.

[34] Joseph Prabhu discusses three of the four categories (religious groups, anthropologists, and those outside the West) in Prabhu, "Human Rights And Cross-Cultural Dialogue," *Religion and Culture Web Forum*, The Martin Marty Centre, University of Chicago Divinity School, April 2006.

[35] Alfreðsson and Eide, "Introduction," in Alfreðsson and Eide (eds.), *The Universal Declaration of Human Rights: A Common Standard of Achievement* (The Hague: Martinus Nijhoff Publishers, 1999), xxix.

The document thus provides ample leeway for different ways of imagining, prioritizing, and interpreting the rights included.[36] Jacques Maritain explained that this would allow "different kinds of music" to be "played on the same keyboard."[37]

The framers would find alien the contemporary notion that the Declaration prescribes a single model of human rights and that the only alternative is a relativistic approach that allows rights to be determined by circumstances. Some of the critiques Western universalists direct toward thick communities and societies would surprise the framers. The 2012 ASEAN Human Rights Declaration is an interesting case. Even though it contains all the civil and political rights that similar documents elsewhere had and includes a wide range of economic, social, and cultural rights as well as innovative provisions related to AIDS sufferers, childbearing mothers, human trafficking, vulnerable groups, and children, it has not been welcomed by organizations such as Amnesty International, the International Commission of Jurists, the UN High Commissioner for Human Rights, and the US State Department because of sections related to implementation that have a regional flavor.[38] Objections center on the Declaration's emphasis that rights must be balanced with duties, and that realization of rights has to take into account the local political and cultural context. But it is these aspects that are most likely to increase the Declaration's legitimacy – and thus the chance that it will be embraced locally.[39] Such elements would have been more readily accepted by Maritain, Chang, and Malik than by Western universalists.

In the end, the framers were able to achieve broad consensus because they crafted a flexible legal document that everyone – whether from thick or thin

[36] Glendon, *A World Made New*, 230.
[37] Jacques Maritain, "Introduction," in UNESCO (ed.), *Human Rights: Comments and Interpretations, A Symposium* (New York, NY: Columbia University Press, 1949), 15–16.
[38] Amnesty International, "Postpone Deeply Flawed ASEAN Human Rights Declaration," Press Release, November 5, 2012, www.amnesty.org/en/press-releases/2012/11/postpone-deeply-flawed-asean-human-rights-declaration/; International Commission of Jurists, "ICJ Condemns Fatally Flawed ASEAN Human Rights Declaration," Press Release, November 19, 2012, www.icj.org/icj-condemns-fatally-flawed-asean-human-rights-declaration/; United Nations Office of the High Commissioner for Human Rights, "Pillay Encourages ASEAN to Ensure Human Rights Declaration is Implemented in Accordance with International Obligations," News Release, November 19, 2012, www.ohchr.org/en/NewsEvents/Pages/DisplayNews.aspx?NewsID=12809&LangID=E; U.S. State Department, "ASEAN Declaration on Human Rights," Press Statement, November 20, 2012, www.state.gov/r/pa/prs/ps/2012/11/200915.htm.
[39] Tom Zwart, "Safeguarding the Universal Acceptance of Human Rights through the Receptor Approach," *Human Rights Quarterly* 36, no. 4 (November 2014): 902–903. The Declaration is available at www.asean.org/news/asean-statement-communiques/item/asean-human-rights-declaration.

societies – could accept[40] and that everyone could believe was morally important. Understanding why this was both necessary to achieve agreement and desirable is crucial to appreciating the vision of the drafters and the success of the UDHR over time. The advancement of human rights, after all, depends much more on moral authority than on legal commitments written on pieces of paper. Unless people around the world accept rights as morally binding such that they become embedded within local values systems, they are unlikely to gain wide acceptance. Universal commitments must allow each culture to flourish as it might see fit. The drafters of the UDHR knew that, as Malik put it, human rights would only be realized when they were defended in each country "in the mind and the will of the people," as reflected in national and local laws and, above all, social practices.[41]

In order to maximize the reach of their creation, the drafters used easy-to-understand language, kept the length short,[42] changed "international" in the title to "universal,"[43] and avoided issues that would in any way be controversial.[44] They also put people and their social institutions front and center, rarely mentioning the state. They understood that ultimately the success of their endeavor depended on inspiring change in how people treated each other – in their relationships – across society.

DIFFERENT FOUNDATIONS

The UDHR, like all international treaties, was a product of intense bargaining, compromise, and pragmatism, producing ambiguity at times instead of precise definitions. Bård Anders Andreassen, in *The Universal Declaration of Human Rights: A Common Standard of Achievement* (UDHR-CSA), argues that "Such results are evidence of the difficulty of framing human rights instruments and of achieving agreement on human rights norms among diverse States Parties."[45] The process, which yielded a "minimum of common principles"[46] that a great

[40] The eight countries that did not formally accede abstained rather than opposed the document.
[41] Glendon and Abrams, "Reflections on the UDHR."
[42] William A. Schabas (ed.), *The Universal Declaration of Human Rights, The Travaux Prépataratoires* (Cambridge: Cambridge University Press, 2013), 161; Morsink, *The Universal Declaration of Human Rights*, 33–34.
[43] Morsink, *The Universal Declaration of Human Rights*, 324.
[44] Zwart, "Re-Rooting International Human Rights by Revisiting the Universal Declaration of Human Rights," 3–4.
[45] Bård Anders Andreassen, "Article 22," in Alfreðsson and Eide (eds.), *The Universal Declaration of Human Rights: A Common Standard of Achievement* (The Hague: Martinus Nijhoff Publishers, 1999), 475.
[46] Ibid., 477.

diversity of different actors could accept, required much horse trading, coalition building, and "a protracted and often excruciating debate about wording and sentence structure."[47]

In the end, the UDHR could pass and become universal precisely because it avoided controversial issues (such as abortion) and because it employed general or vague phrases instead of very specific wording. The delegates could agree to disagree on the basis, use limiting clauses, and balance crosscutting arguments.[48] The goal was to develop a "big tent" that could encompass a wide variety of value systems; calls were repeatedly made to draft a document that would be acceptable to all member states.[49]

Although it promoted a common position, the UDHR stood upon very different philosophical foundations and was to be articulated differently in dissimilar parts of the world.[50] Indeed if not for the acceptance of different foundations and interpretations, it is unlikely that the original UDHR – and subsequent human rights documents – would have been accepted at all.[51] As Jacques Maritain, a prominent drafter of the UDHR, argues in his 1951 book, *Man and the State*,

> As the International Declaration of Rights published by the United Nations in 1948 showed very clearly, it is doubtless not easy but it is possible to establish a common formulation of such *practical conclusions*, or in other words, of the various rights possessed by man in his personal and social existence. Yet it would be quite futile to look for a common *rational justification* of these practical conclusions and these rights. If we did so, we would run the risk of imposing arbitrary dogmatism or of being stopped short by irreconcilable differences.[52]

Or, as he has often been quoted, "Yes, we agree about the rights, but on condition no one asks us why."[53]

---

[47] Sally Engle Merry, *Human Rights and Gender Violence: Translating International Law into Local Justice* (Chicago, IL: University of Chicago Press Books, 2006), 19.
[48] Åshild Samnøy, "The Origins of the Universal Declaration of Human Rights," in Alfreðsson and Eide (eds.), *The Universal Declaration of Human Rights: A Common Standard of Achievement* (The Hague: Martinus Nijhoff Publishers, 1999), 14–20.
[49] Maritain, "Introduction," 9–17; Zwart, "Re-Rooting International Human Rights by Revisiting the Universal Declaration of Human Rights," 1 and 5.
[50] For an overview of the debates related to the theories behind, justifications for, and definitions of human rights, see Amartya Sen, "Elements of a Theory of Human Rights," *Philosophy and Public Affairs* 32, no. 4 (Autumn 2004): 315–356.
[51] This made them legal and not moral commitments.
[52] Maritain, *Man and the State* (Chicago, IL: University of Chicago Press, 1951), 76.
[53] See, for instance, Jeffrey Flynn, "Rethinking Human Rights: Multiple Foundations and Intercultural Dialogue," presented at the Third Berlin Roundtable on Transnationality:

The drafters understood that they had to set aside their assumptions about God, nature, human nature, reason, natural rights, politics, and whatever other metaphysical, theological, and ideological beliefs they had in order to reach agreement. Early on, when they did not, the Commission on Human Rights became paralyzed by foundational differences; the more they brought their suppositions into the open, the more distant became agreement.[54] This led them to, as René Cassin, the French delegate on the Commission, argued, commit to developing a document "that did not require the Commission to take sides on the nature of man and society, or to become immured in metaphysical controversies, notably the conflict among spiritual, rationalist, and materialist doctrines on the origin of human rights."[55]

The result was an agreement on basic principles – laid out in the Preamble, Proclamation, and first two Articles – but not the reasons for them. It was a genuine "overlapping consensus," in the sense that John Rawls meant when he coined this term in his writing on social justice and political liberalism a few decades later.[56] Charles Taylor, professor emeritus of political science and philosophy at McGill University, has argued that this type of agreement is the only way to achieve an "unforced consensus" on human rights across the world today.[57]

The seven paragraphs of the Preamble, setting out the reasons for the Declaration, and Articles 1 and 2 of the thirty-article Declaration, with their principles of dignity, liberty, equality, and brotherhood, show both the multiple foundations of the Declaration as well as the composite nature of its core values. These provide, as Tore Lindholm writes in the UDHR-CSA, a "thin, but indispensable normative basis through which the representatives of a plurality of religions, moral traditions, and ideologies may establish not only a political compromise, but also a non-exclusive and stable moral agreement on human rights."[58] Rejecting attempts to build a religious or natural rights foundation, the drafters used a combination of moral and historical rationales

---

Reframing Human Rights, Berlin, Germany, October 3–7, 2005; Glendon, *A World Made New*, 77; Maritain, "Introduction," 10–11.

[54] Paul Brink, "Debating International Human Rights: The 'Middle Ground' for Religious Participants," in Dennis R. Hoover and Douglas M. Johnston (eds.), *Religion and Foreign Affairs: Essential Readings* (Waco, TX: Baylor University Press, 2012), 475–478.

[55] Glendon, *A World Made New*, 68.

[56] John Rawls, "The Idea of an Overlapping Consensus," *Oxford Journal of Legal Studies* 7, no. 1 (Spring 1987): 1–25.

[57] Charles Taylor, "Conditions of an Unforced Consensus on Human Rights," in Joanne Bauer and Daniel Bell (eds.), *The East Asian Challenge for Human Rights* (Cambridge: Cambridge University Press, 1999), 124–144.

[58] Lindholm, "Article 1," 62.

for human rights[59] to produce "a more complex, more realistic, and more 'open-ended' scheme."[60] Any normative tradition that embodies – or can be made to embody – human rights can thus be used as a basis.[61]

The diverse foundations were seen as an asset during the drafting process. As Malik proclaimed in his speech to the General Assembly, the plurality of views was a strength, not a weakness. It resulted in a document built on a "firm international basis wherein no regional philosophy or way of life was permitted to prevail."[62] After all, a human rights regime could not do without foundations altogether, and a strong grounding in the internal logic of each particular culture was essential to gaining universal moral authority and legitimacy. Indeed, Amy Gutmann has argued, plural foundations make a human rights regime more broadly acceptable than a single foundation.[63]

As reflected in the political process that both gave birth to and shaped the UDHR – and subsequent international agreements – it is better to see human rights as a practical matter involving politics than one deriving from any abstract conception of human nature or reason.[64] Indeed, as William Twining, a leading scholar on international jurisprudence, writes, "nearly all human rights law is the result of hard-won political consensus and compromise at particular moments in time."[65] By accepting that people around the world "adhere to a plurality of more or less rival comprehensive normative traditions," the UDHR's framers could come up with a document that is "both conceptually coherent and politically sustainable across moral divides."[66]

Many Western universalist theorists, such as Jack Donnelly and Johannes Morsink,[67] and activists, such as the major human rights organizations, assume

---

[59] Lindholm, "Prospects for Research on the Cultural Legitimacy of Human Rights: The Cases of Liberalism and Marxism," in An-Na'im and Francis Deng (eds.), *Human Rights in Africa: Cross-Cultural Perspectives* (Washington, DC: Brookings Institution Press, 1990), 399.

[60] Lindholm, "Article 1," 63.

[61] Lindholm, "Prospects for Research on the Cultural Legitimacy of Human Rights," 399.

[62] Glendon, *A World Made New*, 165.

[63] Gutmann, "Introduction," xviii and xxii.

[64] Flynn, "Rethinking Human Rights: Multiple Foundations and Intercultural Dialogue."

[65] "That history is a complex story of reaction to particular contingencies, genuine idealism, opportunism, protracted negotiation (not always unpressured), compromise, adjustment, and power politics." William Twining, *General Jurisprudence: Understanding Law from a Global Perspective* (Cambridge: Cambridge University Press, 2008), 180

[66] Lindholm, "Article 1," 69.

[67] Lindholm, "Prospects for Research on the Cultural Legitimacy of Human Rights," 397–398; Jack Donnelly, "Human Rights and Human Dignity: An Analytic Critique of Non-Western Conceptions of Human Rights," *The American Political Science Review* 76, no. 2 (June 1982): 303–316; Donnelly, "Human Rights as Natural Rights," *Human Rights Quarterly* 4, no. 3

that human rights are a contemporary version of natural rights. This is based on what Twining calls the misconception that human rights as a legal regime "can and should be founded on a coherent philosophy or ideology" – on the straightforward embodiment of moral universalism.[68] Natural law theorists take rights to be self-evident and see them as rigid elements that are unchanging across different contexts, situations, and time. But conflicts inevitably occur over which right(s) should be prioritized and whether competing moral matrices have legitimacy.[69] Although there may have been some justification for a natural rights approach when dealing with a relatively static, homogenous context, such as Europe was a few centuries ago – and even this is questionable given religious differences and the presence of large minorities – the approach is far more controversial and untenable when dealing with a broader geographical space in a dynamic and multipolar era.[70]

Underlying the presumption of universality for natural rights is the belief that all people think in the same fashion. While all human beings tend to have a psychological predisposition to generalize from their own experience – as will be discussed in Chapter 3 – Western philosophers, as Alison Renteln argues, "in particular seem to be prone to projecting their moral categories on others. As a consequence, the presumption of universality is deeply ingrained in Western moral philosophy."[71] For such people, any disagreement calls into question one's moral reasoning, leading to the dismissal of alternative patterns of thought from the beginning.[72]

As the drafters understood and cultural psychologists would later prove, different parts of the world have legitimately different moral priorities and ways of living the good life. As Richard Shweder, the cultural psychologist, explains, "Society is connected to natural moral law, but there are several natural moral worlds. The problem we face, as children and as adults, is that, at any point in time, we can reason and live in only one moral world."[73] Recognizing

---

(Autumn 1982): 391–405; Morsink, "The Philosophy of the Universal Declaration," *Human Rights Quarterly* 6, no. 3 (August 1984): 409–434. Donnelly has grown more flexible over time. His recent work shows greater scope for cultural adaptation than his earlier work.

[68] Twining, *General Jurisprudence*, 180.

[69] Robert Licht, "Introduction," in Licht (ed.), *Old Rights and New* (Washington, DC: The AEI Press, 1993), 14; William Galston, "Between Philosophy and History: The Evolution of Rights in American Thought," in Licht (ed.), *Old Rights and New*, 67–68.

[70] Renteln, *International Human Rights*, 48.

[71] Ibid., 49.

[72] Ibid., 50–51.

[73] Richard Shweder, "In Defense of Moral Realism: Reply to Gabennesch," *Child Development* 61, no. 6 (December 1990): 2066.

the existence of multiple moral matrices is the first step to dialogue and cooperation on human rights issues.

FLEXIBLE IMPLEMENTATION

Such flexibility is especially important if human rights are to retain their legitimacy in an increasingly diverse and multipolar world[74] – when consensus will be the only way to achieve progress. As Tore Lindhom argues in *Human Rights in Cross-Cultural Perspectives*,

> In the years to come some of the most crucial intellectual, moral, and ideological battles about human rights issues may well turn on their cross-cultural intelligibility and justifiability. The open-ended mix of moral and sociohistorical rationales for human rights commitments prefigured by Article I and the Preamble may be employed, I would argue, to enhance the cross-cultural legitimacy of human rights.[75]

The only exception to this flexibility in the UDHR is for a narrow core of "primary rights" that specifies strict restrictions on things like torture, enslavement, degrading punishment, and discrimination.[76] This suggests that although all rights in the UDHR are important and need to be upheld, there was universal agreement that a few have priority. There is less agreement on how to order the remaining rights, which may be emphasized differently across cultures (see Chapter 8).

This has significant implications when distinguishing the relative importance of two or more human rights in practical situations. For instance, in the debate over circumcision that we discuss in Chapter 6, there are conflicts between the right to practice religion and the right to physical integrity; and between the right of parents to determine how to raise their children versus the right of children to be free to determine their own future.[77] Such

---

[74] For more on the philosophical understandings and theories that broaden the scope and interpretations of human rights (and thus make them more flexible to fit into thick contexts), see Allen Buchanan, "The Egalitarianism of Human Rights," *Ethics* 120, no. 4 (July 2010): 679–710; Jürgen Habermas, "The Concept of Human Dignity and the Realistic Utopia of Human Rights," in Claudio Corradetti (ed.), *Philosophical Dimensions of Human Rights: Some Contemporary Views* (Dordrecht, Netherlands: Springer, 2012); Rainer Forst, "The Basic Right to Justification: Toward a Constructivist Conception of Human Rights," *Constellations* 6, no. 1 (March 1999): 35–60; Rainer Forst, "The Justification of Human Rights and the Basic Right to Justification: A Reflexive Approach," *Ethics* 120, no. 4 (July 2010): 711–740.

[75] Lindholm, "Prospects for Research on the Cultural Legitimacy of Human Rights," 399.

[76] Glendon, *A World Made New*, 230.

[77] Children's rights were not emphasized in the UDHR, but in some later documents, such as the Convention on the Rights of the Child. In general, there are two different viewpoints "as to

disagreements touch upon different conceptions of state responsibility for upholding human rights as well as both differences between religious and secular morality and between modern (individualist with universal claims) and postmodern (multicultural and connected to identity politics) discourses on human rights.[78] In the Rwanda example outlined in Chapter 7, there are clashes between retributive justice for criminals that focuses on upholding the law and restorative justice that focuses on peacemaking, healing, and restoring social harmony. For all their similarities, even the United States and Europe have differences in how they interpret and implement human rights: gun rights, religious freedom, property rights, and freedom of speech are all greater in the United States; social and economic rights are greater in Europe. Parts of the former employ the death penalty; the latter finds it inhumane and inconceivable in a developed, rights-based society.[79]

Beyond these two tiers, there is also a third group of rights that may not be shared across countries at all (see Chapter 8 for a full description of these three types of rights). Developments since 1948 reveal that different cultures want to express themselves with different rights that were not included in the original UDHR (or subsequent documents). These include protections for the elderly, the unborn, same-sex marriage, and so on.

This flexibility is paralleled in how the drafters viewed implementation. It was understood that each country's circumstances would dictate how they would fulfill their requirements.[80] Developing countries would have different resources than developed countries. Communist states would emphasize different priorities than capitalist ones. Muslim states' values would vary from those of Western states. Each part of the world would have its particular concerns. As Article 22 of the original Declaration declared, the UDHR would

---

who holds the supreme right over a child. In one view, the state has the primary obligation of shaping children as future citizens, a key value underpinning the European liberal state. In the second view, guaranteeing the religious life of the child, including through circumcision, is the parents' responsibility, that they have an inviolable right to choose the future path of their child." Even within the West, there are differences. Parental autonomy and religious freedom are more highly valued in the U.S. than Europe. Dov Maimon and Nadia Ellis, "The Circumcision Crisis: Challenges for European and World Jewry," The Jewish People Policy Institute, Jerusalem, Israel, 2012, 7–8, http://jppi.org.il/news/117/58/The-Circumcision-Crisis/.

[78] Maimon and Ellis, "The Circumcision Crisis," 7–10.

[79] Glendon, *Rights Talk: The Impoverishment of Political Discourse* (New York: The Free Press, 1991), 1–12, 37, 40, 71, 149, and 161.

[80] Glendon, *A World Made New*, 115–116.

be put into practice "in accordance with the organization and resources of each State."[81] Indeed, as Tom Zwart indicates,

> Southern states can validly make the claim that all efforts made by the state and its people to improve the wellbeing and dignity of the members of society amounts to human rights protection and promotion. Without perhaps using the human rights label, people and government entities everywhere are therefore furthering human rights.[82]

Although the state has the ultimate obligation to fulfill its human rights commitments, any group in society – including the market, social networks, communities, families, and individuals – can play the leading role.[83] It is noteworthy that the UN itself repeatedly acts as if nonstate actors and context matter, such as when it passes resolutions like the "Declaration on Human Rights Defenders," which puts "Individuals, Groups and Organs of Society" at the center of the process to advance human rights.[84] Indeed, given the failures of the statecentric approach in so many areas of human rights, it is hard to imagine anything but an alternative approach working.[85] Thick societies are more likely to have social institutions capable of playing this role – and more likely to prefer to depend upon them for it.

As with other major human rights documents, the UDHR mandates a certain result – though without a clear definition or threshold at times – and it provides great flexibility in how it is achieved.[86] And, while states need to

---

[81] UN General Assembly, *Universal Declaration of Human Rights*, December 10, 1948, 217 A (III), available at: www.un.org/en/documents/udhr/.

[82] Tom Zwart, "Balancing Yin and Yang in the International Human Rights Debate," Paper for the Sixth Beijing Human Rights Forum, Beijing, China, September 12–13, 2013, 5–6.

[83] Andreassen, "Article 22," 484–485; Thandabantu Nhlapo, "The African Customary Law of Marriage and the Rights Conundrum," in Mahmood Mamdani (ed.), *Beyond Rights Talk and Culture Talk: Comparative Essays on the Politics of Rights and Culture* (New York, NY: Palgrave Macmillan, 2000), 136–148; Josiah Cobbah, "African Values and the Human Rights Debate: An African Perspective," *Human Rights Quarterly* 9, no. 3 (August 1987): 320–324; Lakshman Marasinghe, "Traditional Conceptions of Human Rights in Africa," in Claude Welch, Jr. and Ronald Meltzer (eds.), *Human Rights and Development in Africa* (Albany, NY: SUNY Press, 1984), 33.

[84] UN General Assembly, *Declaration on the Right and Responsibility of Individuals, Groups and Organs of Society to Promote and Protect Universally Recognized Human Rights and Fundamental Freedoms*, August 3, 1999, A/RES/53/144, available at: www.ohchr.org/EN/Issues/SRHRDefenders/Pages/Declaration.aspx.

[85] Douglas Donoho, "Human Rights Enforcement in the Twenty-First Century," *Georgia Journal of International & Comparative Law* 35, no. 1 (January 2006): 1; UN General Assembly, *Declaration on the Right and Responsibility of Individuals, Groups and Organs of Society to Promote and Protect Universally Recognized Human Rights and Fundamental Freedoms*.

[86] Andreassen, "Article 22," 484–485.

take immediate steps toward the desired result, it is understood that full realization may take time.[87] There is a crucial distinction in international law between agreeing to fulfill certain standards and implementing them. While states must meet the obligations they sign up to, they have the freedom to determine how.[88] Moreover, as Twining writes, "conceptions of law that are confined to state law leave out too many significant phenomena that deserve to be included in a total picture of law from a global perspective." He argues that "ideas (including rules)" and "institutionalized social practices (involving actual behavior and attitudes as well as ideas)" need to be included.[89]

The Vienna Convention on the Law of Treaties, which codifies several foundations of international law, is widely recognized as the authoritative guide on treaties; its "general rule of interpretation . . . has attained the status of a rule of customary or general international law"[90] and maintains that international agreements between countries are to be interpreted (Article 31.1) "in good faith in accordance with the ordinary meaning to be given to the terms of the treaty in their context and in the light of its object and purpose."[91] No party can impose its particular interpretation upon other parties. As such, while cultural, institutional, and political context cannot be used as excuses for failing to fulfill commitments, they can be taken into account in implementing them.[92]

Although the UDHR is a UN General Assembly resolution rather than a treaty, it was formulated in a treaty-like fashion because its drafters were unsure what status it would eventually be accorded. Moreover, Articles 2.2 and 7–9 of the Vienna Convention make clear that it interprets flexibly what is deemed a "treaty," and thus covers other documents that can be considered to have a similar status internationally.[93] Indeed, the UN's own website states,

---

[87] Ibid., 486.
[88] Zwart, "Safeguarding the Universal Acceptance of Human Rights through the Receptor Approach," *Human Rights Quarterly* 36, no. 4 (November 2014): 900; Manfred Nowak, *UN Covenant on Civil and Political Rights: CCPR Commentary* (Kehl am Rhein: Engel, 2005), 103; O. Schachter, "The Obligation to Implement the Covenant in Domestic Law," in Louis Henkin (ed.), *The International Bill of Rights* (New York, NY: Columbia University Press, 1981), 311–331; Donoho, "Human Rights Enforcement in the Twenty-First Century."
[89] Twining, *General Jurisprudence*, 180.
[90] World Trade Organization Appellate Body Report, *United States – Standards for Reformulated and Conventional Gasoline*, WT/DS2/AB/R, adopted 20 May 1996, DSR 1996:I, p. 17.
[91] United Nations, *Vienna Convention on the Law of Treaties*, May 23, 1969, United Nations, Treaty Series, vol. 1155, p. 331, available at: www.oas.org/legal/english/docs/Vienna%20Convention%20Treaties.htm.
[92] Zwart, "Safeguarding the Universal Acceptance of Human Rights through the Receptor Approach," *Human Rights Quarterly* 36, no. 4 (November 2014): 900.
[93] Zwart, "Re-Rooting International Human Rights by Revisiting the Universal Declaration of Human Rights."

"Some instruments entitled 'declarations' were not originally intended to have binding force, but their provisions may have reflected customary international law or may have gained binding character as customary law at a later stage. Such was the case with the 1948 Universal Declaration of Human Rights."[94]

If there are differing interpretations[95] of a treaty, "any subsequent agreement between the parties" (Article 31.3.a); "any subsequent practice in the application of the treaty which establishes the agreement of the parties" (Article 31.3.b); and "the preparatory work of the treaty and the circumstances of its conclusion" (Article 32) shall all be used to confirm its meaning and application.[96] As such, the discussions and debates that yielded the UDHR, the context in which these took place, and the subsequent global and regional human rights agreements and resolutions that build upon its base all matter for its interpretation.

International human rights agreements have repeatedly recognized that different countries have different ways of implementing commitments. For instance, in the International Covenant on Civil and Political Rights, Article 2.2 obligates states parties "to adopt such laws or other measures as may be necessary to give effect to the rights recognized in the present Covenant." The clause "laws or other measures" clearly recognizes that some countries will use nonstate measures – such as social institutions – to promote human rights.[97] "Furthermore, the Covenant does not require the contracting states to grant individual enforceable rights to those who are under their jurisdiction."

---

[94] See United Nations Treaty Collection, "Definitions," https://treaties.un.org/Pages/overview .aspx?path=overview/definition/page1_en.xml. Moreover, although the UDHR is a UN General Assembly resolution rather than a treaty, it was formulated in a treaty-like fashion because its drafters were unsure what status it would eventually be accorded. Articles 2.2 and 7–9 of the Vienna Convention make clear that it interprets flexibly what is deemed a "treaty," and thus covers other documents that can be considered to have a similar status internationally. Zwart, "Re-Rooting International Human Rights by Revisiting the Universal Declaration of Human Rights."

[95] The logic outlined here follows an "intentionalist" approach to interpreting the UDHR. However, even if one follows a "textualist" or "teleological" approach, the other two methods for interpreting international treaties, the same conclusions can be reached. Indeed, both these methods are used elsewhere in the chapter to make the same points. For more on these "schools" or approaches to treaty interpretation, see American Society of International Law and the International Judicial Academy, "General Principles of International Law: Treaty Interpretation," *International Judicial Monitor* 1, no. 4 (September 2006), available at: www.judicialmonitor.org/archive_0906/generalprinciples.html.

[96] United Nations, *Vienna Convention on the Law of Treaties*; Zwart, "Re-Rooting International Human Rights by Revisiting the Universal Declaration of Human Rights."

[97] UN General Assembly, *International Covenant on Civil and Political Rights*, December 16, 1966, United Nations, Treaty Series, vol. 999, p. 171, available at: www.ohchr.org/en/ professionalinterest/pages/ccpr.aspx.

They are thus allowed to use other arrangements – such as those based on communal ties, religion, and social duties – to fulfill their obligations.[98] The principle of "progressive realization," which is recognized explicitly in the International Covenant on Economic, Social and Cultural Rights – and implicitly elsewhere – also allows states to take their contexts into account when implementing human rights. As Article 2 of the ICESCR affirms, each State Party should "take steps . . . with a view to achieving progressively the full realization of the rights."[99] Outside of a set of core obligations, some rights may be more difficult for some countries to attain; they may provide a temporarily lower level of protection as long as they are working toward full realization.[100]

The drafting and adoption of regional documents such as the African Charter on Human and People's Rights (ACHPR), the ASEAN Human Rights Declaration (AHRD), American Convention on Human Rights, and the European Convention of Human Rights (ECHR) all reflect the understanding that context matters. The preamble of the ACHPR, for instance, states that it "Tak[es] into consideration the virtues of [states'] historical tradition and the values of African civilization which should inspire and characterize their reflection on the concept of human and peoples' rights."[101] Similarly, the AHRD states (Article 7) that "the realisation of human rights must be considered in the regional and national context bearing in mind different political, economic, legal, social, cultural, histor-ical and religious backgrounds."[102] The 1993 Vienna Declaration and Pro-gramme of Action similarly makes clear "the significance of national and regional particularities and various historical, cultural and religious back-grounds" to implementation.[103]

[98] Zwart, "Balancing Yin And Yang in the International Human Rights Debate," 4.

[99] UN General Assembly, *International Covenant on Economic, Social and Cultural Rights*, December 16, 1966, United Nations, Treaty Series, vol. 993, p. 3, available at: www.ohchr.org/EN/ProfessionalInterest/Pages/CESCR.aspx.

[100] Eva Brems, "Reconciling Universality and Diversity in International Human Rights: A Theoretical and Methodological Framework and Its Application in the Context of Islam," *Human Rights Review* 5, no. 3 (2004): 13–14.

[101] Organization of African Unity (OAU), *African Charter on Human and Peoples' Rights* ("Banjul Charter"), June 27, 1981, CAB/LEG/67/3 rev. 5, 21 I.L.M. 58 (1982), available at: www.achpr.org/instruments/achpr/#preamble.

[102] Association of Southeast Asian Nations (ASEAN), *ASEAN Human Rights Declaration*, November 18, 2012, available at: www.asean.org/news/asean-statement-communiques/item/asean-human-rights-declaration.

[103] United Nations, *Vienna Convention on the Law of Treaties*.

Even the European human rights protection system, easily the most developed international human rights judicial protection system, allows a significant degree of flexibility at times with regard to local context. Encompassing forty-seven countries, and considerable historical, religious, ideological, and cultural differences, it has uniquely been able – through the European Court of Human Rights (ECtHR)[104] – to develop a sophisticated set of legal techniques for managing the tensions between culture and human rights standards. The "margin of appreciation" doctrine, its main instrument for doing this, allows the ECtHR to provide greater or lesser flexibility to countries to restrict or limit a particular right agreed to in an international agreement – in Europe's case, the European Convention on Human Rights – depending on the issues involved. A wide margin of appreciation means that the same facts can lead to two different interpretations in two different countries even though the same standard is being applied (i.e., in one country the facts yield a rights violation but in another they yield a legitimate restriction of the right). If only a narrow margin is applied, this is unlikely.[105] The court can thus take into account different contexts and concerns while giving states some discretion when they want to limit particular rights in order to advance the national interest or protect other rights.[106] As the Council of Europe, of which the ECtHR is a part, explains, "Given the diverse cultural and legal traditions embraced by each Member State, it was difficult to identify uniform European standards of human rights. ... The margin of appreciation gives the flexibility needed to avoid damaging confrontations between the Court and the Member States."[107]

European states feel this doctrine is so important that they have proposed adding it to the preamble of the actual Convention.[108] Protocol 15, which

---

[104] I say "uniquely" because there is no other similar supranational institution.
[105] Eva Brems, "The Margin of Appreciation Doctrine of the European Court of Human Rights: Accommodating Diversity within Europe," in David Forsythe and Patrice McMahon (eds.), *Human Rights and Diversity: Area Studies Revisited* (Lincoln, NE: University of Nebraska Press, 2003), 81–82. The Court often states that the "margin will vary according to the nature of the Convention right in issue, its importance for the individual, and the nature of the activities restricted, as well as the nature of the aim pursued by the restrictions." Ingrid Leijten, "The Strasbourg Margin of Appreciation: What's in a Name?," *Leiden Law Blog*, Leiden Law School, Leiden University, April 8, 2014, http://leidenlawblog.nl/articles/the-strasbourg-margin-of-appreciation-whats-in-a-name.
[106] Eva Brems, "Reconciling Universality and Diversity in International Human Rights: A Theoretical and Methodological Framework and Its Application in the Context of Islam," *Human Rights Review* 5, no. 3 (2004): 14.
[107] Council of Europe Lisbon Network, "The Margin of Appreciation," www.coe.int/t/dghl/cooperation/lisbonnetwork/themis/echr/paper2_en.asp.
[108] Previously it was a product of case law.

includes the new recital in Article 1, was adopted in 2013 and is in the process of ratification at the time of writing. The addition also enshrines the principle of subsidiarity, further emphasizing the primacy of national institutions in determining human rights issues (though still allowing the ECtHR to intervene when these fail to sufficiently weigh the issues involved).[109]

UNIVERSAL MINIMUM STANDARDS

Despite the need for flexibility, not all things are acceptable and not all moral systems are equally good. Just as humans never like some tastes, they are never going to find some behaviors admirable, except possibly under conditions of great stress. Similarly, although many moral matrices are possible, some are going to be preferable.

A common evolutionary heritage has produced a finite number of moral receptors and senses for judging the world, and these set clear parameters on the development of human societies.[110] Few groups, at least since the Iron Age, have sanctioned human sacrifice because it is inimical to their sense of rightness. Although there are a few exceptions – some allow the killing of relatives to eat during famines[111]; even many highly developed cultures believe it is admirable for men to sacrifice themselves to save women and children when a boat sinks – these are in extremely stressful circumstances and exceptional when considering the broad scope of human experience.

The development of large sophisticated societies, economies, and religions and the expansion of mass communication and education have broadened the range of what was deemed unacceptable.[112] There are now many more ideas related to acceptable conduct that have wide backing worldwide. Slavery was once widespread; today it is beyond the pale, even if not fully stamped out. Colonialism was once widespread; today it is widely accepted as illegitimate, even if some arguably practice it. Ethnic cleansing, racial discrimination, and

---

[109] Council of Europe, "Protocol No. 15 amending the Convention for the Protection of Human Rights and Fundamental Freedoms," CETS No.: 213, information page on treaty, http://conventions.coe.int/Treaty/Commun/QueVoulezVous.asp?NT=213&CM=7&DF=13/08/2015&CL=ENG.

[110] Jonathan Haidt, *The Righteous Mind: Why Good People Are Divided by Politics and Religion* (New York, NY: Pantheon Books, 2012), 109.

[111] Edward Adamson Hoebel, "Law-Ways of the Primitive Eskimos," *Journal of Criminal Law and Criminology* 31, no. 6 (Spring 1941): 672.

[112] Stephen Pinker, *The Better Angels of Our Nature: Why Violence Has Declined* (New York, NY: Viking, 2011).

torture were all once common; today no regime interested in international legitimacy[113] wants to be caught practicing them (though some do so on a large scale). Although some people in some places never enjoy the full fruits of these advances, many do, and this sets a standard that others can at least aim for.[114]

The result of these transformations in human society and consciousness has certainly not led to a convergence in ways of thinking, moral matrices, and prioritization of rights, but it has arguably led to a convergence of core moral principles that all societies – whether thick or thin – agree ought to be the minimum standard of conduct. Whereas there is little agreement on issues such as circumcision, gay marriage, how to best balance the needs of the group with that of the individual, or what is the acceptable role of religion in public life, today the world has reached a broad consensus that killing without cause, jailing without trial, stealing, rape, and torture are unacceptable.[115] Of course, the interpretations for what these mean may vary a lot at times, and implementation may be weak in many countries.

Despite great differences at times – which lead to the noteworthy intercultural clashes over rights and values that occasionally erupt – there are a large number of human rights around which there is broad consensus.[116] This is especially so if we exclude pariah regimes like North Korea, isolated tribes in places such as the Amazon, and nonstate actors such as drug mafias and terrorist organizations. These common principles can form the basis of human rights agreements that have wide backing, such as the UDHR, and that are both universal and flexible enough to meet the needs of a diverse world.

A THICK SOCIETY AND MORAL MATRIX

As will be discussed in Chapter 4, societies can be organized with thick social institutions and a limited role for government in promoting the human good

---

[113] The only groups that proudly practice these things – most notably the Islamic State – have no interest in international acceptance.

[114] Jack Donnelly makes a similar argument. Jack Donnelly, "Cultural Relativism and Universal Human Rights," *Human Rights Quarterly* 6, no. 4 (November 1984): 404–405.

[115] Empirical research, as suggested by Alison Renteln, would discover exactly what this convergence would look like. See Alison Dundes Renteln, *International Human Rights: Universalism versus Relativism* (Newbury Park, CA: Sage Publications, 1990), 11 and 14–15.

[116] This is evident from the large number of human rights treaties that has already been agreed to by the great majority of countries. See later in the chapter for examples. Jack Donnelly, "The Relative Universality of Human Rights," *Human Rights Quarterly* 29, no. 2 (May 2007): 288.

or vice versa. However, as Morsink, after analyzing the differences between these two types of societies, concludes, when it comes to religion and education, the UDHR adopts a remarkably narrow approach to the "delivery of the human good."[117] It assumes that societies are thick, containing many social institutions essential to advancing human well-being, and that any human rights regime and role for the state must therefore be limited whenever possible. This appears in many places in the UDHR.[118]

The UDHR presents a vision of humanity that is in some important ways more aligned with Southern and religious concern about social context and institutions than contemporary Western and secular emphasis on the individual. The Declaration uses the word *person* to emphasize the social dimension of personhood, recognizing, as Lebanon's Charles Malik put it, that "There are no Robinson Crusoes."[119] The term *person* stands in contrast to an "individual" who is "an isolated knot; a person is the entire fabric around that knot, woven from the total fabric."[120]

The Declaration envisions each person – the "everyone" mentioned throughout the document – as being constituted by and through a variety of relationships. The most important of these are specifically named: families, communities, religious groups, workplaces, associations, societies, cultures, nations, and an emerging international order.[121] Such relationships are to be grounded, as the Declaration recognizes in its prologue, in an understanding of people as both individual and social, and, as it exhorts in Article 1, "in a spirit of brotherhood."[122]

Such concerns echo throughout the structure of the document. The general principles proclaimed in the first two articles encompass dignity, liberty, equality, and brotherhood. The main body (Articles 3 through 27) provides for four sets of rights: those related to the individual (3–11); those related to how individuals relate to each other and to groups (12–17); those related to spiritual, public, and political concerns (18–21); and those related to economic, social, and cultural rights (22–27).[123] These emphasize the

---

[117] Morsink, *The Universal Declaration of Human Rights*, 259.
[118] See just below for examples. Morsink, *The Universal Declaration of Human Rights*, 239 and 259–260.
[119] Glendon, *A World Made New*, 42.
[120] R. Panikkar and R. Panikkar, "Is the Notion of Human Rights a Western Concept?," *Diogenes* 30 (1982): 90.
[121] Glendon, *A World Made New*, 227.
[122] Ibid., 175.
[123] Ibid., 172–174; Marc Agi, René Cassin: Fantassin des Droits de l'Homme (Paris: Plon, 1979), 317.

importance of traditional institutions, such as the family, as the "natural and fundamental group unit of society" (Article 16), religion, and marriage.[124] The last section (Articles 28–30) concludes by linking the person to society and placing the rights within the context of limits, duties, and the order in which they must be realized.[125] It argues that "Everyone is entitled to a social and international order in which the rights and freedoms set forth in this Declaration can be fully realized" (Article 28) and that "Everyone has duties to the community in which alone the free and full development of his personality is possible" (Article 29).[126]

The emphasis on a thick society and limited role for the state is especially evident in the article on the rights of members of religious communities (Article 18),[127] which gives everyone not only the right to freedom of thought, conscience, and religion, but also the "freedom, either alone or in community with others and in public or private, to manifest his religion or belief in teaching, practice, worship and observance." It also appears in the sections dealing with family (Article 16) and education (Article 26). The state is only mentioned twice as an active actor, once for the protection of family (Article 16) and once for cooperating with other countries to create a world order able to see the rights outlined realized (Article 22). The focus is on a democratic society not a democratic state (Article 29), implying that there are many ways to create participatory systems of governance besides that embodied in the Western normative of competitive politics and elections.[128]

The UDHR articulates a set of rights that are connected to – even interdependent with – each other. Freedom links to solidarity. Rights imply responsibilities. Institutions matter. Each of the ideas balances against the others as part of a larger whole. As such, the Declaration does not see the specific rights as items to be isolated from the others and propagated on their own.[129]

The body of principles is meant to be read as an integrated whole, indivisible, interdependent, and interrelated, with an organic unity.[130] As Morsink points out,

[124] Zwart, "Using Local Culture to Further the Implementation of International Human Rights: The Receptor Approach," *Human Rights Quarterly* 34, no. 2 (May 2012): 553.

[125] Glendon, *A World Made New*, 172–174.

[126] UN General Assembly, *Universal Declaration of Human Rights*.

[127] Morsink, *The Universal Declaration of Human Rights*, 259–260.

[128] Ibid., 239.

[129] David Blankenhorn, *The Future of Marriage* (New York, NY: Encounter Books, 2007), 182.

[130] Eide, "Article 28," in Alfreðsson and Eide (eds.), *The Universal Declaration of Human Rights*, 606.

the drafters wanted the readers of the Declaration to interpret each article in light of the others. Most of them believed that the exact place of an article was not crucial to its meaning since it needed to be interpreted in the context of the whole anyway. This organic character of the text applies both to how it grew to be what it now is, as well as to a deeper interconnectedness of all the articles.[131]

Indeed, as Glendon and others argue, one of the surest ways to misconstrue – or misuse – human rights is to think that any particular right is absolute, or that all the diverse rights can ever wholly be in harmony with each other. On the contrary, every distinct right must have certain limitations and boundaries and exist within a community of other rights that often conflict with each other for it to have any real meaning. There is no clear blueprint for how to deal with conflicts of this nature. Communities balance the weight of claims of one right versus another – recognizing that no particular right has preponderance over all the rest – before determining the best course of action.[132] Given these conditions, Richard Nisbett suggests that the holistic thinking of Asians may actually be more suitable than the analytic thinking used by Westerners for interpreting human rights documents like the UDHR because of the need to balance different elements against each other and to take into account social context in doing so.[133]

THE IMPORTANCE OF DUTIES

Duties play an impressively prominent role in the Declaration. In Article 1, the "foundation and cornerstone of the entire Declaration,"[134] there is, according to Chang, "a happy balance" between "the broad statement of rights in the first sentence and the implication of duties in the second,"[135] indicating that each is meant to be kept as a distinct concern and not conflated.[136] Article 29, one of the three articles at the end of the Declaration that provide the pediment that binds the structure together in Cassin's overall design, acts as

---

[131] Morsink, *The Universal Declaration of Human Rights*, 232.

[132] Glendon, *Rights Talk*, x; Glendon, *A World Made New*, 239; Blankenhorn, *The Future of Marriage*, 187–188 and 302; Lindholm, "Prospects for Research on the Cultural Legitimacy of Human Rights," 422 (footnote 17). Isaiah Berlin often wrote about this problem. See Chapter 4 for a discussion and references.

[133] Richard Nisbett, *The Geography of Thought: How Asians and Westerners Think Differently . . . and Why* (New York, NY: The Free Press, 2003).

[134] Lindholm, "Article 1," 58.

[135] Ibid., 54 and 62.

[136] Ibid., 62.

a general limiting provision. It states (in 29.1) that "Everyone has duties to the community in which alone the free and full development of his personality is possible." It also makes clear (in 29.2) that an individual's rights can be limited by the "rights and freedoms of others and . . . the just requirements of morality, public order, and the general welfare in a democratic society."

The phrase "meeting the just requirements of morality, public order and the general welfare in a democratic society"[137] in the second paragraph was included because delegates "liked the transcendent character of morality as a separate standard over systems of domestic law and over the calculations of the general welfare." This attitude is more analogous to a community- or divinity-based moral orientation found in thick societies than an autonomy-based one found in thin societies. No such similar consensus could be found on exactly what "democracy" stood for.[138]

The UDHR outlines, according to Morsink, five different communities toward which an individual has duties[139] and which "contribute to the free and full development of the human person."[140] "The first group, which the drafters of the Declaration were especially solicitous of," is the family, the place where morality, values, and beliefs are first learned. Next in importance "must surely rank religious and educational communities." The different communities to which an individual is attached "spread themselves out in concentric circles of communities from the individual and his or her imme-diate community of birth and growth" in the first paragraph of Article 29 all the way through to the world community in the third paragraph, with many intermediate groups playing a role in between these two.[141]

These layers of community create a vast system of reciprocal rights and duties.[142]

Article 29 "reminds us that the individual has not only rights, but also duties (paragraph 1), and that limitations on rights not only may, (paragraph 2) but also must, (paragraph 3) be drawn."[143] Rights proclaimed in previous articles come with three caveats: (1) the corollary of rights is duties, (2) rights are not unlimited, (3) the exercise of rights must be balanced against the needs of the world community. The first two are essential to balance the various needs of a

---

[137] UN General Assembly, *Universal Declaration of Human Rights.*
[138] Morsink, *The Universal Declaration of Human Rights*, 250.
[139] Ibid., 241.
[140] Ibid., 258.
[141] Ibid., 241.
[142] Ibid., 258.
[143] Torkel Opsahl and Vojin Dimitrijevic, "Article 29 and 30," in Alfreðsson and Eide (eds.), *The Universal Declaration of Human Rights*, 633.

society and to ensure that social harmony can be maintained. The third makes it clear that humanity as a whole has some interests that must at times override the rights of any particular individual or country.[144]

The article goes further away from individualism when it adds the word *alone* to the first paragraph: "Everyone has duties to the community in which alone the free and full development of his personality is possible."[145] This amounts, as Morsink explains,

> to the announcement of an organic connection between the individual and the community to which he or she owes duties, not unlike Confucius would have had it . . . [As such, it] may well be the most important single word in the entire document, for it helps us answer the charge that the rights set forth in the Declaration create egotistic individuals who are not closely tied to their respective communities . . . solidarity and mutuality [are a] . . . part of the possession of every human right.[146]

Many delegates emphasized the importance of duties in the debates that yielded the document. Brazil's De Athayde, for instance, told the Third Committee (covering social, humanitarian, and cultural affairs), which reviewed the draft prepared by the Commission, "It was impossible to draw up a declaration of rights without proclaiming the duties implicit in the concept of freedom which made it possible to set up a peaceful and democratic society. Article 27 [which later became Article 29] was of great importance because without such a provision all freedom might lead to anarchy and tyranny." Similarly, the Netherlands' Beaufort observed that "the debate on Article 27 [29] had shown that the rights of the individual were not absolute. It was necessary to define the restrictions demanded by respect for the rights of other individuals and of different social groups."[147]

Duties are also a common part of regional documents, supporting their importance in the UDHR. Part I of the ACHPR is entitled "Rights and Duties." A whole chapter (2) is dedicated to them.[148] Article 6 of the AHRD states that "The enjoyment of human rights and fundamental freedoms must be balanced with the performance of corresponding duties as every person has responsibilities to all other individuals, the community and the society where

---

[144] Opsahl and Dimitrijevic, "Article 29 and 30," 634.
[145] UN General Assembly, *Universal Declaration of Human Rights.*
[146] Morsink, *The Universal Declaration of Human Rights*, 246 and 248.
[147] Both quoted in Morsink, *The Universal Declaration of Human Rights*, 249.
[148] Organization of African Unity, *African Charter on Human and Peoples' Rights* ("Banjul Charter").

one lives."[149] Duties also receive recognition in the ACHR, which declares that (Article 32.1) "Every person has responsibilities to his family, his community, and mankind" and (32.2) "The rights of each person are limited by the rights of others, by the security of all, and by the just demands of the general welfare, in a democratic society."[150] Even the ECHR makes clear (10.2) that the exercise of rights "since it carries with it duties and responsibilities, may be subject to such formalities, conditions, restrictions or penalties as are prescribed by law and are necessary ... in the interests of national security ... the prevention of disorder or crime, for the protection of health or morals ..."[151]

The UDHR is often presented as if its rights were absolute and unqualified, but Torkel Opsahl and Vojin Dimitrijevic argue that the document's limitations were "crucial" and note, "While the UDHR saves limitations to the end ... they turn up in the front line in all the conventions and in the practice of the implementation bodies."[152]

LEGAL NOT MORAL COMMITMENTS

The flexibility that the UDHR and subsequent human rights agreements provide for each society to prioritize and interpret human rights commitments show that the authors of these documents do not presume a uniform moral matrix across countries. While they seek to promote minimum universal standards throughout the world, they do not uphold one universal value system. As such, the agreements that are legal documents, such as the International Covenant on Civil and Political Rights and the International Covenant on Economic, Social and Cultural Rights, only need to be fulfilled; they are not binding commitments to a particular way of life. The UDHR is not legally binding at all, as it was a UN resolution not a treaty; it only has power from its moral weight, and as such can only have influence through popular support.

---

[149] Association of Southeast Asian Nations (ASEAN), ASEAN *Human Rights Declaration.*

[150] Organization of American States (OAS), American Convention on Human Rights, "Pact of San Jose, Costa Rica," November 22, 1969, available at: www.oas.org/dil/treaties_B-32_ American_Convention_on_Human_Rights.htm.

[151] Council of Europe, *European Convention for the Protection of Human Rights and Fundamental Freedoms, as amended by Protocols Nos. 11 and 14,* November 4, 1950, ETS 5, available at: www.hrcr.org/docs/Eur_Convention/euroconv3.html.

[152] Opsahl and Dimitrijevic, "Article 29 and 30," 642.

TABLE 2.1 *Comparing traditional, Western universalist, and UDHR views of human rights*[153]

Attitudes toward	Traditional view (thick societies)	Western universalist view (thin societies)	The UDHR
Foundations	Depends on context; often just positive law	Natural rights	Various; agree to disagree
Treaties	Legal commitments	Moral commitments	Minimal standards
Flexibility of implementation	Extensive	Limited	Extensive
Duties	Important; linked to rights	Not emphasized	Important; balanced to some extent with rights
Role of the state	Important but limited	Very important	Needed; does not act alone
Social institutions	Foundational and crucial	Secondary; not highly appreciated	Primary
Traditions	To be cherished and protected; part of identity	To be minimized or adapted to new norms	To be respected
Religion	Very important; part of identity; basis for human dignity	Not important; only freedom of conscience warrants protection	Important; in need of protection
Differences across cultures	Natural; essential	Limited	Natural; to be expected and respected
Conflicting rights	Common; different contexts, different weighting	Not so common because hierarchy of values	To be expected
Individual relationship with society	Interdependent with others; collaboration	Autonomous of society; consumption	Part of society; connection

Table 2.1 compares how thick societies, which make up the great majority outside the West and include religious groups within the West; thin societies, which are mainly the liberal modernist West; and the Declaration advance

---

[153] I created this typology to show how the thick/thin society lens, explored in Chapter 4, advances our understanding of human rights promotion. It demonstrates the UDHR's potential as a flexible middle way.

human rights. As discussed above, the UDHR tilts toward a thick conception of society and a limited role for the state and legal regime in enforcing human rights rules. This is clear from the differing attitudes towards the treaties, implementation, role of the state, traditions, religion, and so forth. If anything, culture and social institutions are seen as important launching pads for human rights protection and promotion.

Human rights obligations are best understood as binding on states not because they flow from a particular philosophy, belief system, etc. but because they are rooted in positive (human-made) law. They are legal commitments resulting from the treaties that have been ratified and do not presume any particular ordering of rights, except for the few primary rights mentioned earlier; any particular way of implementing the rights; or any particular lifestyle.[154] On the contrary, they are designed to be a minimum standard that can be flexibly interpreted and implemented across cultures.[155]

As Zwart writes in a *Human Rights Quarterly* article,

> All contracting states parties, regardless of their philosophical views on human rights, have decided to put their eggs in the treaty mechanism basket ... By ratifying these treaties, Western states also have accepted that law rather than the accomplishments of the Enlightenment, serve as the basis of human rights obligations. Human rights treaties are neither Western nor Eastern, neither Northern nor Southern. Instead, states parties must live up to the obligations to which they have committed themselves, nothing more, and nothing less.[156]

Of course, states can refuse to sign or even opt out of agreements that they have previously agreed to (because human rights are positive not natural law). The United States, for instance, has never ratified the International Covenant on Economic, Social and Cultural Rights (ICESCR), one of the two most important follow-on agreements to the UDHR, even though 164 other countries have.[157] Nor has it ratified the Convention on the Elimination of all Forms of Discrimination against Women (CEDAW) even though all but

---

[154] Twining, *General Jurisprudence*, 180.

[155] Jerome Shestack, "The Philosophic Foundations of Human Rights," *Human Rights Quarterly* 20, no. 2 (May 1998): 209. Zwart, "Using Local Culture to Further the Implementation of International Human Rights," 552.

[156] Zwart, "Using Local Culture to Further the Implementation of International Human Rights," 552.

[157] The US signed the ICESCR in 1977. United Nations Treaty Collection, "Chapter IV: Human Rights, 3. International Covenant on Economic, Social and Cultural Rights," Status, accessed on August 24, 2015, https://treaties.un.org/pages/viewdetails.aspx?chapter=4&lang=en&mtdsg_no=iv-3&src=treaty.

8 UN member countries – 189 in all – have.[158] A number of African countries
have threatened to leave the Rome Statute, which established the International Criminal Court, because of what they perceive as bias in its functioning. All cases as of 2015 were against Africans. Many countries commit to treaties
but with reservations. Over fifty have ratified CEDAW but with certain declarations, reservations, and objections.[159] However, the strong international
consensus on the importance of human rights – whatever the disagreements
over implementation – provide ample external and internal pressure on the
great majority of countries to join and, at least at the rhetorical level, support
major human rights treaties. Virtually all countries accept the authority of the
UDHR. As of mid-2015, an average of 88 percent (175 out of 197) had ratified
the six core international human rights treaties (which cover civil and political
rights; economic, social, and cultural rights; racial discrimination; women;
torture; and children).[160] As such, even states that have often showed little
regard for human rights – such as Syria – sign, ratify, and accede to many
agreements and do their best to show the world that they are actually following
them – even if the reality is substantially different.[161]

Despite these qualifications and reservations, many Western universalists
believe that the international agreements bind signatories to a number of
prescribed thin society values, as will be explored in Chapter 5. The strong
emphasis on the individual in contemporary Western thought – especially
pronounced since the 1960s – accentuates a thin society perspective and leads
to an underemphasis on the social context, the role of institutions, and the
relationship between the rights articulated in the original Declaration. This
has significantly contributed to the differing perceptions on implementation
that exist between Western governments and human rights organizations that
focus on individual rights and the Southern and religious (thick society)
preference for broader concerns involving the needs of community and
religion. These perceptions will be discussed at length in Chapters 6 and 7.[162]

[158] The US signed the CEDAW in 1980. United Nations Treaty Collection, "Chapter IV: Human
Rights, 8. Convention on the Elimination of All Forms of Discrimination against Women,"
Status, accessed on August 24, 2015, https://treaties.un.org/Pages/ViewDetails.aspx?src=
TREATY&mtdsg_no=IV-8&chapter=4&lang=en.
[159] United Nations Treaty Collection, "Chapter IV: Human Rights, 3. International Covenant on
Economic, Social and Cultural Rights," Status, accessed on August 24, 2015.
[160] Jack Donnelly, "The Relative Universality of Human Rights," *Human Rights Quarterly* 29,
no. 2 (May 2007): 288. Ratification data is available at http://indicators.ohchr.org/.
[161] University of Minnesota, Human Rights Library, "Ratification of International Human Rights
Treaties – Syria," accessed on August 24, 2015, www1.umn.edu/humanrts/research/ratification-
syria.html.
[162] Glendon, *A World Made New*, xix–xx and 228–230.

Part of the problem is that the history of how the UDHR was developed and the intention of its drafters is not widely known. There was a large gap between when it was written and passed by the United Nations (1947–48) and when it started to be actively used by the human rights movement in the late 1960s. The architects of the Declaration, who came from all over the world, passed from the scene before the UDHR's major promoters, which came from only one part of the world, were firmly established. Glendon describes how major human rights organizations presume an understanding of rights that stems from the American judicial rights revolution of the 1950s and 1960s. She argues,

> The Declaration itself began to be widely, almost universally, read in the way that Americans read the Bill of Rights, that is, as a string of essentially separate guarantees. Alas, that misreading of the Declaration not only distorts its sense, but facilitates its misuse.[163]

The human rights field is limited in its current orientation by a discourse shaped by Western values and institutions. Yet the enduring relevance of the UDHR demonstrates that there is potential for a return to consensus on human rights, if actors move toward a flexible universalism that reflects differences among societies. Understanding these differences – and the role of different moral matrices in producing them – is the subject of the next chapter.

[163] Glendon and Abrams, "Reflections on the UDHR."

3

Cultural Psychology's Contribution

If one were to offer men to choose out of all the customs in the world such as seemed to them the best, they would examine the whole number, and end by preferring their own; so convinced are they that their own usages far surpass those of all others.[1]
                                        – Herodotus

Although cultural relativism is often discussed in the human rights field, it has rarely been used as an explanatory construct for differences in how people think, how societies organize themselves, and how values might be ordered differently across cultures. Yet, as the two case studies will show, such differences can be quite stark, both between thick communities within thin society Western countries and between thick societies in the West and thin societies in the South. There are, for instance, strong differences in opinion across cultures with regard to the role of women in society, parent–child relationships, religion and schooling, the appropriate balance between social cohesion and individual rights, and what makes for a legitimate government.[2]

Cultural psychology offers a unique way to assess the legitimacy of such differences, especially when they lead to vastly different interpretations of the role and weighting of various human rights. Even though humanity is understood to have a common underlying framework or grammar of morality, making some actions or goals wrong regardless of context, some customs or sociopolitical systems may simply be different – a product of another history,

---

[1] Herodotus, *The Histories of Herodotus*, translated by George Rawlinson (New York, NY: Digireads, 2009), Book III, chapter 38, page 121.
[2] For a more complete list of contested practices within Western countries, see Richard Shweder, Martha Minow, and Hazel Rose Markus, "Engaging Cultural Differences," in Shweder, Minow, and Markus (eds.), *Engaging Cultural Differences: The Multicultural Challenge in Liberal Democracies* (New York, NY: Russell Sage Foundation, 2002), 2–3.

environment, and set of values.[3] Better understanding where to draw the line between these is essential to resolving many seemingly unresolvable debates within the field – and to revitalizing the Universal Declaration's original role as a unifying bridge across both thick and thin societies.

Cultural psychology research[4] offers both a novel way to interpret cultural differences and to reexamine the long-standing universality–relativity debate. It suggests, first, that there are real and substantial differences in human cognition – and thus what people innately value. Second, new research suggests that Westerners are the real outliers. Third, cultural psychology provides a framework that can be used to undertake empirical research on how different cultures prioritize and interpret human rights, adding a scientific basis to debates over human rights. Recent studies suggest that most psychologists – and other social scientists, especially economists[5] – assume cognition, perception, and behavior are universal.[6] A 2008 survey of the top six psychology journals, for instance, indicated that more than 96 percent of the subjects used in psychological tests between 2003 and 2007 were Westerners, even though these countries made up only one-eighth of the world population.[7] Conclusions were assumed to reveal traits common to all humans.

These assumptions result in a Platonic view of human nature that cannot but influence how other cultures are perceived. The differences that individuals exhibit – differences in religion, rituals, values, meanings, knowledge, institutions, technologies, contexts – are assumed to be incidental or secondary "noise" to the thinking that goes on within their head.[8] When persons

---

[3]   See, for instance, Jonathan Haidt, *Righteous Mind: Why Good People Are Divided by Politics and Religion* (New York, NY: Pantheon Books, 2012).

[4]   Anna Wierzbicka argues that "it is impossible for a human being to study anything . . . from a totally extra-cultural point of view . . . we are inevitably guided by certain principles and certain ideals which we know are not necessarily shared by the entire human race." Wierzbicka, *Cross-Cultural Pragmatics: The Semantics of Human Interaction* (Berlin: Mouton de Gruyler, 1991), 9.

[5]   Ethan Watters, "We Aren't the World," *Pacific Standard*, March/April 2013, www.psmag.com/books-and-culture/joe-henrich-weird-ultimatum-game-shaking-up-psychology-economics-53135.

[6]   The main exceptions are historians and philosophers of science who have raised the possibilities that at least ancient Greek and Chinese scientists and philosophers were different. Richard Nisbett and Takahiko Masuda, "Culture and Point of View," *Proceedings of the National Academy of Sciences* 100, no. 19 (September 16, 2003): 11163.

[7]   Joseph Henrich, Steven Heine, and Ara Norenzayan, "The Weirdest People in the World?," *Behavioral and Brain Sciences* 33, no. 2–3 (June 2010): 63.

[8]   Shweder, "Cultural Psychology – What Is It?," in James Stigler, Schweder, and Gilbert Herdt (eds.), *Cultural Psychology: Essays on Comparative Human Development* (Cambridge: Cambridge University Press, 1990), 4–5; Alan Page Fiske, Shinobu Kitayama, Hazel Rose

perform badly according to the standards of a particular culture or subculture – such as psychological tests and tasks – either they (or their minds) are assumed to be less than fully developed or the standards are assumed to have baffled or bewildered them.[9] Given that it sets the terms for its own assessment, this view of humankind is difficult to change or expand.[10]

PSYCHOLOGICAL PROCESSES AND CULTURAL DIFFERENCES

Challenging these assumptions about the universality of human experience, cultural psychology asserts that even though everyone starts with the same core psychological capacities and propensities, "'basic' psychological processes depend substantially on cultural meanings and practices," as Alan Page Fiske, Shinobu Kitayama, Hazel Markus, and Richard Nisbett explain[11] in the fourth edition of the *Handbook of Social Psychology*, the standard reference work in the field.[12]

Based on an understanding that "culture and psyche make each other up,"[13] cultural psychology is, according to Richard Shweder,

> the study of the way cultural traditions and social practices regulate, express, and transform the human psyche, resulting less in psychic unity for human-kind than in ethnic divergences in mind, self, and emotion ... It does not presume the premise of psychic unity, that the fundamentals of the mental life are by nature fixed, universal, abstract, and interior ... Psyche and culture are thus seamlessly interconnected. A person's psychic organization is largely made possible by, and expressive of, a conception of itself, society, and nature.[14]

Markus, and Richard Nisbett, "The Cultural Matrix of Social Psychology," in Susan Fiske, Daniel Gilbert, and Gardner Lindzey (eds.), *The Handbook of Social Psychology*, Volume 2, 4th ed. (New York, NY: McGraw-Hill, 1998), 915–919.
9   Shweder, "Cultural Psychology – What Is It?," 11; Fiske, Kitayama, et al. "The Cultural Matrix of Social Psychology," 915–919.
10   Shweder, "Cultural Psychology – What Is It?," 6; Fiske, Kitayama, et al. "The Cultural Matrix of Social Psychology," 915–919.
11   Fiske, Kitayama, et al. "The Cultural Matrix of Social Psychology," 915–916.
12   Whereas cultural psychology looks at the way cultural traditions and social practices affect the mind, social psychology examines how people's thoughts, feelings, and behaviors are influenced by the actual, imagined, or implied presence of others. There is some overlap, and the two fields inform each other.
13   Shweder, "Cultural Psychology – What Is It?," 1–43; Fiske, Kitayama, et al. "The Cultural Matrix of Social Psychology," 915–919.
14   Shweder, "Cultural Psychology – What Is It?," 1, 22, and 26.

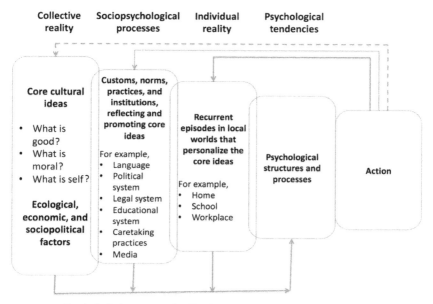

FIGURE 3.1 Psychological process and cultural content
Source: Fiske, Kitayama, et al., "The Cultural Matrix of Social Psychology," 918

Psychological processes, in turn, generate and transform cultural processes, shaping the very social institutions, practices, and meanings that will in turn influence them (see Figure 3.1).[15] The cycle operates in such a way as to intensify its unique features: "the environments influence perception and the resulting perceptual preferences prompt people to produce different environments."[16] As such, the field of cultural psychology combines anthropology's focus on context with psychology's focus on mental processes.[17]

In some ways, this is a return to an older way of thinking. When the modern social sciences began to take shape in the nineteenth century, most scholars stressed that the "human psyche is a product of the social (and, as we would now say, cultural) milieu in which it develops and functions."[18] But the social sciences have largely neglected to develop the insights of these earlier thinkers, especially since the 1960s. American researchers tend to be biased

---

[15] Shweder, "Cultural Psychology – What Is It?," 1–43; Fiske, Kitayama, et al. "The Cultural Matrix of Social Psychology," 916.
[16] Nisbett and Masuda, "Culture and Point of View," 11170.
[17] Haidt, *Righteous Mind*, 99.
[18] Fiske, Kitayama, et al. "The Cultural Matrix of Social Psychology," 917.

against the role of groups, discussing forms of social influence over individuals with derogatory labels such as conformity, groupthink, and obedience.[19]

There is now evidence that even though the mind starts with a predisposition toward a limited number of moral frameworks (see following), it molds itself to its cultural environment far more than previously thought. As a result, the largest impact culture has on people is not in the visible things they do – how they eat, what rituals they follow, what their moral beliefs are, and so on – but in how it shapes their most fundamental thinking and perception.[20] As the article in the *Handbook of Social Psychology* explains, "Humans have evolved unique psychological capacities and propensities to take adaptive advantage of cultures, but in the course of development these proclivities also make their psyches dependent on their own particular cultures."[21]

Joseph Henrich goes one step further, pointing out that such processes may be a prerequisite for the development of sophisticated civilizations, as the amount of knowledge in any culture is far greater than any individual could ever learn on their own. People tap their culture's storehouse of knowledge simply by unconsciously mimicking the ways of behaving and thinking of those around them. Their taboos and value systems are thus more a product of their cultural environments than their own calculations.[22]

As a result, influenced by distinctive ecologies, economies, social structures, and histories, the way brains perceive and analyze their environments differs substantially across cultures.[23] Richard Nisbett, Kaiping Peng, Icheol Choi, and Ara Norenzayan explain, "It should not be surprising if it turned out to be the case that members of markedly different cultures, socialized from birth into different world views and habits of thought, might differ even more dramatically in their cognitive processes."[24]

There are differences in a wide range of cognitive processes. Research has, for instance, found wide cultural differences in visual perception, spatial reasoning, induction, memory, how we perceive the motivations of others,

---

[19] Ibid., 918–919.
[20] Ethan Watters, "We Aren't the World."
[21] Fiske, Kitayama, et al., "The Cultural Matrix of Social Psychology," 915–916.
[22] Ethan Watters, "We Aren't the World."
[23] No one knows for sure. A few have speculated. See, for instance, Richard Nisbett, *The Geography of Thought: How Asians and Westerners Think Differently ... and Why* (New York, NY: The Free Press, 2003), 29–45.
[24] Richard Nisbett, Kaiping Peng, Incheol Choi, and Ara Norenzayan, "Culture and Systems of Thought: Holistic vs. Analytic Cognition," *Psychological Review* 108, no. 2 (April 2001): 291.

categorization, moral reasoning, the boundaries between the self and others, and many other areas.[25]

DIFFERENT CULTURES, DIFFERENT MORAL MATRICES

Cultural psychology shows that different cultures – as well as different groups within societies – develop different moral matrices. This is not to say that all possible moral frameworks are possible or that all societies have equally good moral codes. Some customs – such as human sacrifice – are undesirable and should obviously be considered unacceptable in any society (see later). But, as flexible universalists argue, moral diversity within and across countries ought to be considered natural, a normal product of human evolution. This diversity should include the weight given to one set of rights over another or the degree to which obligation supersedes personal freedom. Indeed, societies that limit such diversity or that try to reduce all of morality to a single principle – moral monism – risk both becoming unattractive to large numbers of people and reducing their competitiveness versus other more morally pluralistic societies.[26]

People are born with a fixed set of "moral receptors,"[27] whose volumes are turned up or down depending on their cultures. As Jonathan Haidt, a moral psychologist researching complex social systems at New York University, describes:

> Our minds have the potential to become righteous about many different concerns, and only a few of these concerns are activated during childhood. Other potential concerns are left undeveloped and unconnected to the web of shared meanings and values that become our adult moral matrix.[28]

Environments shape the volume of these receptors from birth, beginning quite literally in the crib. For example, while American and Northern European parents train their babies to sleep in their own bed or even room – setting up a pattern by which they will repeatedly encourage independence throughout childhood – most parents elsewhere sleep with their babies in the same bed, and act in ways that emphasize interdependence throughout childhood. While Western parents constantly ask their children to make their

---

[25] Henrich, Heine, and Norenzayan, "The Weirdest People in the World?," 36–37; Nisbett and Masuda, "Culture and Point of View," 11163–11170; Nisbett, *The Geography of Thought*, xix and 44–45; and Watters, "We Aren't the World."

[26] Haidt, *The Righteous Mind*, 113.

[27] Ibid., 184.

[28] Ibid., 109.

own decisions and require them to do things on their own, other parents often make decisions for their children and are more likely (in the mother's case) to accompany their children.[29]

Moral expectations are communicated through routine family, school, and social life practices including eating, sleeping, possessing objects, and distributing resources (and reinforced through advertising, television, social media, and other media). They are further conveyed through the commands, threats, sanctions, explanations, justifications, and excuses necessary to maintain these routine practices. In the end,

> children's emerging moral understandings are the product of continuous participation in social practices (the mundane rituals of everyday life), and those socially produced and reproduced understandings are the grounding for later attempts reflectively or self-consciously to reconstruct their own moral code.[30]

Such training so influences moral development that between substantially different cultures, such as American and Indian, five-year-olds show limited correlation in their judgments of right and wrong. For instance, while both Oriya (a mostly Hindu ethnic group in eastern India) and American five-year olds agree that it is wrong to break a promise or kick a harmless animal, the former think it is wrong to eat beef or use one's father's first name when addressing him while the latter think it is wrong to cane a naughty child or open a letter sent to one's teenager.[31] "Human infants come into the world possessing a complex emotional keyboard; yet as they become Eskimo, Balinese, or Oriya only some keys get played."[32]

As Shweder puts it, "there is no homogenous 'backcloth' to our world. We are multiple from the start."[33] As a result, different societies – and different groups within societies – emphasize different combinations of moral goods.[34]

---

[29] Nisbett, *The Geography of Thought*, 57–61.

[30] Shweder and Nancy Much, "Determinations of Meaning: Discourse and Moral Socialization," in Shweder, *Thinking through Cultures: Expeditions in Cultural Psychology* (Cambridge, MA: Harvard University Press, 1991), 191.

[31] Shweder and Much, "Determinations of Meaning," 190; Nisbett, *The Geography of Thought*, 57–61; Markus and Conner, *Clash!*, xix.

[32] Shweder, *Thinking through Cultures*, 7; Nisbett, *The Geography of Thought*, 57–61; Markus and Conner, *Clash!*, xix.

[33] Shweder, *Thinking through Cultures*, 5.

[34] He explains that, "Different cultural traditions try to promote human dignity by specializing in (and perhaps even exaggerating) different ratios of moral goods. Consequently, they moralize about the world in somewhat different ways and try to construct the social order as a moral order in somewhat different terms." Shweder, Nancy Much, Manamohan Mahapatra, and Lawrence Park, "The 'Big Three' of Morality (Autonomy, Community, and Divinity) and the

Further, there is a clear distinction between what Roy D'Andrade calls "institutionalized values" (or "normative or social values"), which people believe "should be valued in enacting some role or performing in some group," and personal values. Everyone recognizes that those in the military, for instance, should uphold certain institutionalized values – such as obedience, respect for rank, courage, and patriotism – no matter what their personal values are. Similarly, most people understand that their personal preferences (e.g., self-interest) may often stray from societal preferences (e.g., altruism) but that it would be problematic if every person catered only to personal preferences. Indeed, conflict over how to balance social obligations with personal goals is a challenge for people everywhere.[35]

The biggest difference among moral matrices across groups involves the balance between the needs of individuals and the needs of communities. Whereas thick sociocentric communities such as those in East Asia place the interest of groups and institutions first, individualistic thin societies such as those in Europe and North America place individuals at the center, with society organized toward personal fulfillment.[36]

MAPPING MORAL DIVERSITY

Cultural psychologists have developed a number of frameworks to map and analyze moral diversity – operating with an understanding that all humans share a basic moral sensibility, if not identical emphases. For instance, Haidt believes evolution has yielded six moral receptors – much like it has yielded five different taste sensors on the tongue with a "hard-wired" connection with the brain[37] – which all people share. These are: care/harm; liberty/oppression; fairness/cheating; loyalty/betrayal; authority/subversion; and sanctity/degradation. Just as childhood socialization in a particular culture shapes each person's taste buds, it also shapes our moral matrices. And, just as our taste buds limit what any particular cuisine might look like – it cannot, for instance, be based

'Big Three' Explanations of Suffering," in Allan Brandt and Paul Rozin (eds.), *Morality and Health* (New York, NY: Routledge, 1997), 141.

[35] Roy D'Andrade, *A Study of Personal and Cultural Values: American, Japanese, Vietnamese* (New York, NY: Palgrave Macmillan, 2008), 43, 121, and 137.

[36] Hazel Rose Markus and Shinobu Kitayama, "Culture and the Self: Implications for Cognition, Emotion, and Motivation," *Psychological Review* 98, no. 2 (1991): 224–253.

[37] The five taste categories are salty, bitter, sour, sweet, and umami. See Robert Barretto et al., "The Neural Representation of Taste Quality at the Periphery," *Nature* 517 (January 15, 2015): 373–376, www.nature.com/nature/journal/v517/n7534/full/nature13873.html.

on tree bark or primarily bitter flavors – human mores are limited to how these six moral receptors are calibrated.[38]

In another framework, Alan Fiske, a professor of anthropology at UCLA, argues that all social relationships, duties, and moral responsibilities can be classified according to four models: communal sharing, authority ranking, equality matching, and market pricing.[39] These form the basis, Fiske says, of every aspect of social activity, "from the exchange of goods and services to the organization of work and the social meaning of objects, land, and time. They organize ideas about social justice, moral judgment, political ideology, religious observance, and social conflict." Different combinations of the four models produce different cultures.[40]

Shweder diverges from these two frameworks and develops a theory based on research in India showing that people have three moral clusters of conceptually linked themes – the ethics of autonomy, community, and divinity.[41] Shweder's more elemental framework is the most helpful for navigating human rights debates regarding universality and relativity because its three ethics illuminate the bases on which cultural disputes arise in an easy to understand fashion.

The autonomy ethic emphasizes that individuals are highly independent and thus have the right to pursue their personal preferences as they see fit, without much outside interference. This ethic stresses moral concepts such as rights, harm, liberty, and justice to help regulate behavior and organize society. The majority cultures in Europe and especially the United States heavily stress this ethic.

The community ethic emphasizes that people are part of larger entities such as families, clans, ethnic groups, religions, and nations, which have their own identity, standing, history, and reputation to be safeguarded. Individuals have important roles and obligations stemming from their membership in

---

[38]   Haidt, *The Righteous Mind*, 113–114, 184, and 302.
[39]   Alan Page Fiske, "The Four Elementary Forms of Sociality: Framework for a Unified Theory of Social Relations," *Psychological Review* 99, no. 4 (1992): 689–723.
[40]   Meg Sullivan, "Four Systems to Describe Human Motives," *UCLA College Report* Volume 3 (Winter 2005), www.sscnet.ucla.edu/anthro/faculty/fiske/pubs/UCLA_College_Report_4_ Systems_2005.pdf. The Chinese scholar Kwang-Kuo Hwang developed his own model of four kinds of interpersonal ties – expressive ties, mixed ties, instrumental ties, and vertical ties – that roughly corresponds to Fiske's four elementary forms of social behavior. He argues that the Western ideal of individualism emphasizes and exaggerates market pricing and instrumental ties, neglecting or ignoring the others. Hwang, *Foundations of Chinese Psychology: Confucian Social Relations* (New York: Springer, 2012), xiv and 21–40.
[41]   Haidt, *The Righteous Mind*, 99; Shweder, Much, et al., "The 'Big Three' of Morality (Autonomy, Community, and Divinity) and the 'Big Three' Explanations of Suffering," 138.

these groups. This ethic stresses moral concepts such as duty, hierarchy, interdependency, respect, reputation, and patriotism. Societies that make it a strong part of their moral matrices – such as those in East Asia – naturally see highly individualistic societies as promoting behaviors that weaken the social fabric and destroy important social institutions on which order depends.

The divinity ethic emphasizes the role of the divine and the relationship of people to it. Individuals are spiritual entities connected to a sacred order, and they must behave in ways that responsibly uphold a legacy that is elevated and divine. Their bodies play a role in this order and should not be treated as a playground. This ethic, which plays an important role in the Middle East and South Asia and within religious communities in the West, stresses moral concepts such as sanctity and sin, purity and pollution, and elevation and degradation; and it aims to protect the soul, spirit, spiritual aspects of human activity, and nature from debasement. In such societies, Western culture may be perceived as libertinism, hedonism, and a celebration of humanity's baser instincts.[42]

Although "cognized reality is incomplete if described from any one point of view,"[43] cultures cannot equally appreciate all three moral "frames" all of the time, forcing them to specialize.[44] Whereas in the United States individualism dominates discourse, in East Asia the community ethic is strongest, and in the Middle East the divinity ethic is strongest. In Hindu society and in Africa, the community and divinity discourses are both prioritized over the individual.

For religious people within the West, the divinity ethic is the strongest, but its influence is compromised considerably by the surrounding culture's bias toward individual fulfillment.[45] Through church attendance and other group activities, community plays an important role in the lives of adherents, but beliefs and practices have been to some extent "debased" by the growing individualism in the broader society.[46] Prosperity preachers, self-esteem gurus, and therapeutic spiritual leaders have thrived while institutional Christianity has lost its influence.[47] Whereas once religion constrained and balanced

---

[42] Haidt, *The Righteous Mind*, 99–100; Shweder, Much, et al., "The 'Big Three' of Morality (Autonomy, Community, and Divinity) and the 'Big Three' Explanations of Suffering," 138.

[43] Shweder, Much, et al., "The 'Big Three' of Morality (Autonomy, Community, and Divinity) and the 'Big Three' Explanations of Suffering," 141; Fiske, Kitayama, et al. "The Cultural Matrix of Social Psychology," 915–919.

[44] Fiske, Kitayama, et al. "The Cultural Matrix of Social Psychology," 943.

[45] Ross Douthat, *Bad Religion: How We Became a Nation of Heretics* (New York, NY: Free Press, 2012), 62–64, 77, and 88.

[46] Ibid., 1–16.

[47] Ibid., 59–65, 104–105, and 132–135.

individual choice, now the latter runs rabid in what has become "a nation of heretics" (to use the term of a 2012 book describing the process).[48]

Shweder's three themes can be thought of as coexisting moral discourses that work together on multiple planes simultaneously. They offer alternative solutions to the practical problems individuals face and societies must deal with. It is "often advantageous to have more than one discourse for interpreting a situation or solving a problem."[49]

THE PERSISTENCE OF MORAL MATRICES

Differences between cultures can stay in place for hundreds of generations because, as Nisbett describes in his book, *The Geography of Thought*, "Each of these orientations ... is a self-reinforcing, homeostatic system. The social practices promote the worldviews; the worldviews dictate the appropriate thought processes; and the thought processes both justify the worldviews and support the social practices."[50]

Contemporary differences between the West and East, for instance, parallel differences in ancient times. As Nisbett, Peng, Choi, and Norenzayan write, the social and cognitive differences that scholars have found in ancient China and Greece are remarkably similar to those among contemporary peoples. And such differences are both "quantitatively very large and even qualitatively distinct."[51]

The philosophies and worldviews of the ancient Greeks and Chinese were remarkably different, as were their social structures and conceptions of themselves. Whereas the Greeks emphasized personal agency and individual identity, the Chinese emphasized collective agency, the individual's prescribed roles in a larger grouping, and living in harmony with others. Whereas the Greeks treasured the ability to debate and sought to control their environments, the Chinese treasured family and social ties and self-control. Whereas Ionic philosophy emphasized understanding the fundamental nature of the world, Confucianism emphasized a system of elaborate obligations between emperor and subject, parent and child, husband and wife, and so on.[52]

Although modernization and rising incomes are accompanied by a predictable shift in beliefs and values – with priorities moving from an overwhelming

[48] Ibid., 1–16.
[49] Shweder, Much, et al., "The 'Big Three' of Morality (Autonomy, Community, and Divinity) and the 'Big Three' Explanations of Suffering," 140–141.
[50] Nisbett, *The Geography of Thought*, xx.
[51] Nisbett, Peng, et al., "Culture and Systems of Thought," 292.
[52] Nisbett, *The Geography of Thought*, 1–28.

emphasis on economic and physical security to an emphasis on subjective well-being, self-expression, participation in decision making, and a relatively trusting and tolerant outlook – it does not produce convergence. As the World Values Survey, a global research project that has conducted representative national surveys in almost 100 countries, shows, cultural change is path dependent; a society's cultural heritage determines how its values evolve on the global cultural map. Distinctive clusters of countries includes those from Protestant Europe, Catholic Europe, ex-communist Europe, the English-speaking states, Latin America, South Asia, the Islamic world, East Asia, and Africa.[53]

Even though Japan has had a capitalist economy for well over a century and a stable democracy for three generations, there are "numberless signs that Japan has changed little in many social respects and we find large differences between the way Japanese and Westerners perceive the world and think about it."[54] Similarly, although Chinese are becoming more individualistic and Africans less patriarchal as their countries develop, their cultures are still notably different than those in the West. A sophisticated statistical analysis of survey data collected in China and Taiwan, for instance, shows that despite significant economic development, democratization (in the case of Taiwan), institutional transformation, and social change, cultural attitudes toward authority remain unchanged. Due to the influence of traditional culture, Chinese are more trustful of and less confrontational toward authority than Westerners, and their cultural conception of democracy remains fundamentally different. While Westerners define democracy in procedural terms and emphasize the role of public participation and regular elections, Chinese tend to see it as "guardianship" and emphasize the qualifications and performance of rulers.[55]

This reflects broader dynamics across the region. Whereas in the West, democratic movements have focused on promoting rights and liberating people from authoritarian government, and in Latin America and Africa, they

[53] Ronald Inglehart and Christian Welzel, "How Development Leads to Democracy: What We Know about Modernization," *Foreign Affairs* 88, no. 2 (March/April 2009): 40–41. As Ronald Inglehart, the director of the World Values Survey, and Wayne Baker conclude, "The broad cultural heritage of a society … leaves an imprint on values that endures despite modernization." Ronald Inglehart and Wayne Baker, "Modernization, Cultural Change, and the Persistence of Traditional Values," *American Sociological Review* 65, no. 1 (February 2000): 19.
[54] Nisbett, *The Geography of Thought*, 222–223.
[55] Tianjian Shi, *The Cultural Logic of Politics in Mainland China and Taiwan* (Cambridge: Cambridge University Press, 2014), 197–200.

have focused on particularistic ethnic and class demands, in East Asia, they have positioned themselves as "redeemers of the state and as vessels of a *shared* national purpose," reflecting different histories and cultures.[56] There is an overarching "Asian Governance Model" based on "a strong state tradition embedded in social accountability pressures" that operates whether a country is authoritarian or democratic, ensuring much greater continuity across regime types than is typical elsewhere[57] (or that Western political theory, which generally does not recognize such overarching societal dynamics, allows for). Only six of the sixteen countries in East and Southeast Asia are functioning democracies, a significantly lower rate than the global average; many of the nondemocracies are among the world's most resilient authoritarian regimes.[58]

In general, as Bruce Gilley writes in *The Nature of Asian Politics*, in East Asia,

> rights claims have been taken not as absolute values but as political values that must compete against others and should never be put above politics. If liberalism is an ideology that, in Crick's words, wishes to "honour the fruit but not the tree," in [East] Asia, preserving and sustaining the tree itself has remained paramount.[59]

These differences in how people think can produce conflicts over morality that persist over thousands of years, as we shall see later in the circumcision case. Even if everything on the surface about a place has changed – its technology, its economy, its level of development – deeply rooted cultural traits may not. Modernity and modernization are not necessarily synonymous.

Descriptive fieldwork from around the world has demonstrated that moral judgments are ubiquitous in human groups, and that when people make a moral judgment (such as "circumcision is an outrage" or "abortion is evil"), "they themselves believe there are matters of objective fact to which their judgment refers and that they are making a truthful claim about some impersonal or independently existing domain of moral reality."[60] As Ernest Gellner,

---

[56] Bruce Gilley, *The Nature of Asian Politics* (Cambridge: Cambridge University Press, 2014), 104–105.

[57] Ibid., 99.

[58] Doh Chull Shin, *Confucianism and Democratization in East Asia* (Cambridge: Cambridge University Press, 2011).

[59] Gilley, *The Nature of Asian Politics*, 139. The quote comes from Bernard Crick, *In Defence of Politics* (Chicago, IL: University of Chicago Press, 1962), 98.

[60] Shweder, "Relativism and Universalism," in Didier Fassin (ed.), *A Companion to Moral Anthropology* (Malden, MA: Wiley-Blackwell, 2012), 89; Fiske, Kitayama, et al. "The Cultural Matrix of Social Psychology," 915–919.

the well-known philosopher and social anthropologist, argues, "Men and societies frequently treat the institutions and assumptions by which they live as absolute, self-evident, and given."[61]

The influence of moral matrices over how people think is so strong that they act as a deterrent to understanding the behavior of those from other cultures, who are naturally living with a different "operating system." As Haidt concludes,

> Moral matrices bind people together and blind them to the coherence, or even existence, of other matrices. This makes it very difficult for people to consider the possibility that there might really be more than one form of moral truth, or more than one valid framework for judging people or running a society.[62]

Understandably, as Haidt suggests, it is easy to condemn practices in another culture without fully understanding the rationale embedded within that culture for the particular behavior. This explains to some extent the challenges Western universalists face when they encounter moral matrices in thick societies.

THE WEST AS OUTLIER

Cultural psychology's most startling discovery is how much of an outlier Westerners in general – and Western, secular, middle and upper classes in particular – are from everyone else. Research has repeatedly shown that this group of people is, as one magazine reporting on the work describes, "particularly unusual when compared to other populations – with perceptions, behaviors, and motivations that were almost always sliding down one end of the human bell curve."[63]

In a paper called "The Weirdest People in the World?," psychologists Joseph Henrich, Steven Heine, and Ara Norenzayan argue that the very way this group thinks and perceives things make them remarkably distinct from other humans.

---

[61] Ernest Gellner, *Plough, Sword, and Book: The Structure of Human History* (Chicago, IL: University of Chicago Press, 1988), 11.

[62] Haidt, *The Righteous Mind*, 110. As Michel de Montaigne, one of the most important philosophers in the French Renaissance, wrote, "I think there is nothing barbarous and savage in that nation, from what I have been told, except that each man calls barbarism whatever is not his own practice; for it seems we have no other test of truth and reason than the example and pattern of the opinions and customs of the country we live in. There [in the country we live in] is always the perfect religion, the perfect government, the perfect and accomplished manners in all things."

[63] Watters, "We Aren't the World."

A large body of evidence shows that the habitual use of what are considered 'basic' cognitive processes ... vary systematically across populations ... highlighting the difference between the West and the rest. Several biases and pattern are not merely differences in strength or tendency, but show reversals of Western patterns.[64]

Americans were particularly unusual "even within the unusual population of Westerners – outliers among outliers."[65]

Western, educated, industrialized, rich, and democratic – WEIRD – minds have a number of unique characteristics. They are far more individualistic, far more likely to assume that each person is working as a free agent able to determine and follow their own personal preferences, and far more likely to be concerned with fairness and equality than people elsewhere. They are far more likely to assume that people and objects can be understood and categorized according to a relatively limited set of rules, and far more likely to play down the significance of context and the complexity of situations when making judgments and decisions. They emphasize logic in their problem solving and think more analytically than others, who tend to think more holistically.[66] And "the WEIRDer you are, the more you see a world full of separate objects, rather than relationships."[67]

Such differences create divergent priorities. Westerners assume that each individual is a free agent able to determine his or her own path, and thus ought to be concerned with fairness and self-awareness. Only WEIRD people, for instance, can frequently believe an action that bothered or disgusted them was permissible or even right if done in private – for example, having sex with a chicken.[68] In contrast, East Asians – and most non-Westerners – generally believe they live in an interdependent world in which each individual is part of a greater whole and ought to make sacrifices to maintain group harmony.[69] They are much more likely to see objects within their broader contexts, emphasize the complexity of situations, and see particular events as a product of a wide number of factors that influence each other in intricate, not easily determined ways.[70]

[64] Henrich, Heine, and Norenzayan, "The Weirdest People in the World?," 26–27.
[65] Ibid., 61–135.
[66] Nisbett, *The Geography of Thought*, xvi.
[67] Haidt, *The Righteous Mind*, 96.
[68] Haidt, *The Righteous Mind*, 96.
[69] Nisbett, *The Geography of Thought*, 76.
[70] Ibid., xvi.

The conclusions of Henrich and his colleagues converge with ethnographic observation and research across a wide range of fields, including history and the philosophy of science.[71] As noted cultural anthropologist Clifford Geertz stated in 1974:

> The Western conception of the person as a bounded, unique, more or less integrated motivational and cognitive universe, a dynamic center of awareness, emotion, judgment, and action organized into a distinctive whole and set contrastively both against other such wholes and against its social and natural background, is, however, incorrigible it may seem to us, a rather peculiar idea within the context of the world's cultures.[72]

Of course, as Melfred Spiro has argued, differences are more relative than absolute. Both the West and South have independent and interdependent characteristics, albeit in differing amounts. Societies exist along a continuum and are not simply polar opposites. But as Henrich and his colleagues' work shows, there are real differences in the extent that individual and communal concerns are emphasized in morality and what is considered normative behavior between WEIRD populations and everyone else. The self exists as a separate entity in both contexts – as Spiro argues it should – but is significantly more likely to be influenced by relationships in the latter, due to society's emphasis on obligations, duties, social ties, etc.[73]

Generalizations based on exclusively WEIRD or other particular cultural norms – whether in the field of psychology or economics or human rights – thus need to be undertaken very carefully. As Henrich, Heine, and Norenzayan conclude,

> There are no obvious a priori grounds for claiming that a particular behavioral phenomenon is universal based on sampling from a single subpopulation. Overall, these empirical patterns suggests that we need to be less cavalier in addressing questions of human nature on the basis of data drawn from this particularly thin, and rather unusual, slice of humanity.[74]

---

[71] Nisbett and Masuda, "Culture and Point of View," 11163.

[72] Clifford Geertz, "'From the Native's Point of View': On the Nature of Anthropological Understanding," *Bulletin of the American Academy of Arts and Sciences* 28, no. 1 (Oct. 1974): 26–45.

[73] Melfred Spiro, "Is the Western Conception of the Self 'Peculiar' within the Context of the World Cultures?," *Ethos* 21, no. 2 (June 1993): 107–153.

[74] Henrich, Heine, and Norenzayan, "The Weirdest People in the World?," 2.

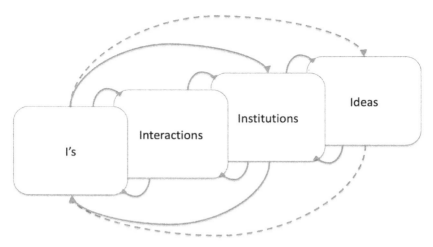

FIGURE 3.2 The culture cycle
Source: Markus and Conner, *Clash!*, xix

DIFFERING CONCEPTS OF THE SELF

Other cultures have a markedly different view of the self and its relationship with others. As a seminal 1991 article by Hazel Rose Markus, from Stanford University, and Shinobu Kitayama, who is now based at the University of Michigan, concluded, most cultures foster an "interdependent self" that is connected to others in a social group. Such cultures favor social harmony over an assertion of individual preferences. WEIRD cultures, in contrast, foster an "independent self" that exists apart from the group pursuing one's own needs and wants.[75]

In both cases, the culture cycle (see Figure 3.2) strongly influences the most important ideas that answer the big questions about the self:

> What, exactly, is a person? What is a *good* person? and What is her or his relationship to other people, the past, and the environment? ... The [culture] cycles that feed and flow from the big idea that the self is independent are quite distinct from the cycles that feed and flow from the big idea that the self is interdependent.[76]

---

[75] Markus and Kitayama, "Culture and the Self," 224–253.
[76] Markus and Conner, *Clash!*, 18.

TABLE 3.1 *Summary of key differences between an independent and an interdependent construal of self*

Feature compared	Independent	Interdependent
Definition	Separate from social context	Connected with social context
Structure	Bounded, unitary, stable	Flexible, variable
Important features	Internal, private (abilities, thoughts, feelings)	External, public (statuses, roles, relationships)
Tasks	Be unique	Belong, fit in
	Express self	Occupy one's proper place
	Realize internal attributes	Engage in appropriate action
	Promote own goals	Promote others' goals
	Be direct; "say what's on your mind"	Be indirect; "read other's mind"
Role of others	*Self-evaluation*: others important for social comparison, reflected appraisal	*Self-definition*: relationships with others in specific contexts define the self
Basis of self-esteem*	Ability to express self, validate internal attributes	Ability to adjust, restrain self, maintain harmony with social context

* Esteeming the self may be primarily a Western phenomenon, and the concept of self-esteem should perhaps be replaced by self-satisfaction, or by a term that reflects the realization that one is fulfilling the culturally mandated task.
Source: Markus and Kitayama, "Culture and the Self," 230

The differences between the two concepts of self – which are really poles between which a continuum of possible combinations exist – can be stark.[77] Whereas an independent construal of the self promotes an individualist, egocentric, separate, autonomous, idiocentric, and self-contained worldview, an interdependent construal of the self promotes a sociocentric, holistic, collective, allocentric, constitutive, contextualist, connected, and relational worldview.[78] The former leads to an emphasis on uniqueness, influencing others, freedom, and equality; the latter leads to an emphasis on being similar, adjusting to others, seeking rootedness, and ranked status.[79] (See Table 3.1 and Figure 3.3.) The different construals "can influence, and in many cases

[77] Markus and Kitayama, "Culture and the Self," 224–253.
[78] Markus and Kitayama, "Culture and the Self," 226–227.
[79] Markus and Conner, *Clash!*, xii–xiii.

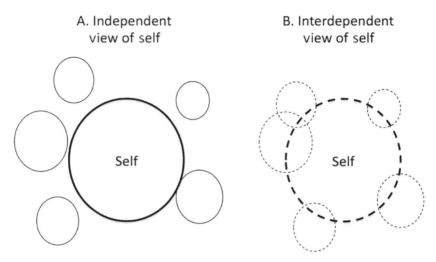

A. Independent
view of self

B. Interdependent
view of self

Self

Self

FIGURE 3.3 Conceptual representations of the self (A: independent construal. B: interdependent construal)
Source: Markus and Kitayama, "Culture and the Self," 226; Markus and Conner, *Clash!*, xv

determine, the very nature of individual experience, including cognition, emotion, and motivation."[80]

For the Akan people in Ghana, for instance, "a human person is essentially the center of a thick set of concentric circles of obligations and responsibilities matched by rights and privileges revolving around levels of relationship."[81] The Dinka in South Sudan emphasize "social consciousness" and "efforts to harmonize one's own interests with those of others in the community" in their ideas regarding human relations. "The fundamental goal of traditional Dinka society is a social order envisaging ideal human relations expressed in the quest for unity, harmony, cooperation, and mutual support."[82]

In highly sociocentric Japan, which has a culture whose essence anthropologists have described as an "ethos of social relativism,"[83] the word for self – *jibun* (自分) – refers to one's share of the whole. Harmony, peace, and balance are so valued that the character used to denote this meaning is used for the

[80] Markus and Kitayama, "Culture and the Self," 224.
[81] Kwasi Wiredu, "The Moral Foundation of an African Culture," in Pieter Hendrik Coetzee and A. P. J. Roux (eds.), *Philosophy from Africa: A Text with Readings* (Oxford: Oxford University Press, 2002), 291.
[82] Francis Deng, *Identity, Diversity, and Constitutionalism in Africa* (Washington, DC: United States Institute of Peace Press, 2008), 92.
[83] Takie Sugiyama Lebra, *Japanese Patterns of Behavior* (Honolulu, HI: University of Hawaii Press, 1976).

name of the country, *wa* (和). Self-assertion is considered immature; an individual focuses on controlling his or her inner self instead of embellishing his or her personality to better take advantage of their social situations.[84] As such, when Japanese describe themselves, they tend to describe their relationships instead of their qualities. In emails and text messages, they use (^_^;), which depicts cold sweat rolling down a nervous face, to express worry that they have done something wrong and disturbed a relationship as often as they use smiling and frowning emoticons – the two most commonly used in the United States – because of the high importance placed on harmony and relationships.[85]

In such thick society cultures, the individual may actually cease to be the primary unit of consciousness at times. Instead, the sense of belongingness to a social relation may be so strong that it becomes the functional unit of conscious reflection.[86]

Indeed, as Shweder writes, "To members of sociocentric organic cultures the [thin society] concept of the autonomous individual, free to choose and mind his or her business, must feel alien, a bizarre idea cutting the self off from the interdependent whole, dooming it to a life of isolation and loneliness."[87]

Similarly, to religious believers, the idea of living without faith is not only alien to their identities and worldviews, but also in conflict with their understanding of human nature. In fact, some scholars argue that belief and religion are a natural part of the human psyche, the product of evolution (see Chapter 4). As such, "thwarting religious impulses could be as wrong as thwarting any other basic human need or interest."[88]

Of course, even if thick and thin societies show substantial differences, cultures are not monolithic; they can be divided into an endless number of components. Ethnic backgrounds, religious affiliation, economic status, education level, place of upbringing – there are countless differences that individually and in endless combinations influence us.[89] Some Chinese may be quite independent – masking it at times if necessary – even if their society as a whole is quite interdependent; some Americans may be quite

---

[84] Markus and Kitayama, "Culture and the Self," 228.
[85] Markus and Conner, *Clash!*, xiv.
[86] Markus and Kitayama, "Culture and the Self," 226.
[87] Shweder and Edmund Bourne, "Does the Concept of the Person Vary Cross-Culturally?," in Shweder, *Thinking through Cultures*, 154.
[88] Roger Trigg, *Equality, Freedom, and Religion* (Oxford: Oxford University Press, 2012), 18.
[89] Watters, "We Aren't the World."

interdependent even if their society as a whole is quite independent.[90] Chinese Americans combine, as one person writes, elements of the two societies, "tempering raw individualism with a sense of community; adding a corrective dose of duty and propriety to a society rooted in rights and self-expression; paying heed to context and history, not just what's shiniest here and now."[91] Research shows that Northern Chinese – which, unlike the rest of East Asia, cultivate wheat, a simpler crop requiring less shared labor and group cooperation than rice, the region's staple – are more individualistic and analytical than Southern Chinese.[92]

We are all "bicultural" in the sense that we combine both independent and interdependent traits; different circumstances bring out different aspects of ourselves.[93] But in general, WEIRD thin society cultures have moral matrices that are unusually narrow, with a strong emphasis on the autonomy ethic. No other part of the world seems to share the same degree of emphasis. More sociocentric thick society cultures have broader moral matrices, combining the three ethics of autonomy, community, and divinity identified by Shweder in a more balanced fashion.[94] These cultural and cognitive differences explain much of the conflict over values and rights that exist between countries from very different cultural zones as well as those that exist between groups with very different moral matrices in the same country. When religious and secular groups clash over things like male circumcision or abortion, it is most likely a reflection of the two very different cultures that these groups inhabit.

The result, as will be discussed in Chapter 4, is two radically different approaches to creating a society – one with thin ties between people, a limited role for social institutions, and limited constraints on the individual, and the other with thick ties between people and a large role for social institutions to bind people together, regulate behavior, and encourage actions that promote the success of the group.

---

[90] Tom Zwart, Professor of Human Rights, Utrecht School of Law, conversation with author, November 2014.

[91] Eric Liu, "Why I Just Can't Become Chinese," *Wall Street Journal*, August 29, 2014, http://online.wsj.com/articles/why-i-just-cant-become-chinese-1409333549.

[92] Thomas Talhelm, Xuemin Zhang, et al., "Large-Scale Psychological Differences within China Explained by Rice versus Wheat Agriculture," *Science* 344, no. 6184 (May 9, 2014): 603–608, www.sciencemag.org/content/344/6184/603.

[93] Nisbett, *The Geography of Thought*, 228–229.

[94] Haidt, *The Righteous Mind*, 110.

4

Thick versus Thin Societies

Philosophers have [long] been divided into those who wished to tighten social bonds and those who wished to relax them ... It is clear that each party to this dispute – as to all that persist through long periods of time – is partly right and partly wrong. Social cohesion is a necessity, and mankind has never yet succeeded in enforcing cohesion by merely rational arguments. Every community is exposed to two opposite dangers, ossification through too much discipline and reverence for tradition, on the one hand; on the other hand, dissolution, or subjection to foreign conquest, through the growth of an individualism and personal independence that makes co-operation impossible.[1]
                                        – Bertrand Russell

All large societies must enable unrelated persons to live together peacefully. Cultural psychology research shows that there are, broadly speaking, two different approaches to meeting this challenge: one focused on maximizing personal freedoms and the other on maximizing the robustness of relationships and institutions. The first centers on the individual and emphasizes the independence of each person as long as they do nothing to harm anyone else; the second centers on the well-being of society as a whole, emphasizing the interdependence of each person within the groups and networks they belong to.

These approaches assume and promote different definitions of the good life. Individualistic societies highly value choice and fairness, and they emphasize moral concepts such as rights, liberty, and justice. Sociocentric societies highly value order, hierarchy, and tradition; they emphasize moral concepts such as duty, respect, reputation, patriotism, sanctity, and purity.

---

[1]   Bertrand Russell, *History of Western Philosophy* (Milton Park, UK: Routledge, 2009), 8.

The two can be, respectively, characterized as "thin societies" and "thick societies,"[2] depending on how extensive a role they provide for social institutions to regulate behavior. Thin societies provide little role; thick societies provide a substantial role.

These two social orders have different conceptions of human rights and the role of the state in enhancing human welfare.[3] Thin societies prefer a human rights framework that offers broad protections for individual choice and that gives the state a large role in enforcing rules. Cultural differences, traditions, and social institutions can be set aside if they conflict with human rights goals. Thick societies, in contrast, prefer a human rights framework that includes a few core rules that ensure certain minimum standards are met while providing flexibility for local adaptation. The state is still important but plays a narrower role in enforcing rules. Traditions and social institutions, considered crucial to identity and feelings of dignity, are given a relatively large role. Human rights are seen as but one of many ways to better lives and improve how societies work.

---

[2] The "thick"/"thin" dichotomy has occasionally been employed in the social sciences. Michael Walzer, for instance, uses "thick" and "thin" to discuss different types of moral reasoning. In the former, in-depth assessments are made of all aspects of a problem. In the latter, easy-to-recognize slogans and terms predominate. Thin goods, such as ending poverty, are easy to reach a consensus on. But thick goods, such as how to achieve such goals, are much more difficult. See Walzer, *Thick and Thin: Moral Argument at Home and Abroad* (South Bend, IN: University of Notre Dame Press, 1994). There is little overlap between Walzer's use of "thick" and "thin" and their use here. Clifford Geertz uses the term to refer to different types of ethnographic descriptions. Thin descriptions are factual accounts that focus mainly on behavior; thick descriptions include interpretations that take into account many details of the context. See Geertz, "Thick Description: Toward an Interpretive Theory of Culture," in *The Interpretation of Cultures: Selected Essays* (New York, NY: Basic Books, 1973), 5–6 and 9–10. Richard Shweder has used "thick" ethnicity to describe something similar to what is explored here but not in any detail. See Shweder, "Moral Maps, 'First World' Conceits, and the New Evangelists," in Lawrence Harrison and Samuel Huntington (eds.), *Culture Matters: How Values Shape Human Progress* (New York, NY: Basic Books, 2000), 158–176. He also discusses how morality is much broader and thicker in India than the United States. See Shweder, Nancy Much, Manamohan Mahapatra, and Lawrence Park, "The 'Big Three' of Morality (Autonomy, Community, and Divinity) and the 'Big Three' explanations of Suffering," in Allan Brandt and Paul Rozin (eds.), *Morality and Health* (New York, NY: Routledge, 1997), 119–169. The only place I have observed "thick" and "thin" in the human rights context is in three references Johannes Morsink makes to describe how involved government is in society in *The Universal Declaration of Human Rights: Origins, Drafting, and Intent* (Philadelphia, PA: University of Pennsylvania Press, 1999), 259. These references appear in the sections on "Religious and Educational Communities" (7.3) and "The Omission of a Special Minority Rights Article" (7.4). In contrast, this book concentrates on the substantial differences between thick and thin societies and the consequences of these differences for human rights.

[3] Morsink, *The Universal Declaration of Human Rights*, 259.

TWO DIFFERENT BASES FOR SOCIETY

Thick and thin societies are exemplified, respectively, by the approaches of British philosopher John Stuart Mill and French sociologist Émile Durkheim.[4]

In Mill's vision, the individual is the basic social unit (and *Gesellschaft* social ties predominate).[5] Society strongly emphasizes fairness and equality, and it gives maximum liberty to everyone to develop their talents and relationships as they see fit. It is based on a social contract designed for the mutual benefit of all individuals. Groups form and disband voluntarily and often quickly. Diversity and self-expression are not only valued, but even favored at times, over preference for one's own group. In such places, as Mill wrote in *On Liberty*, "the only purpose for which power can be rightly exercised over any member of a civilized community, against his will, is to prevent harm to others."

In Durkheim's vision, the family or clan/community is the basic social unit (and *Gemeinschaft* social ties predominate). Society is the product of a slow, organic process through which people develop ways of living with each other. In such places, social institutions play a much greater role binding people together, regulating behavior, suppressing selfishness, penalizing free riders, and encouraging actions that promote the success of the group. Relationships matter much more, with loyalty, respect for authority, and concern for upholding what is considered sacred all highly valued. Individuals are born into a network of relationships, groups, and commitments that constrain their autonomy and reshape their behavior to fit established norms. Self-control is valued, as are duty and loyalty to one's group and traditions. As Durkheim

---

[4]   Jonathan Haidt makes the same comparison. See Haidt, *The Righteous Mind: Why Good People Are Divided by Politics and Religion* (New York, NY: Pantheon Books, 2012), 164, 185, and 272. Johann Gottfried von Herder, an eighteenth-century German philosopher and to some degree an precursor to Durkheim, argued that there were no universal values, only groups of people bound together by common language, traditions, customs, and history. These social entities work like independent organisms and have their own unified spiritual essence. Each group or nation has its own values; none are better than anyone else's, just different. One group's values cannot be judged by another's. See Hans Adler and Wulf Koepke (eds.), *A Companion to the Works of Johann Gottfried Herder* (Rochester, NY: Camden House, 2009).

[5]   The *Gemeinschaft-Gesellschaft* dichotomy was first proposed by Ferdinand Tönnies. *Gemeinschaft* (generally translated as community) refers to groups of people that are sustained by feelings of togetherness, and which produce roles, values, and beliefs that are designed to nurture and maintain such ties. On the other hand, *Gesellschaft* (generally translated as society) refers to groups that are designed to be instrumental for their members' individual aims and goals and are sustained by indirect interactions, impersonal roles, formal values, and beliefs. Tönnies, *Gemeinschaft und Gesellschaft* (Leipzig: Fues's Verlag, 1912).

wrote, "man cannot become attached to higher aims and submit to a rule if he sees nothing above him to which he belongs. To free himself from all social pressure is to abandon himself and demoralize him."[6]

Speaking simply, Mill's thin society is that of the WEIRD world. Durkheim's thick society is that of most of the rest of the world – including religious groups living in Western countries. In Millian societies, morality encompasses a relatively small number of behaviors. In Durkheimian societies, in contrast, morality is much broader and thicker, encompassing a much greater set of practices than in the former.[7] Durkheim believed that people have two distinct sets of "social sentiments," one for the individual, and one for the larger society. The first set of sentiments

> bind[s] each individual to the person of his fellow-citizens: these are manifest within the community, in the day-to-day relationships of life ... The second are those which bind me to the social entity as a whole ... The first [set of emotions] leave[s] my autonomy and personality intact ... When I act under the influence of the second, by contrast, I am simply a part of the whole, whose actions I follow, and whose influence I am subject to.[8]

WEIRD utilitarians such as Mill and Jeremy Bentham focused intently on improving the welfare of society by enabling individuals as much scope as possible to fulfill their own utility. In contrast, a Durkheimian perspective argues that human flourishing depends on the robustness of the broader social order, which is extraordinarily important yet hard to nourish and sustain.[9]

In many ways, these two different visions echo those of the eighteenth-century giants Thomas Paine and Edmund Burke, arguably the most important political philosophers on the left and right in the Anglo-American world. Paine, the progressive liberal, believed that "human beings are best understood apart from the community and the past, as complete and sufficient individuals endowed with natural rights whose interactions are functions of their individual choices and actions." On the other hand, Burke, the "forward-looking traditionalist," argued that "human beings are best understood in their social and historical settings, as members of their

---

[6]   Haidt, *The Righteous Mind*, 164–166.
[7]   Ibid., 17.
[8]   Emile Durkheim, "Review of Guyau's L'irreligion de l'avenir," in Anthony Giddens (ed.), *Emile Durkheim: Selected Writings*, translated by Anthony Giddens (Cambridge: Cambridge University Press, 1972), 219–220.
[9]   Haidt, *The Righteous Mind*, 272.

communities with obligations to each other and as the recipients of a valuable inheritance from the past."[10]

For Paine, a product of the Enlightenment and a great believer in rationalism, universal political principles could be discovered by reason and applied to all countries – as Western universalists assert. Everything should promote the cause of rational politics so as to "rescue man from tyranny and false systems and false principles of government, and enable him to be free and establish government for himself."[11] Tradition and society should be disregarded when establishing institutions to govern.[12] For Burke, the opposite was true: every society is different and needs to build on its own institutions, history, and prejudices to advance – as flexible universalists argue.[13] He thought that governing human communities was "much too complex a task to be simplified into a series of pseudoscientific questions and resolved by logical exercises."[14]

While Paine remains highly influential, especially in left-leaning political philosophy, Burke's legacy is more ambivalent. Although he is considered the founder of the conservative movement (in the Anglo-American world), conservatism has gradually evolved to embrace the prevailing individualism, and according to Yuval Levin, it now "lacks his emphasis on community and on the sentiments." He continues, "Today's conservatives are thus too rhetorically strident and far too open to the siren song of hyperindividualism."[15] As a result, Burkean politics has all but collapsed; there is no strong political force pushing for policies that strengthen local communities, traditional institutions, and the moral character of human beings. These are all apparently off limits in thin societies.

When non-WEIRD philosophers and traditions develop moral systems, they are more likely to be based on relationships rather than rules, duties rather than rights, and virtues rather than freedoms.[16] Confucius' Analects, for instance, focuses on relationship-specific duties and virtues and contains a broader set of moral foundations than its Western counterparts. There is no attempt, as there is often in Western philosophy (and Christianity), to reduce

---

[10] Yuval Levin, *The Great Debate: Edmund Burke, Thomas Paine, and the Birth of Right and Left* (New York, NY: Basic Books, 2014), 220.
[11] Thomas Paine, *The Complete Writings of Thomas Paine*, edited by Philip Foner (New York, NY: Citadel Press, 1945), Volume 2, p. 1480.
[12] Yuval Levin, *The Great Debate*, 220.
[13] Ibid., 159.
[14] Ibid., 128.
[15] Ibid., 229.
[16] Haidt, *The Righteous Mind*, 97.

teachings to a single golden rule.[17] In addition, religious teachings such as the Muslim Koran, Hebrew Bible, Christian Bible, and the Hindu religious texts all emphasize moral concepts such as purity, virtuousness, self-sacrifice, tradition, and hierarchy that have no or a limited place in an individualistic rights-based moral code. "In the Hindu moral universe, obligations to people you know rank higher than obligations to such abstract principles as 'justice,' 'individual rights,' and 'rule of law.'"[18]

Of course, "thick" and "thin" are ideal types. Cultures are contested and ever changing, not fixed and uniform. Thick societies contain thin elements and vice versa. Thick and thin elements within a single community or society are often in tension or competition with each other, being more or less important depending on the context, issue, and time. The balance can thus shift between the two even if the overall characteristic of a community or society does not change. For instance, the populist backlash in the United States and elsewhere can be interpreted as a shift toward thicker elements such as conservative nationalism in reaction to attempts to make society too individualistic and secular universalist. But it does not change the fact that the country is, on the whole, much more thin than thick – a prototypical WEIRD society and highly individualistic. Similarly, all societies have a wide range of groups with different combinations of thick and thin elements. The balance of influence between these can ebb and flow, affecting how the society evolves without fundamentally altering its fundamentally thick or thin orientation, except possibly over many generations and severe changes in the environment in which the society exists.

There can also be very different combinations of thick and thin elements even within a set of societies that are all thick or all thin. For instance, some European countries have a much thicker understanding of identity (e.g., Italy, Poland, Hungary) than the United States because of their basis in ethnic ties, rather than immigration. In such countries, it is much harder to be naturalized and accepted as an insider than in the United States, which better absorbs and integrates newcomers. On the other hand, the influence of religion – and with it a thicker understanding of human institutions – in the United States has produced much more opposition to abortion and gay

---

[17] Ibid., 97 and 336–337. The single golden rule is originally religious. Jesus summarizes all of the Hebrew Law in Matthew 7:12 "So whatever you wish that others would do to you, do also to them, for this is the Law and the Prophets."

[18] Hazel Rose Markus and Alana Conner, *Clash! 8 Cultural Conflicts That Make Us Who We Are* (New York, NY: Hudson Street Press, 2013), 188.

marriage in parts of the country (e.g., the south) than one would find in places such as Scandinavia, arguably the thinnest part of Europe.

TWO DIFFERENT APPROACHES TO SOCIAL INSTITUTIONS AND THE STATE

These two visions of society exhibit dissimilar perceptions vis-à-vis social institutions. Thin, individualistic societies see little role for social norms that constrain individual behavior, such as abstention from premarital sex and tithing, and the enforcement mechanisms, such as houses of worship and traditional clan structures, operating alongside or even in lieu of the state. A flourishing civil society is valued, but only if it does nothing to limit the autonomy of individuals. Thick, sociocentric, interdependent societies, on the other hand, highly value social institutions, seeing them as the key to human flourishing. And they have fewer qualms limiting individual freedom in the name of social harmony.

Two definitions of social institutions are useful for the discussion here. According to Nobel Prize winner Douglass C. North, institutions are "the humanly devised constraints that structure human interaction. They are made up of formal constraints (e.g., rules, laws, constitutions), informal constraints, (e.g., norms of behavior, conventions, self-imposed codes of conduct), and their enforcement characteristics."[19] Social institutions are the informal "rules of the game" that "define the incentive structures of society."[20] They operate independently of the formal rules and laws made up by and enforced by the state.

For English social anthropologist A. R. Radcliffe-Brown, social institutions are "the ordering by society of the interactions of person in social relationships." Instead of "haphazard conjunctions of individuals," social institutions ensure that "the conduct of persons in their interactions with others is controlled by norms, rules, or patterns." As a result, they ensure that "a person knows that he is expected to behave according to these norms and that other persons should do the same."[21]

As such, social institutions, also known as intermediate institutions, are a pattern of rules and structures that seek to better the human condition – much

---

[19] Douglass C. North, "Economic Performance through Time," *American Economic Review* 84, no. 3 (June 1994), 360–361.

[20] Douglass C. North, "Institutions," *The Journal of Economic Perspectives* 5, no. 1 (Winter 1991): 97–112.

[21] A. R. Radcliffe-Brown, *Structure and Function in Primitive Society* (Glencoe, IL: Free Press, 1992), 10–11.

like a rights-based system might, but in a very different way. Whereas rights reduce restraints and regulations to enhance individual opportunity, institutions impose rules and obligations to meet social needs and promote public goods. While both are essential components of any good society, they are qualitatively different, like apples and oranges, and cannot work in lieu of each other.[22] Both are needed, which is why the flexible universalist approach to rights promotion is so promising.

Neither social institutions nor individual rights can succeed in a vacuum. Rights depend heavily on institutions to be realized. Treaties, laws, and regulations have limited influence when societies do not provide an institutional ecosystem that supports their fulfillment. The framers of the UDHR understood this, and they crafted the Declaration to support both individual rights and thick social realities. Freedom of speech, for instance, requires "more than mere absence of government censorship or prohibition to thrive; [it] also require[s] institutions, practices, and technological structures that foster and promote [it]." Intermediate institutions such as newspapers, political parties, interest groups, libraries, universities, and churches all play an important infrastructural role nurturing the civil society space and social norms that allow an individual's right to freedom of speech to be exercised.[23] Similarly, the well-being of children depends not only on rights but also on parents, families, communities, schools, and neighborhoods.

In thick societies, social institutions and relationships play a central role in daily life, influencing where one lives, what life choices one makes, who one socializes with, and what one believes and values. They bring people together, set rules for how they should behave, and create dense networks of mutual support and obligation. In such places, individuals feel a strong sense of responsibility to bend for the sake of groups and relationships. Sacrifices must be made to maintain harmony and sacredness. Traditions, rituals, and time-consuming activities tied to beliefs and relationships are highly valued. Even today, more than four-fifths of marriages are arranged in India because the extended family is considered such an important part of the relationship.[24]

---

[22] Mary Ann Glendon, *Rights Talk: The Impoverishment of Political Discourse* (New York, NY: The Free Press, 1991), 75; Daniel Bell, "East Asian Challenge to Human Rights: Reflections on an East West Dialogue," *Human Rights Quarterly* 18, no. 3 (August 1996): 641–644; William Galston, "Between Philosophy and History: The Evolution of Rights in American Thought," in Robert Licht (ed.), *Old Rights and New* (Washington, DC: The AEI Press, 1993), 73.

[23] Jack Balkin, "The Infrastructure of Religious Freedom," *Balkinization Blog*, May 5, 2007, http://balkin.blogspot.com/2007/05/infrastructure-of-religious-freedom.html.

[24] Markus and Conner, *Clash!*, 191–192.

Whereas in thin societies the relationship between the state and the individual is predominant, in thick societies intermediate institutions are equally or even more important at times. People "view societies not as aggregates of individuals but as molecules, or organisms."[25] In such places, morality is very broad and encompassing; almost every practice is tied to it. For instance, whereas in the individualistic West it is common to place one's personal needs and preferences above those of family and friends when they conflict, in an interdependent place like India duty is more important. If your brother needs help with something – say a move to a new apartment – you have an obligation to help even if you do not have a warm and affectionate relationship with him. It is not a matter of choice or preference or dependent on how close you are, but a moral obligation. Whether you like your brother or not, helping him is a matter of right and wrong.[26] "The social order is a moral order."[27]

In such contexts, individuals do not "opt in" to a social institution; membership is an integral part of one's identity and beliefs. Though Shweder differentiates between a social ethic and divinity ethic, it is worth noting that in many societies the two are intertwined. Indeed, for religious believers,

> The terms "preference" and "choice" ... suppose a "world" occupied by a plurality of objects whose measure is scalar. Invocation of these terms supposes that all desires may be brought into proximity and set side by side, as if they could be weighed and compared in the marketplace using a common currency of exchange ... Religious experience is of a different order than having "preferences" and making "choices." Religious experience cannot be understood as a "preference," because the God who stands before man is not among the plurality of scalar objects among which he prefers this over that. Religious experience pertains not to the extant plurality in the created "world," but rather to the Creator who is the source of that plurality.[28]

Of course, dominant social institutions can also undermine the rule of law in countries with weak government, a common problem in less-developed countries. In such places, cronyism, which at times is a natural product of a "millennia-old moral code that stresses interpersonal duties over abstract notions of justice, law, and individual rights," is very hard to root out. In India, for example, obligations to people you are related to or know well rank

[25] Richard Nisbett, *The Geography of Thought: How Asians and Westerners Think Differently ... and Why* (New York, NY: The Free Press, 2003), 198.
[26] Markus and Conner, *Clash!*, 190.
[27] Haidt, *The Righteous Mind*, 17.
[28] Joshua Mitchell, "Religion Is Not a Preference," *The Journal of Politics* 69, no. 2 (May 2007): 354.

higher than obligations to any abstract principle implemented by a government with which you have no personal relationship.[29] The same is true in much of the Middle East and Africa.[30] Corruption – or at least some aspect of it – may not be seen as evil in these countries, but as part of the normal functioning of society. It may even play a constructive role lubricating trade, promoting stability and investment, and protecting property rights.[31]

Partly as a consequence, in most of the world, the state is not nearly robust enough to fulfill the substantial role that thin societies require of it. On the contrary, in most of Africa, Asia, the Middle East, and even Latin America, people must depend much more on their family, social networks, and communal or religious ties for security and help getting ahead than any formal state-centered regime. Governments are corrupt, captured by powerful interests, not terribly capable, and unable to enforce the law equitably. Even if they sign all human rights treaties, pass all requisite human rights laws, and declare repeatedly in public fora and international meetings their commitment to human rights principles, states may be unable to enforce the great majority of their commitments in practice. As Gary Haugen and Victor Boutros, two human rights practitioners, write,

> The failure to build effective public justice systems in the developing world ... has made the great victories of the modern human rights movement largely irrelevant for addressing the most pressing human rights challenge of [the poor's] daily lives – to be free from unchecked criminal violence.[32]

Regulations are complicated and costly, making them hard to follow for anyone but the well off. Most employment exists in the informal sector, and

---

[29] Markus and Conner, *Clash!*, 188.

[30] See, for instance, Markus and Conner, *Clash!*, 196–198.

[31] There are many examples from the literature. Here I quote two: "Most educated Africans are citizens of two publics in the same society. On the one hand, they belong to a civic public from which they gain materially but to which they give only grudgingly. On the other hand they belong to a primordial public from which they derive little or no material benefits but to which they are expected to give generously and do give materially. Their relationship to the primordial public is moral, while that to the civic public is amoral." Peter Ekeh, "Colonialism and the Two Publics in Africa: A Theoretical Statement," *Comparative Studies in Society and History* 17, no. 1 (January 1975): 91–112. "Western language about 'corruption' in Pakistan suggests that it can and should be cut out of the political system; but in so far as the political system runs on patronage and kinship, and corruption is intertwined with patronage and kinship, to cut it out would mean gutting Pakistan's society like a fish." Anatol Lieven, *Pakistan: A Hard Country* (New York, NY: Public Affairs, 2011), 27.

[32] Gary Haugen and Victor Boutros, *The Locust Effect: Why the End of Poverty Requires the End of Violence* (Oxford: Oxford University Press, 2014), 159.

large swathes of some countries may see little government presence. Such environments do little to inspire confidence that the state can promote human rights on its own – and much to encourage an interdependency that everyone takes for granted in any case. In such places, intermediate institutions are arguably the only game in town. As a result, human rights are more likely to be advanced, at least in the short term, by leveraging the intermediate institutions that dominate people's lives rather than assuming than the state can play a strong role.[33]

This is not to say that thick societies must necessarily have weak governments. Japan, Korea, Singapore, and China are among the most developed or most successful developing countries in the world at least partly due to their robust state apparatuses. These have played a pivotal role guiding markets, allocating resources, educating citizens, and creating the incentives necessary for high growth.[34] And, reflecting their Confucian cultures and long histories of strong government – China had the first modern state 2200 years ago, almost two millennia before any European country[35] – the people in these East Asian countries naturally trust the state and expect it to play an important role in development in ways that would seem foreign in much of the thin West (especially the Anglo-Saxon part). Nevertheless, social institutions still matter much more in these thick societies than in the West, and attitudes toward social change are much more conservative, in the Burkean sense. More is expected of the family with regard to children, marriage, the elderly, and so on. Much less is expected of government in terms of welfare and social change. People want the state to be capable and responsive but in ways that nurture and strengthen social institutions, not in ways that undermine them. (The Communist Party in China has historically veered most from this course due to its ideology – imported from the West – about the importance of the state and the deficiencies of religious and other independent social institutions. That has, however, gradually

---

[33] See, for instance, Tom Zwart, "Using Local Culture to Further the Implementation of International Human Rights: The Receptor Approach," *Human Rights Quarterly* 34, no. 2 (May 2012): 546–569.

[34] See, for instance, Peter Evans, "Transferable Lessons? Re-examining the Institutional Prerequisites of East Asian Economic Policies," *Journal of Developmental Studies* 34, no. 6 (August 1998): 66–83; Robert Wade, *Governing the Market: Economic Theory and the Role of Government in East Asian Industrialization* (Princeton, NJ: Princeton University Press, 1990); Alice Amsden, *Asia's Next Giant: South Korea and Late Industrialization* (Oxford: Oxford University Press, 1992).

[35] Francis Fukuyama, *The Origins of Political Order* (New York, NY: Farrar, Straus and Giroux, 2011), 290–317.

changed over time as the country sinifies Marxism and the Party slowly embraces Confucianism to shore up its legitimacy.)

In the individualistic West, in contrast, the state is both strong enough to play a constructive role and increasingly expected to intervene to ensure a certain vision of human rights is upheld – even if that means weakening social institutions in the process. In such places, human rights are aimed at augmenting individual choice. Institutions and the obligations they impose are generally ignored as possible solutions to social problems and sometimes even denigrated as relics that need to be eliminated.[36] "Lacking an adequate linguistic or conceptual apparatus to deal with the intermediate institutions that stand between the individual and the state," Western countries regularly overlook the social ecosystem within which individuals (and state institutions) develop.[37] As a result, family stability, communal cohesion, social norms, trust, and civic engagement are all in decline in the West. Even though the United States still has a richer reservoir of nongovernmental organizations – what might be termed "visible" social institutions – among its population than most other countries (thick or thin), the institutions that influence individual behavior – what might be termed "invisible" social institutions – have severely deteriorated, especially among the working class.[38]

This is not to say that thin societies in the West expect the state to be all-powerful. On the contrary, a significant number of people want to limit the role of government in the economy, marriage, privacy, and choices about sexual orientation and sex.[39] Ideas about civil liberties; political freedom; the rule of law; representative democracy, which ostensibly holds government on a tight leash; and economic freedom underpin Western concepts about the appropriate relationship between state and society.[40] All the same, most countries in the West have ceded many of the key roles traditionally played by social institutions to the state (e.g., social welfare, rules circumscribing marriage, taking care of the elderly). Now there is growing tension within the West over how proactive government should be in upholding and enforcing

[36] David Blankenhorn, *The Future of Marriage* (New York, NY: Encounter Books, 2007), 96–98.
[37] Glendon, *Rights Talk*, 75.
[38] Nicholas Eberstadt, "Our Miserable 21st Century," *Commentary*, February 15, 2017.
[39] Libertarians are the best example of this. See, for instance, Peter Vallentyne, "Libertarianism," in Edward Zalta (ed.), *The Stanford Encyclopedia of Philosophy* (Stanford, CA: Stanford University, 2009).
[40] See, for instance, Freedom House, "Freedom in the World 2012: Methodology," https://freedomhouse.org/report/freedom-world-2012/methodology; Mark Dickerson, Thomas Flanagan, and Brenda O'Neill, *An Introduction to Government and Politics: A Conceptual Approach* (Toronto, Ontario: Nelson College Indigenous, 2009).

certain liberal modern ideas about human rights.[41] In some places, a growing majority already strongly supports a proactive role for government. In many European countries, for example, the state increasingly seeks to limit the ability of religious groups to practice their faith, intervening in ancient customs such as circumcision, the ritual slaughter of meat, and the running of private schools (as discussed in Chapter 6).

In some cases, vital social institutions have been converted into a bundle of rights – changing their very meaning in the process – because of the inability of Western societies to think in any other terms.[42] Marriage, for instance, was once a pillar institution in society, promoting procreation, the well-being of children, the buildup of wealth, and self-discipline. Today it is primarily a legal contract that provides rights to the two parties involved, and the obligations underpinning it have dissolved. Other objectives that this institution once held have been made less important in order for individuals to have maximum freedom to pursue their own goals.[43] Although this has brought many benefits to some, future generations will inherit a weaker social institution and receive fewer benefits from the public goods it provides.

Although civil society is considered important in Western countries, it is generally understood as comprised of certain types of nongovernmental organizations that play a visible role in the public sphere and not something much broader.[44] Many expressions of citizen action – such as religious, traditional, village-, or clan-based social institutions – contribute mightily to social capital and communal well-being, but are downplayed.[45]

A thin society's focus on individual rights means that there is often under-investment in nourishing and maintaining the social ecosystem – including families, neighborhoods, workplace associations, religious bodies, and other communities of obligation[46] – that cultivates the social capital, social networks, experiences in self-governance, and democratic norms upon which

---

[41] See, for instance, Chris Cillizza, "How Unbelievably Quickly Public Opinion Changed on Gay Marriage, in 5 Charts," *Washington Post*, June 26, 2015, www.washingtonpost.com/news/the-fix/wp/2015/06/26/how-unbelievably-quickly-public-opinion-changed-on-gay-marriage-in-6-charts/.

[42] Blankenhorn, *The Future of Marriage*, 94–105.

[43] Blankenhorn, *The Future of Marriage*, 94–105.

[44] Mike Edwards, *Civil Society*, 3rd ed. (Cambridge: Polity Press, 2014), 1–17 and 72–92.

[45] Duncan Green, "Civil Society and the Dangers of Monoculture: Smart New Primer from Mike Edwards," *From Poverty to Power Blog*, January 15, 2015, http://oxfamblogs.org/fp2p/civil-society-and-the-dangers-of-monoculture-smart-new-primer-from-mike-edwards/.

[46] Glendon, *Rights Talk*, 120.

a free society depends. As Alexis de Tocqueville, the nineteenth-century
political thinker, warned, "in a community in which the ties of family, of
caste, of class, and craft fraternities no longer exist, people are far too much
disposed to think exclusively of their own interests, to become self-seekers
practicing a narrow individualism and caring nothing for the public good."[47]
Durkheim notes that the state alone is "too remote from individuals"; it is
insufficient for maintaining the social fabric. He continues,

> A nation can be maintained only if, between the State and the individual,
> there is intercalated a whole series of secondary groups near enough to the
> individuals to attract them strongly in their sphere of action and drag them, in
> this way, into the general torrent of social life.[48]

Although the legal and political vocabularies of Western countries can easily
handle issues related to rights, markets, and the state, they do not provide an
easy way to value and make use of the smallish groups and systems that
inculcate the values and practices that shape how societies and countries as
a whole evolve and how effectively their democracies and governments will
work.[49] Many of the problems Western democracies such as the United States
now face – such as rising partisanship and inequality – are arguably the
product of a decaying social ecosystem.[50]

Many of the elements of modernization – including urbanization,
bureaucratization, marketization, centralization, and increased mobility[51] –
may have made the weakening of social institutions like marriage inevitable as

---

[47] Alexis de Tocqueville, *The Old Regime and the French Revolution*, translated by Stuart Gilbert
(New York, NY: Doubleday Anchor, 1955), xiii.
[48] Emile Durkheim, *The Division of Labor in Society*, translated by George Simpson (New York,
NY: Free Press, 1964), 28.
[49] Glendon, *Rights Talk*, 120.
[50] There has been a lot of discussion on how a decaying social system disadvantages large
segments of the population, increasing inequality. See, for instance, Robert Putnam, *Our Kids:
The American Dream in Crisis* (New York, NY: Simon & Schuster, 2015); Charles Murray,
Coming Apart: The State of White America, 1960–2010 (New York, NY: Crown Forum/
Random House, 2012); David Brooks, "The Wrong Inequality," *The New York Times*, October
31, 2011, www.nytimes.com/2011/11/01/opinion/brooks-the-wrong-inequality.html; and Brooks,
"The Inequality Problem," *The New York Times*, January 16, 2014, www.nytimes.com/2014/01/
17/opinion/brooks-the-inequality-problem.html. There is much less discussion on how the
decaying social ecosystem affects politics, but there is ample commentary on the decline of
social capital, bridging institutions, and a sense of community across different parts of the
population, which is directly related to rising partisanship. See, for instance, Putnam, *Bowling
Alone: The Collapse and Revival of American Community* (New York, NY: Simon & Schuster,
2000); and Robert Nisbet, *The Quest for Community: A Study in the Ethics of Order and
Freedom* (Wilmington, DE: ISI Books, 2010).
[51] Glendon, *Rights Talk*, 119.

societies industrialized. But secularization and individualization – which have gone further in the West than modernization required (see later)[52] – have substantially accentuated the general trend, with many social and political consequences. Western countries, for instance, have far greater rates of children born out of wedlock than Asian and Middle Eastern countries because of the weakening of the institutions around marriage. While two out of every five children are born out of marriage in the United States, only one out of fifty are in Japan, which is just as modern. In China, India, Indonesia, Egypt, and Saudi Arabia, it is 1 percent or less.[53]

MODERNIZATION VERSUS MODERNITY

In analyzing differences among societies, the impact of the tumultuous changes over the past two centuries must be considered. But it is important to distinguish between modernity – often known as Westernization to people outside the West – and modernization.[54] Modernity implies the introduction of secular, individualistic, rational values typically associated with Western societies. Modernization is the development of sophisticated institutions, technologically advanced industries, and complex, efficient divisions of labor. Societies and communities can modernize while keeping their traditional values and ways of living, as shown by East Asian countries such as Japan and by highly successful religious groups in the West and elsewhere. What Peng-chun Chang, the Chinese delegate who played a prominent role in the drafting of the UDHR (as discussed in Chapter 2), wrote in 1923 is what the great majority of such societies and groups would argue today:

> Modernization is a process. It will call for certain indispensable modern products in the development of the process. But it does not commit itself

---

[52] See, for instance, The Editors, "Contending Modernities," *The Immanent Frame*, 2010, http://blogs.ssrc.org/tif/2010/11/17/multiple-modernities/.

[53] W. Bradford Wilcox and Carlos Cavallé, "The Sustainable Demographic Dividend: What Do Marriage and Fertility Have to Do with the Economy?," Social Trends Institute, New York, 2011, Table 2, page 32, http://sustaindemographicdividend.org/articles/international-family-indicators/global-childrens-trends. Interestingly, the main exception in Asia is a highly Christian country – the Philippines – probably because Christianity in that context has promoted a much more individualistic outlook over time.

[54] Many authors, especially outside the West, have made this argument. In the West, Samuel Huntington is probably most well known for it. Huntington, "The West: Unique, Not Universal," *Foreign Affairs* 75, no. 6 (November/December 1996); Shmuel Noah Eisenstadt, *Comparative Civilizations and Multiple Modernities*, 2 vols. (Boston, MA: Brill, 2003); Gerard Delanty, "Modernity," in George Ritzer (ed.), *Blackwell Encyclopedia of Sociology*, 11 vols. (Malden, MA: Blackwell Publishing, 2007).

to uphold any crystallized formulations of the modern West to the entire detriment of the norms and formulations of the old [non-Western] culture. It emphasizes the process rather than the products.[55]

Cultures are ever changing, flexible, and to some extent contested.[56] This is especially true today, when social change is much more rapid than in the past due to both modernization, which reorders ways of working and governing and the institutions related to these, and globalization, which gives people much greater exposure to other cultures around the world. Cultures are not homogenous and static; they are hybrid, porous, dependent, and full of internal contradictions.[57]

Yet, as discussed in the previous chapter, cultures retain their core features over long time periods, even millennia in some cases. Change happens but is usually incremental, building on what people know and prioritize. Consequently, importing liberal modern frameworks will not result in fundamental change unless accompanied by very long periods of education and immersion in the new methods that completely dissolves preexisting social patterns. As North argues, "... the single most important point about institutional change, which must be grasped if we are to begin to get a handle on the subject, is that institutional change is overwhelmingly incremental."[58]

Economic development may shift many beliefs and values – bringing, for instance, increasing emphasis on self-expression and greater demand for responsive behavior from leaders – but it does not lead to a common result. International values surveys show that "cultural change is path dependent; a society's cultural heritage also shapes where it falls on the global cultural map." Similar societies evolve along similar paths, creating distinctive clusters of countries: Protestant Europe, Catholic Europe, ex-communist Europe, the English-speaking countries, Latin America, South Asia, the Islamic world, and Africa. "The values emphasized by different societies fall into a remarkably coherent pattern that reflects both those societies' economic development and their religious and colonial heritage."[59]

---

[55] Peng-chun Chang, *Education for Modernization in China* (New York, NY: Teachers College, Columbia University, 1923), 15.

[56] Sally Engle Merry, *Human Rights and Gender Violence: Translating International Law into Local Justice* (Chicago, IL: University of Chicago Press Books, 2006), 8–11

[57] Ibid., 8–11.

[58] North, *Institutions, Institutional Change and Economic Performance* (Cambridge: Cambridge University Press, 1990), 87 and 89.

[59] Ronald Inglehart and Christian Welzel, "How Development Leads to Democracy: What We Know about Modernization," *Foreign Affairs* 88, no. 2 (March/April 2009): 41.

Thick societies are unlikely to become thin – and vice versa – as evidenced by the continuities between ancient and contemporary Chinese and Western societies despite thousands of years of change and upheaval in between. The rise and fall of countries did not alter the basic pattern because the fundamental producers of culture continued much as before. There may have been movement in one direction or another depending on the levels of prosperity and stability – the West shifted toward a more sociocentric dynamic in the Middle Ages when chaos and poverty was common and back to a more individualistic dynamic when these declined dramatically – but the great differences between cultures remained. Nationalism, communism, and fascism all contributed to a relatively thick period in the West starting in the mid to late nineteenth century, products of the great social changes wrought by industrialization, urbanization, and modernization, but each weakened its grip after the devastations caused by the great wars and the gains from these changes spread more evenly across populations. The great majority of Southern countries are going to retain their thick societies even as they modernize because the institutions that acculturate their future generations will be based on those they already have today. The only possible exceptions are countries that are very small and highly exposed to foreign influences, such as some island states whose education and media are dominated by the United States or another Western country.[60] Changes over time in the thickness or thinness of a population depend on the unit of analysis: some parts of a country may change faster or slower than the broader society (e.g., WEIRD groups have changed faster and religious groups have changed slower than the rest of Western populations).

Religion can reproduce its own sociocentric values and institutions even if it is surrounded by a highly individualistic culture as long as it retains firm control of the environment that children grow up in – education, family and communal life, places of worship, and media – the main acculturating institutions. But when it fails to do this, a faith will suffer defections or a certain loss of integrity, as has happened to certain religious groups in the West as the strength of communal ties dissipated and new media such as television proliferated since the 1950s. Mainline Protestantism and non-Orthodox Jewish groups have seen large declines in membership. Catholicism and evangelicalism have retained their numbers, but have

---

[60] The effect, at least culturally, can be similar to what happens when small tribal societies get exposed to foreign influences. See John Bodley, *Victims of Progress* (Lanham, MD: Rowman & Littlefield, 2008).

become more individualistic in the West[61] than their Southern counterparts –
despite being more groupish than the rest of the West – precisely because of
the limitations they have on controlling their surroundings. Western media,
popular entertainment, and many schools send a very individualistic message.
A few exceptional communities exist: the Amish, a significant portion of the
orthodox Jewish community, Mormons, and parts of the Catholic and evangelical communities.

It is important to repeat, as noted in the cultural psychology chapter, that
thin societies can play host to thick communities. These minority groups are
naturally influenced by their surroundings, becoming more like their home
cultures than comparable groups elsewhere. However, if they remain vigilant
about passing on their cultures, customs, and norms, they can maintain their
core identities over time. They may end up having significant tension if
the gap between the community and broader society grows too large, as is
happening in parts of the West today. Although thick societies could theoret-
ically play host to thin communities, the latter by definition lack the dense
relationships and institutions that are essential to maintaining their integrity
over many generations in a foreign environment. Instead, they assimilate.

Globalization, and the technological change that drives it, challenges both
thick and thin societies, but in different ways. The more churn there is within
society – from population movements, job losses, the proliferation of media,
family breakdown, and increased competition – the less the state is able to
provide answers and the more important social institutions and communal
cohesion become. This partly explains the rise of secessionism in even well-
governed states such as the United Kingdom and Spain, and desecularization
in many parts of the world, especially outside the West.[62] But even when
urban and local governments – and a robust private sector – can play more
constructive roles, they are limited in their ability to address many problems
such as broken families, bad schools, and the proliferation of drugs. Countries
with weak states are even more vulnerable, even if they have thick societies:
they are systematically disadvantaged in competing internationally for investment and have great difficulties addressing transnational crime, capital flight,
and the pilfering of natural and state resources, all of which make them more
likely to lose from globalization. The rare combination of capable state *and*

---

[61] Ross Douthat, *Bad Religion: How We Became a Nation of Heretics* (New York, NY: Free Press,
2012).

[62] Peter Berger uses this term when asserting that "the assumption we live in a secularized world is
false ... The world today is as furiously religious as it ever was." Berger (ed.), *The
Desecularization of the World: Resurgent Religion and World Politics* (Grand Rapids, MI: Wm.
B. Eerdmans Publishing Co., 1999), 2.

thick society – such as those that exist in East Asia – will likely fare best amid the great disruptions these forces bring.

THE EVOLUTION OF BINDING SOCIAL INSTITUTIONS

There is great potential in a healthy social ecosystem. Social institutions have played a central role in human evolution by providing a groupish overlay onto a mostly selfish human nature. A product of communal or religious life (and often both), these institutions encompass all the various norms that Shweder identified with the community and divinity ethics. Individuals compete with each other, but so do groups, and competition favors the collection of people that have genuine team players. As such, group-level natural selection has long worked on humans to encourage the development of social institutions that promoted social cohesion in much the same way that evolution worked on individual organisms.[63]

Religion, which builds on the natural spirituality deeply embedded in the human psyche,[64] has historically been the best producer of social institutions, and it has evolved in conjunction with groups, reinforcing groupishness and being strengthened by the solidity of its communal adherents. As such, it has been the source of morality, dignity, and the rule of law for human societies worldwide.[65] But a similar origin does not guarantee similar products: Depending on the context, belief system, and competition, different societies ended up with very different mixtures of the divinity, social, and autonomy ethics.

---

[63] There is not a consensus on group-level selection, and it remains controversial among some evolutionary theorists. Although Darwin certainly believed in it, and a lot of academic research since the 1970s has supported it, some academics continue to think competition only exists at the level of the individual. Whether this has anything to do with how WEIRD people think – with their obvious preference for the individual over the community – is hard to say. Haidt, *The Righteous Mind*, 199 and 218–220. The most important supporters of group-level selection include Edward O. Wilson, David Sloan Wilson, Elliot Sober, and Michael Wade. Sober and D. S. Wilson, *Unto Others: The Evolution and Psychology of Unselfish Behavior* (Cambridge, MA: Harvard University Press, 1998); D. S. Wilson and E. O. Wilson, "Rethinking the Theoretical Foundation of Sociobiology," *Quarterly Review of Biology* 82, no. 4 (December 2007): 327–348; D. S. Wilson and E. O. Wilson, "Evolution 'for the Good of the Group,'" *American Scientist* 96, no. 5 (September/October 2008): 380–389.

[64] Many have made this argument. See, for instance, Roger Trigg, *Equality, Freedom, and Religion* (Oxford: Oxford University Press, 2012). I will leave it to the reader to determine whether this natural spirituality latent in the human psyche stems from natural selection, divine intervention, or a combination of the two.

[65] For a discussion on the role of religion in the development of the rule of law, see Francis Fukuyama, *The Origins of Political Order* (New York, NY: Farrar, Straus and Giroux, 2011).

Groups that can suppress selfishness and encourage sacrifice on behalf of the larger collective have crucial advantages over those that do not.[66] As a result, social institutions that could bind groups together, regulate behavior, and promote desirable social outcomes evolved as a complement to individualistic impulses over time. By increasing cooperation and a desire to work on behalf of the group and reducing slacking, cheating, or a desire to leave, such mechanisms strengthened groups and reproduced themselves, growing in importance over time.[67] Groups with such institutions were more likely to flourish. Groups without them were more likely to deteriorate or go extinct.[68] As Charles Darwin argues in *The Descent of Man*:

> When two tribes of primeval man ... came into competition, if (other circumstances being equal) the one tribe included a great number of courageous, sympathetic and faithful members, who were always ready to warn each other of danger, to aid and defend each other, this tribe would succeed better and conquer the other ... Selfish and contentious people will not cohere, and without coherence nothing can be effected.[69]

Morality can thus be understood as mainly a "tribal phenomenon," at least in its geneses. It "binds us into groups, in order to compete with other groups."[70] Over time, social orders backed by moral codes grew stronger and more prevalent, establishing their dominant role across the world. Eventually, according to the biologist Edmund O. Wilson, ethics were even wired into our genes – "biologicized" – as a result of natural selection.[71] The more moral intuitions worked on a biological level, the more effective they were, creating a feedback mechanism that impacted how the mind works.

The importance of religion – as well as other especially binding social institutions – can be understood in this context.[72] As Haidt puts it, "groupishness – despite all of the ugly and tribal things it makes us do – is

[66] George Christopher Williams, *Adaptation and Natural Selection: A Critique of Some Current Evolutionary Thought* (Princeton, NJ: Princeton University Press, 1966), 92–92.
[67] Haidt, *The Righteous Mind*, 189–220.
[68] Ibid., 191–192.
[69] Charles Darwin, *The Descent of Man, and Selection in Relation to Sex* (New York, NY: D. Appleton and Company, 1882), 130.
[70] Haidt, "A New Science of Morality, Part 1," Edge.org, September 17, 2010, https://edge.org/conversation/a-new-science-of-morality-part-1.
[71] Edmund Wilson, *Sociobiology: The New Synthesis* (Cambridge, MA: Harvard University Press, 1975), 27.
[72] Niraj Chokshi, "Fear of a Vengeful God May Explain Humanity's Global Expansion," *Washington Post*, February 12, 2016, www.washingtonpost.com/news/acts-of-faith/wp/2016/02/12/fear-of-a-vengeful-god-may-explain-humanitys-global-expansion/.

one of the magic ingredients that made it possible for civilization to burst forth."[73] Religion's uniquely strong ability to help groups cohere, divide labor, and work together to promote well-being made it a powerful force in the development of human societies – the strongest social institution of all.[74] In essence, religion emerged, survived, and thrived because it conferred benefits on those groups and individuals that adopted it. Those religions that made groups more cohesive and cooperative – through various forms of cultural innovation – outcompeted their peers and expanded at their expense.[75] Groups of people did not necessarily get wiped out as much as they adopted either the more effective religions or the most effective components of other religions.

As David Sloan Wilson explains in *Darwin's Cathedral*, "religions exist primarily for people to achieve together what they cannot achieve on their own."[76] Gods effectively reduced selfishness and divisiveness and built trust and the complex forms of cooperation that depended on it. Seeing everything and possessing the ability to discipline cheaters and oath breakers, belief in gods convinced people to cheat and break their oaths less frequently. Angry gods were especially effective, using shame and collective punishment as tools of discipline. Sacralizing rituals, laws, and other constraints were costly, inefficient, and irrational – at least to outsiders – but proved to be the most successful mechanisms for promoting cooperation without kinship invented.[77] These practical implications of religious belief are worth noting for the discussion here; religious adherents could argue that the origin of a given faith was divinely orchestrated, or even that a secular academic perspective cannot grasp the sacred roots of belief and morality.

Robert Putnam and David Campbell quantify contemporary effects of religious belief, showing in *American Grace* that even today religion has a strong positive influence on the groupishness of people. Those who frequently attend church or some other place of worship are more likely to donate money to charity, volunteer, help the homeless, donate blood, spend time with a

---

[73] Haidt, *The Righteous Mind*, 199.
[74] Scott Atran and Joseph Henrich, "The Evolution of Religion: How Cognitive By-Products, Adaptive Learning Heuristics, Ritual Displays, and Group Competition Generate Deep Commitments to Prosocial Religions," *Biological Theory* 5, no. 1 (2010): 18–30.
[75] Nicholas Wade, *The Faith Instinct: How Religion Evolved and Why It Endures* (New York, NY: Penguin Press, 2009); Robert Wright, *The Evolution of God* (New York, NY: Little, Brown and Company, 2009).
[76] David Sloan Wilson, *Darwin's Cathedral: Evolution, Religion, and the Nature of Society* (Chicago, IL: University of Chicago Press, 2002), 136.
[77] Scott Atran and Joseph Henrich, "The Evolution of Religion," 18–30; Haidt, *The Righteous Mind*, 255–258.

person who is depressed, offer a seat to a stranger, or help someone find a job. Religiosity is a better predictor of altruism and empathy than education, age, income, gender, or race.[78] Frequent worshippers are also more likely to belong to community organizations, neighborhood and civic groups, and professional associations. Within these, they are more likely to be active on committees and in a leadership role. They take a more active role in public life, participating more often in elections, public meetings, and even demonstrations. They are disproportionately represented among those working to promote social and political change. In short, they get more involved in more ways and are more likely to play a leadership role in their communities. "And the margin of difference between them and the more secular is large."[79]

Other studies show that regular attendance at religious services is linked to strong marriages; stable family life; well-behaved children; reductions in the incidences of domestic abuse, crime, and addiction; and increases in physical health, mental health, education levels, and longevity.[80] And, as Patrick Fagan summarizes, "these effects are intergenerational, as grandparents and parents pass on the benefits to the next generations."[81]

Putnam's work shows that too much individualism weakens social cohesion while "religion creates community, community creates altruism, and altruism turns us away from self and toward the common good."[82] Societies without any religion risk over many generations losing the very mechanisms –

[78] Jonathan Sacks, "The Moral Animal," *The New York Times*, December 24, 2012, www.nytimes.com/2012/12/24/opinion/the-moral-animal.html; Robert Putnam and David Campbell, *American Grace: How Religion Divides and Unites Us* (New York, IL: Simon & Schuster, 2010).

[79] Sacks, "Regular Worship Is the Mortar of the Big Society," *The Times*, November 5, 2010, www.rabbisacks.org/credo-regular-worship-is-the-mortar-of-the-big-society/; Putnam and Campbell, *American Grace*.

[80] Patrick Fagan, "Why Religion Matters Even More: The Impact of Religious Practice on Social Stability," Heritage Foundation Backgrounder No. 1992, December 18, 2006. See also W. Bradford Wilcox, "The Latest Social Science Is Wrong. Religion Is Good for Families and Kids," *Washington Post*, December 15, 2015. Both these articles provide an ample list of sources for their conclusions. For instance, see Amy Burdette, Christopher Ellison, Darren Sherkat, and Kurt Gore, "Are There Religious Variations in Marital Infidelity?," *Journal of Family Issues* 28 (December 2007): 1553–1581; W. Bradford Wilcox and Brad Wilcox, *Soft Patriarchs, New Men: How Christianity Shapes Fathers and Husbands* (Chicago, IL: University Of Chicago Press, 2004); Daniel Lichter and Julie Carmalt, "Religion and Marital Quality Among Low-income Couples," *Social Science Research* 38, no. 1 (March 2009): 168–187; John Bartkowski, Xiaohe Xu, and Martin Levin, "Religion and Child Development: Evidence from the Early Childhood Longitudinal Study," *Social Science Research* 37, no. 1 (March 2008): 18–36.

[81] Fagan, "Why Religion Matters Even More.".

[82] Sacks, "Regular Worship Is the Mortar of the Big Society"; Putnam and Campbell, *American Grace*.

embedded in social institutions – that have held them together and enabled them to thrive historically.[83]

Of course, religion can also be a destabilizing force if it promotes violence or bonding social capital among adherents at the expense of bridging social capital with other members of society. These dangers are much greater when the state is weak and society is fragmented because in such contexts there may be no other mechanism to bring different groups together.[84] The difference between moderate and extremist groups and between integrationist and isolationist groups in their balance of positive and negative influences on society varies tremendously depending on the nature of the group and society.

But, in general, social institutions – as exemplified through religion – have been essential to human well-being since time immemorial. This is as true in thin as it is in thick societies – though in a more limited fashion. Even where state institutions play a much larger role, they depend to a great extent on the nature of visible and invisible social institutions to function effectively. If all the organizations that hold government officials to account and all the norms that encourage civility, trust, compromise, and acceptance of the rule of law deteriorated, so would the quality of state institutions.

TWO DIFFERENT APPROACHES TO HUMAN RIGHTS

Thin societies can have a state-mandated human rights framework that downplays context and diminishes differences between groups because of their strong focus on the individual and their relative dearth of social institutions. In contrast, thick societies are better off using a more constrained human rights framework, with limited state involvement. Such a framework ensures minimum standards but does not preclude differences across groups and provides ample room for robust social institutions to play a constructive role in people's lives.

The former – which corresponds to the framework adopted by Western universalists and nearly all human rights actors – assumes a uniform moral matrix across countries and groups within the West.[85] It generally views culture as fixed and unchanging, and thus as an obstacle to human rights

---

[83] Trigg, *Equality, Freedom, and Religion*, 22–23 and 139.

[84] Seth Kaplan, "Identifying Truly Fragile States," *The Washington Quarterly* 37, no. 1 (Spring 2014), 49–63.

[85] See, among others, Jack Donnelly, "Human Rights and Human Dignity: An Analytic Critique of Non-Western Conceptions of Human Rights," in Frederick Snyder and Surakiart Sathirathai (eds.), *Third World Attitudes toward International Law: An Introduction* (Dordrecht, The Netherlands: Martinus Nijhoff Publishers, 1987), 341–357.

that needs to be re-formed through education and the intervention of national and international authorities.[86] This may work in WEIRD societies, which are not only highly individualistic but also a product of the same culture that has developed the Western-dominated international human rights system (see Chapter 5). In this case, modernization has really yielded modernity; a human rights framework based on it finds easy acceptance, especially among the highly educated, secular elites who often formulate policy.

But in thick societies – whether in the South or within religious groups in the West – a framework that assumes a strong role for state or international enforcement of a uniform set of thin society values makes little sense. Practices labeled as harmful and traditional are really essential pillars of a culture operating according to fundamentally different principles.[87] Wider systems of kinship and community are deeply embedded in patterns of family and religion and unlikely to change unless forced to do so.[88] And state capture poses risks for implementing rights laws; Western universalist ideas may be imposed unevenly so as to advantage elites.

Instead of recognizing differences between societies as potentially beneficial for both groups, Western human rights discourse assumes that thick societies are at an earlier evolutionary stage and that traditional practices ought to fade away as the countries or groups modernize, moving "from a primitive form to something like civilization."[89] This risks repeating the pattern of colonialism, when the "law was seen as the gift of the colonizers to societies viewed as chaotic and arbitrary."[90]

As Charles Taylor argues, the Western approach leaves even those outside the West who are eager to espouse universal norms feeling "uneasy by the underlying philosophy of the human person in society. This seems to give pride of place to autonomous individuals, determined to demand their rights, even (indeed especially) in the face of widespread social consensus."[91] Taylor highlights the difficult position those from the East and South find themselves in:

---

[86] Merry, *Human Rights and Gender Violence*.
[87] Erika George, "Virginity Testing and South Africa's HIV/AIDS Crisis: Beyond Rights Universalism and Cultural Relativism toward Health Capabilities," *California Law Review* 96, no. 6 (2008): 1447–1518.
[88] Markus and Conner, *Clash!*, 188.
[89] Merry, *Human Rights and Gender Violence*, 10–12.
[90] Ibid., 226.
[91] Charles Taylor, "Conditions of an Unforced Consensus on Human Rights," in Joanne Bauer and Daniel Bell (eds.), *The East Asian Challenge for Human Rights* (Cambridge: Cambridge University Press, 1999), 128–129.

Can people who imbibe the full Western human rights ethos, which reaches its highest expression in the lone courageous individual fighting against all the forces of social conformity for her rights, ever be good members of a "Confucian" society? How does this ethic of demanding what is due us fit with the Theravada Buddhist search for selflessness, for self-giving and *dana* (generosity)?[92]

Flexible universalism – as discussed in Chapter 2 – conceptualizes thick social practices as being both deeply embedded in local cultures and malleable to some extent. Sociocentric cultures are not going to become individualistic, but they certainly can adapt new ways of expressing themselves. Women's rights, for instance, can be advanced by working with traditional institutions and not just seeking to eliminate them. Even if there is significant resistance in patriarchic societies, there will be social forces and ideas embedded within local cultures that can be leveraged to promote change (and which are unlikely to favor the wholesale discarding of local traditions).[93] As Celestine Nyamu argues, "Proponents of gender equality must appropriate positive openings presented by cultural and religious traditions, instead of dismissing culture as a negative influence."[94] Indeed, giving social institutions a prominent role to play in promoting change is probably one of the best ways to achieve it. Attacking cultural practices, on the other hand, will likely invite a backlash and lead to human rights being viewed with suspicion. Unfortunately, as Erika George argues, "the normative commitments of classical liberal universalism in which human rights are grounded," make it much easier for Western universalists to call for the elimination of social institutions than to consider how they might leverage "existing opportunities within a given cultural normative order for actually facilitating women's empowerment."[95]

On a practical level, the difference between the two approaches to human rights can be seen in how each type of society tackles inequality. Thin societies prefer a state-led approach that aims to reduce inequality through progressive taxation, income transfers, social security, and positive discrimination. Thick societies, on the other hand, are more likely to emphasize the role of non-state

[92] Taylor, "Conditions of an Unforced Consensus on Human Rights," 128–129.
[93] "Traditional worldviews can't be negated, abolished, or banned; they have to be engaged." Michael Walzer, *The Paradox of Liberation: Secular Revolutions and Religious Counterrevolutions* (New Haven, CT: Yale University Press, 2015), 121.
[94] Celestine Nyamu, "How Should Human Rights and Development Respond to Cultural Legitimization of Gender Hierarchy in Developing Countries?," *Harvard International Law Journal* 41, no. 2 (Spring 2000): 382.
[95] George, "Virginity Testing and South Africa's HIV/AIDS Crisis," 1507.

actors in addressing the sources of disadvantage (e.g., family or communal breakdown, weak social networks, discrimination) while seeking to build inclusiveness and social cohesion into every aspect of how society functions.[96] Religious actors were on the forefront of the civil rights movement, led by Reverend Martin Luther King in the United States and leaders of reconciliation in South Africa after apartheid ended. Many of the countries with the lowest Gini coefficient – the most commonly used measure of inequality – are thick East Asian nations with limited social welfare spending[97]; their success is due to an egalitarian ethos that pervades society, leading to a wide range of state and nonstate institutions – for example, education systems that are especially good at educating the bottom rungs of society and norms that ensure that almost all children grow up with two parents.

The two types of societies also differ as to who is entitled to rights as well as how rights are framed. Whereas thick societies may give rights to fetuses and the dead, thin societies may give rights to the environment and some animals.[98] The scope of rights that children and parents enjoy can differ substantially between the two groups. Thick societies, for instance, may strengthen the social institutions around marriage and family in order to protect the rights of children to be raised in a stable environment with robust social support. In contrast, thin societies may only focus on the rights of children to receive a certain standard of education and upbringing that does not limit their choices as adults. The former may limit the freedoms of parents to ensure the sanctity of marriage, but do nothing to constrain how they educate or bring up their children; the latter may limit the freedom of parents to pass on their values and traditions to their children, but do nothing to constrain their autonomy and ability to leave relationships even if children may be negatively impacted by such freedoms.[99]

---

[96] See, for instance, Brooks, "The Wrong Inequality"; Brooks, "The Inequality Problem"; Brooks, "The Opportunity Gap," *The New York Times*, July 9, 2012, www.nytimes.com/2012/07/10/opinion/brooks-the-opportunity-gap.html; and Henry Rowen, "The Political and Social Foundations of the Rise of East Asia: An Overview," in *Behind East Asian Growth: The Political and Social Foundations of Prosperity*, ed. Rowen (New York, NY: Routledge, 1998), 1–31.

[97] See, among others, The World Bank, *The East Asian Miracle: Economic Growth and Public Policy* (New York, NY: Oxford University Press, 1993).

[98] Licht, "Introduction," 14–15; Galston, "Between Philosophy and History," 68–70.

[99] Douthat, "The Liberalism of Adult Autonomy," *The New York Times*, June 4, 2015, http://douthat.blogs.nytimes.com/2015/06/04/the-liberalism-of-adult-autonomy/?_r=0.

LIBERAL PLURALISM

A flexible universalism that builds on the liberal pluralism articulated by political philosophers such as Isaiah Berlin provides a practical way to bridge these gaps and thus advance human rights. In his writings, Berlin argued that philosophers[100] – like many contemporary Western human rights advocates – have long believed that they could find absolute truth, such that all "true questions" have "one answer and one only." According to those who think this way, "a perfect life can be conceived" even though people, cultures, moral and political views, doctrines, religions, moralities, and ideas differ tremendously.[101] But this is impossible to achieve. In the end, "men choose between ultimate values; they choose as they do because their life and thought are determined by fundamental moral categories and concepts that are, at any rate over large stretches of time and space, a part of their being and thought and sense of their own identity; part of what makes them human."[102]

"Berlin's moral pluralism offers," as William Galston from the Brookings Institution writes,

> the best account of the moral universe we inhabit. He depicts a world in which fundamental values are plural, conflicting, incommensurable in theory, and uncombinable in practice – a world in which there is no single, univocal summum bonum that can be defined philosophically, let alone imposed politically.[103]

Moral philosophers such as Galston, Charles Taylor, Joseph Raz, and John Gray have in recent years developed Berlin's thinking into a full-fledged

---

[100] He did not say so, but in light of Berlin's context and what we have learned from cultural psychology, it is obvious he meant Western philosophers.

[101] Isaiah Berlin, "My Intellectual Path," in Henry Hardy (ed.), *The Power of Ideas* (Princeton, NJ: Princeton University Press, 2002), 5–7.

[102] Berlin, "Two Concepts of Liberty," *Four Essays on Liberty* (Oxford: Oxford University Press, 1969), 31. Most disagreements on what choices to make in a particular circumstance can be overcome if the focus is on the practical action (and not the abstract) and the perspective of the one deciding what to do. This requires really putting oneself in the shoes of another and assimilating their culture, history, and life experience.

[103] Galston, *Liberal Pluralism: The Implications of Value Pluralism for Political Theory and Practice* (Cambridge: Cambridge University Press, 2002), 30.

value-pluralist movement,[104] clarifying many of the complex issues his approach raised, and dealing with objections.[105]

Liberal pluralism recognizes that although there is a clear distinction between good and bad, and between good and evil, there is no supreme good, definitive ranking of goods, or common measure of goods (liberal monism) for all individuals, communities, or societies because they are qualitatively heterogeneous. There are a range of public goods and virtues for which the relative importance depends on both circumstances and the values held by those involved. As Berlin wrote, "we are faced with choices between ends equally ultimate, and claims equally absolute, the realisation of some of which must inevitably involve the sacrifice of others."[106] As a result, "the possibility of conflict – and of tragedy – can never wholly be eliminated from human life, either personal or social."[107] Many choices are not between good and bad, but between good and good (or, at times, between bad and bad). "To live well is to choose a good life, which inevitably means excluding other good possibilities. The philosophical justification for social pluralism is the diversity of legitimate human goods."[108] The moral life of a nun, for instance, is incompatible with that of a mother, yet there is no purely rational measure of which is preferable.

These conditions are true whether you are living in a thick or thin society. Both Burke (who argued for the constant balancing, reconciling, and compensating between multiple forces and needs within a society) and Mill (who argued for constant experimenting with different aspects of life, with the understanding that error was very possible) understood that it is impossible to formulate clear and certain answers to life's most important questions, or to build a definitive ranking of goods that works in all contexts and times.[109]

Within the liberal pluralist framework, some types of goods are so basic that they always matter, while the importance of others depends on the context. A relatively tiny number are basic in the sense that they form part of any choiceworthy conception of human life. Beyond these, there is a wide range

---

[104] Galston gives a five-part definition of value pluralism: not relativism; objective goods cannot be fully rank-ordered; some goods are basic in that they form a necessary core in every worthy conception of life; beyond this small core, there is a wide range of possibilities that are legitimate; different from monism, which believes there is a common standard to judge values. See Galston, *Liberal Pluralism*, 5–6.
[105] Galston, *Liberal Pluralism*, 5.
[106] Berlin, "Two Concepts of Liberty," 29–30.
[107] Ibid.," 30.
[108] Galston, *The Practice of Liberal Pluralism* (Cambridge: Cambridge University Press, 2004), 181.
[109] Berlin, "Two Concepts of Liberty," 31.

of possibilities that are legitimate.[110] These depend on individual or community-specific conceptions of what is true, good, beautiful, and efficient (which is also one way to define culture).[111] Whereas the ancient Greeks subsidized the theatre, the ancient Jews subsidized education. In the European Middle Ages, curing souls was so important that it was socialized; curing bodies was less important and privatized.[112] The range of legitimate diversity defines the zone of individual liberty and should include everything beyond a necessary common core.[113]

Liberal pluralism thus differentiates between three types of rights: (1) a small group of basic rights that everyone agrees are important and need to be prioritized (and thus are natural rights); (2) a longish list of rights that everyone shares but may prioritize and implement differently; and (3) a set of rights that are unique to particular cultures or communities and not commonly shared (only some cultures see them as true, good, beautiful, or efficient).[114] Thick and thin societies will both readily accept the importance of the first set of rights, but will have clear differences in how they prioritize the second set. They may also each have a set of rights that the other does not think are important; this is the third set.

Liberal pluralism is based on practical philosophy and an acute awareness of the diversity and messiness of the moral universe we inhabit. As Galston explains,

> Practical philosophy is (or ought to be) the theory of our practice. When we are trying to decide what to do, we are typically confronted with a multiplicity of worthy principles and genuine goods that are not neatly ordered and that cannot be translated into a common measure of value. This is not ignorance but, rather, the fact of the matter. That is why practical life is so hard.[115]

---

[110] Galston, *Liberal Pluralism*, 5–6. Walzer makes a similar point. See Walzer, "Justice, Justice Shalt Thou Pursue," in Michael Harris, Daniel Rynhold, and Tamra Wright (eds.), *Radical Responsibility: Celebrating the Thought of Chief Rabbi Lord Jonathan Sacks* (Jerusalem: Maggid Books, 2013), 79–93.

[111] Berlin, *Vico and Herder* (London: Hogarth Press, 1976), 194–195; Shweder, "Moral Maps, 'First World' Conceits, and the New Evangelists," in Harrison and Huntington (eds.), *Culture Matters*, 163.

[112] Walzer, "Justice, Justice Shalt Thou Pursue," 85–87; Walzer, *Spheres of Justice: A Defense of Pluralism and Equality* (New York, NY: Basic Books, 1983), 69–74 and 87.

[113] Galston, *Liberal Pluralism*, 5–6.

[114] Galston differentiates between two types of rights when discussing liberal pluralism in Galston, *Liberal Pluralism*, 5–6. Teraya Koji nicely summarizes the debates that surround differentiating between the importance of different rights in Koji, "Emerging Hierarchy in International Human Rights and Beyond: From the Perspective of Non-Derogable Rights," *European Journal of International Law* 12, no. 5 (2001): 917–941.

[115] Galston, *Liberal Pluralism*, 131.

State constitutions work according to this conception of the moral universe. They are characterized by a large variety of goals, none of which is overriding in all contexts. Implementation, whether through the executive, legislative, or judicial branches of government, depends on weighing and comparing competing rights and public interests without clear guidelines.[116]

Shweder's "moral universalism without the uniformity"[117] reflects a similar disposition. It is based on the belief that there are simply too many universally binding values to be reduced to a single common measurement, trade-offs are inevitable,[118] and human reason has limits. Differences in "local beliefs, interests and social facts" inevitably lead to differences in how values or goods are prioritized and applied.[119] As Michael Walzer writes, "Goods have different meanings in different societies. The same 'thing' is valued for different reasons, or it is valued here and disvalued there."[120] There are pluses and minuses to most actions and value systems, whether based on long-standing cultural traditions or liberal modernity. There is a lot of space for alternative discourses and ideologies regarding progress and how one judges who is better or worse off.[121] Walzer concludes, "There is no way to rank and order these worlds with regard to their understanding of social goods. . . . To override those understandings is (always) to act unjustly."[122]

OVERCOMING REACTIVE CYCLES

Liberal pluralism provides a framework that can enable a much wider range of actors to play a constructive role in promoting human rights. It establishes universal standards and principles, yet works across both thick and thin groups, countries, continents, and cultures in a way that current practice cannot. This framework avoids the vicious, reactive cycles that have become all too common today.

When Western universalists urge the South (and religious actors within the West) to discard tradition or heterodox ways of living or adopt a one-size-fits-all approach to various challenges that states face, it engenders ill will and undermines the existing consensus around the UDHR and related

---

[116] Ibid., 88–89.
[117] Shweder, "Relativism and Universalism," in Didier Fassin (ed.), *A Companion to Moral Anthropology* (Malden, MA: Wiley-Blackwell, 2012), 94.
[118] Berlin, "Two Concepts of Liberty," 29–30.
[119] Shweder, "Relativism and Universalism," 97.
[120] Walzer, *Spheres of Justice*, 7.
[121] Berlin, "Two Concepts of Liberty," 29–30; Galston, *Liberal Pluralism*, 5–6.
[122] Walzer, *Spheres of Justice*, 314.

documents – consensus that holds power to bridge differences and improve human well-being. Western universalists too often incite resistance from thick societies and communities to even those reforms that ought to be acceptable to them. Such a dynamic yields a cycle whereby Western condemnation helps feed a negative reaction, which leads to further condemnation, more reaction, and so on.[123] Such a pattern is apparent in the relationship between the West and the Middle East, and, to a lesser degree, parts of Asia.[124] It has seeped into the relationship with Africa as the latter has grown rapidly and become less dependent on Western largesse.[125] And it is increasingly present within the West itself, as thick community religious actors fight the actions of the thin society state to narrow the definition of freedom of religion to freedom of conscience and to eliminate traditions and institutional practices contrary to a Western universalist interpretation of human rights.

This unhealthy dynamic prevents cooperation that could advance the cause of human rights. It holds back any meaningful discussion on issues – such as those to do with globalization, the elderly, future generations, the environment, communal control of land, and so on – that concern rights not included or not well articulated within the current international human rights regime and that affect everyone – East and West, South and North.[126] It prevents some countries from forging a consensus among a broad range of different actors to promote human rights because it blocks the use of alternative approaches. These approaches are often better rooted in local value systems and enjoy wider legitimacy than the narrow approach pursued by Western human rights actors.

The thin society West's narrow view of human rights also holds back efforts aimed at separating legitimate thick society cultural concerns from criticisms that merely advance the interests of self-serving leaders and governments abroad (and paternalistic figures in Western countries). This distinction is possibly the biggest long-term question in the human rights field. Cultural

---

[123] See, among others, Taylor, "Conditions of an Unforced Consensus on Human Rights," 140–144; Bauer and Bell, "Introduction," in Bauer and Bell (eds.), *The East Asian Challenge for Human Rights*, 4.

[124] Bauer and Bell (eds.), *The East Asian Challenge for Human Rights*.

[125] Karen Alter, James Thuo Gathii, and Laurence Helfer, "Backlash against International Courts in West, East and Southern Africa: Causes and Consequences," iCourts Working Paper Series, No. 21; Duke Law School Public Law & Legal Theory Series, May 12, 2015, http://papers.ssrn .com/sol3/papers.cfm?abstract_id=2591837. See, for instance, Norimitsu Onishi, "American Support for Gay Rights May Leave Africans Vulnerable," *The New York Times*, December 21, 2015, www.nytimes.com/2015/12/21/world/africa/us-support-of-gay-rights-in-africa-may-have-done-more-harm-than-good.html.

[126] Bauer and Bell, "Introduction," 4 and 23.

concerns, when articulately expressed by those that have little power to lose, do not challenge the need for human rights like those in the Universal Declaration; these concerns respond to how inflexibly they are often construed. The ability to outlaw certain groups, increase limits on free speech, jail opponents, introduce special security measures, limit the rights of women, keep a tight rein on divorce, and teach certain values in school are all legitimate topics of attention. Yet, today too many Eastern and Southern governments (and religious actors in the West) can hide behind the cultural card when criticized by Western universalists in such areas – precisely because of the unease created by the approach adopted by Western governments, organizations, and activists. The defensiveness that people in these communities feel may weaken the overall case for human rights – reducing their legitimacy and moral authority as a result.

For instance, instead of rebuking Southeast Asian governments for adopting the ASEAN Human Rights Declaration (discussed in Chapter 2) Western institutions should have submitted how it might be improved. Sharp criticism is more likely to back the region into a corner, setting off a backlash as happened during the "Asian values" debates during the 1990s, than lead to any improvement.[127] Yet, leading international human rights organizations "called for the postponement of the adoption of the ASEAN Human Rights Declaration" because it "falls short of existing international human rights standards and risks creating a sub-standard level of human rights protection in the region."[128]

The "Asian values" debate – which has echoes elsewhere – is really a question of tradeoffs between competing rights or needs. Whereas the thin society West emphasizes civil and political rights, the thick society South prefers to give higher priority to economic, social, and cultural needs.[129] Indeed, as Asbjørn Eide and Gudmundur Alfredsson argue,

---

[127] For the complete set of references to the rebukes, see the footnote in Chapter 2. Tom Zwart, "Safeguarding the Universal Acceptance of Human Rights through the Receptor Approach," *Human Rights Quarterly* 36, no. 4 (November 2014): 903–904; Paula Gerber, "ASEAN Human Rights Declaration: A Step Forward or a Slide Backwards?," *The Conversation*, November 20, 2012, http://theconversation.com/asean-human-rights-declaration-a-step-forward-or-a-slide-backwards-10895; and Yohanna Ririhena and Bagus BT Saragih, "Despite Criticism, ASEAN Set to Adopt Rights Declaration," *The Jakarta Post*, November 17, 2012, www.thejakartapost.com/news/2012/11/17/despite-criticism-asean-set-adopt-rights-declaration.html.

[128] Amnesty International, "Postpone Deeply Flawed ASEAN Human Rights Declaration," Press Release, November 5, 2012), www.amnesty.org/en/press-releases/2012/11/postpone-deeply-flawed-asean-human-rights-declaration/.

[129] Bauer and Bell, "Introduction," 22.

to the degree that these differences are substantive in nature, rather than transparent attempts to hold on to power and privilege, they raise the question as to whether human rights should constitute a priority over other elements considered necessary for sustainable development and social justice.[130]

Southern states and religious actors in the West can legitimately argue that all efforts made to improve the well-being and dignity of their citizens or community members amount to the promotion of human rights or at least better human lives. In the 1993 Bangkok Declaration, Asian countries did just this when they reaffirmed their commitment to the UDHR while calling for a greater stress on economic, social, and cultural rights – especially, the right to economic development over civil and political rights.[131] "Without perhaps using the human rights label, people and government entities everywhere are therefore furthering human rights."[132]

Whereas it is perfectly legitimate to criticize China (or other states) for treating minorities inequitably, torturing prisoners, limiting the right to a fair hearing, or locking up citizens without due process, the success the government has had developing the country and improving the lives of hundreds of millions should limit criticism of its political system. In fact, if you compare its success versus the failure of many democracies in Africa and elsewhere – states that cannot even preserve the right to a secure social order in some cases – it is hard to say the country's leadership is less accountable and responsive despite its very different form from the Western norm.[133] It thus should not be surprising that China's government generally outperforms many democracies on surveys of public satisfaction.[134] Other Southern developmental states such as Ethiopia, Rwanda, Singapore, and, in an earlier era, South

---

[130] Asbjørn Eide and Gudmundur Alfredsson, "Introduction," in Guðmundur Alfreðsson and Asbjørn Eide (eds.), *The Universal Declaration of Human Rights: A Common Standard of Achievement* (The Hague: Martinus Nijhoff Publishers, 1999), xxix.

[131] "Bangkok Declaration," Final Declaration of the Regional Meeting for Asia of the World Conference on Human Rights, Bangkok, April 7, 1993, UNGA A/CONF.157/ASRM/8A/ CONF.157/PC/59, www.hurights.or.jp/archives/other_documents/section1/1993/04/final-declaration-of-the-regional-meeting-for-asia-of-the-world-conference-on-human-rights.html#_edn1.

[132] Zwart, "Balancing Yin and Yang in the International Human Rights Debate," Paper for the *Sixth Beijing Human Rights Forum*, Beijing, China, September 12–13, 2013, 5.

[133] See World Bank, *World Development Report 2017: Governance and the Law* (Washington, DC: World Bank, 2017).

[134] Wenfang Tang, Michael Lewis-Beck, and Nicholas Martini, "Government for the People in China?," *The Diplomat*, June 17, 2013, http://thediplomat.com/2013/06/government-for-the-people-in-china/.

Korea and Taiwan have worked hard to satisfy their publics even if they haven't met Western political norms. However, if, as these countries develop, their populations' expectations of their governments increase, yielding greater pressure from within for a different form of government – as was the case in South Korea and Taiwan – then external advocacy for change may be warranted.

As we'll see in the next chapter, Western universalist human rights organizations – reflecting Western cultural orientation and autonomy-centered moral matrices – have strongly identified civil and political rights with human rights in general. This tendency limits the more nuanced approach that the UDHR originally allowed for.[135] Makau Mutua contends, "They claim to practice law, not politics. Although their mandates seek to promote paradigmatic liberal values and norms, they present themselves as neutral, universal, non-ideological, non-partisan, and unbiased."[136] This bias is reflected in the reports of Amnesty International, Human Rights Watch, and others, which lack a comprehensive set of standards to judge countries based on the full gambit of rights agreed upon in international human rights documents, including the UDHR, ICESCR, ICCPR, and Vienna Declaration.[137]

Narrowing the scope of human rights to a core that is widely accepted across cultures and moral matrices – a universal minimum standard – is key to bridging the ever-greater gaps between thick and thin societies and reestablishing the overlapping consensus on human rights that once existed.

---

[135] Yasuaki Onuma "Towards an Intercivilizational Approach to Human Rights," in Joanne Bauer and Daniel Bell (eds.), *The East Asian Challenge for Human Rights* (Cambridge: Cambridge University Press, 1999), 112.

[136] Makau Mutua, "Savages, Victims, and Saviors: The Metaphor of Human Rights," *Harvard International Law Journal* 42, no. 1 (Winter 2001): 240–241.

[137] Onuma, "Towards an Intercivilizational Approach to Human Rights," 113–114.

5

The Limits of Western Human Rights Discourse

Western normative assumptions undergird much of the current human rights discourse[1], and many human rights campaigners believe that "all states parties to human rights treaties have committed themselves to the Western view on human rights."[2] There are both historical and contemporary reasons for this. Western universalists' understanding of human rights has been shaped by Enlightenment ideals, notions about natural rights, and the rights revolution of the 1960s.[3] Today, Western universalists play an extraordinarily large role as funders and conveners of human rights organizations and scholarly debates, directly and indirectly shaping agendas, frameworks of analysis, and evaluation methods in the process.

This approach holds that "human rights are part of a distinctive modernist vision of the good and just society that emphasizes autonomy, choice, equality, secularism, and protection of the body,"[4] and it converts cultural norms in one part of the world into universal rights.[5] As they prioritize individual rights and rely on what Sally Engle Merry calls a "cultural system ... rooted

---

[1] As William Twining writes, "In much of the discourse about human rights, there is a tendency to conflate human rights law and human rights as moral or political rights." Twining, *General Jurisprudence: Understanding Law from a Global Perspective* (Cambridge: Cambridge University Press, 2008), 178.

[2] Tom Zwart, "Using Local Culture to Further the Implementation of International Human Rights: The Receptor Approach," *Human Rights Quarterly* 34, no. 2 (May 2012): 553.

[3] Charles Taylor, "Conditions of an Unforced Consensus on Human Rights," in Joanne Bauer and Daniel Bell (eds.), *The East Asian Challenge for Human Rights* (Cambridge: Cambridge University Press, 1999), 128.

[4] Sally Engle Merry, *Human Rights and Gender Violence: Translating International Law into Local Justice* (Chicago, IL: University of Chicago Press Books, 2006), 220–221.

[5] They can also be seen as "the moralized expression of a political ideology." Although depicted as nonideological, impartial, and the "quintessence of human goodness," human rights are merely a way to extend Western liberal modernity across the world. Makau Mutua, "The Ideology of Human Rights," *Virginia Journal of International Law* 36 (1996): 592–593.

in secular transnational modernity,"[6] Western governments and human rights actors are prone to undervalue thick society activities that promote community or involve religion. This limits the ability of practitioners to adapt human rights principles (such as those found in the UDHR, discussed in Chapter 2) to specific circumstances and cultures, reducing both their effectiveness and appeal in the process.[7] It diminishes the ability of human rights organizations to embed themselves within local cultures and gain legitimacy in the eyes of local people. And, by focusing on the state as the mechanism of change, the Western human rights framework strengthens the very power that human rights are supposed to limit.[8]

Western universalists, like all people, are a product of their context. As David Bentley Hart, an American Eastern Orthodox theologian notes, "modernity is itself an ideology, pervasive and enormously powerful," which Westerners have adopted and espoused – sometimes unknowingly.[9] Organizations and governments may simultaneously triumph their commitment to "free expression" and "diversity" while subtly discriminating against those who do not share their perspective.[10]

Working with this singular worldview, Nikitah Okembe-Ra Imani contends that Western universalist human rights actors and scholars both create "the parameters of legitimate discussion concerning global issues" and then serve "as the de facto 'ideal type' and standard for evaluative judgments relative to those issues." They develop and sustain a system of international and state institutions to judge and sanction those who do not conform. "Not surprisingly to anyone, except perhaps the West itself, non-Western forms, ideas, and concepts are found wanting and deficient and therefore subject to exclusion from the theater of debate and communicative legitimacy."[11] Seeing thick Southern and religious "customs" as harmful practices rooted in traditional culture; as excuses for noncompliance with international obligations;[12] and even as barbaric, odious, and detestable,[13] Western universalists have difficulty

---

[6]   Merry, *Human Rights and Gender Violence*, 90, 220–221.
[7]   Ibid., 222.
[8]   Ibid., 223; Twining, *General Jurisprudence*, 184.
[9]   David Bentley Hart, *Atheist Delusion: The Christian Revolution and Its Fashionable Enemies* (New Haven, CT: Yale University Press, 2009), 32.
[10] Ross Douthat, "Diversity and Dishonesty," *The New York Times*, April 13, 2014, www.nytimes.com/2014/04/13/opinion/sunday/douthat-diversity-and-dishonesty.html.
[11] Nikitah Okembe-Ra Imani, "Critical Impairments to Globalizing the Western Human Rights Discourse," *Societies without Borders* 3, no. 2 (2008): 270–271.
[12] Merry, *Human Rights and Gender Violence*, 10.
[13] Shweder, "Relativism and Universalism," in Didier Fassin (ed.), *A Companion to Moral Anthropology* (Malden, MA: Wiley-Blackwell, 2012), 92.

contemplating alternative visions of social justice that are less individualistic and more focused on religion, communities, social institutions, and duties.[14] This tendency has torn the overlapping consensus that once existed on human rights, and it stands in the way of repairing it.

INDIVIDUALISM AND RIGHTS PROMOTION IN THE WEST

The evolution of the rights discourse within the West[15] – alongside growing secularization and individualization[16] – has prompted many of the growing disagreements over human rights. Whereas liberty was once thought to depend on a healthy body politic and a careful balance of rights and obligations – a modern understanding[17] – since the triumph of the civil rights movement, it has increasingly meant individual rights and freedom from constraints, especially those of any particular group – a postmodern understanding.[18] As a result, whereas thick societies see social institutions as crucial to protecting or advancing rights, thin societies such as those in the West see them as in natural conflict with rights. Jack Donnelly, one of the most prominent Western human rights scholars, argues that rights are "inherently 'individualistic,'" the "inalienable entitlements of individuals held in relation to state and society."[19]

Governments, once seen as crucial providers of law and order, and social institutions, once seen as essential to maintaining the social fabric, have been redefined to serve the needs of the individual.[20] As Daniel Elazar writes, whereas in the colonial period it was understood that "the fabric of society

---

[14] Merry, *Human Rights and Gender Violence*, 3–4.

[15] Twining differentiates between three different modern visions of human rights that have appeared in succession. The first is based on a legal regime, the second on a set of universal moral standards that apply to all people all the time, and the third on discourse ethics, which provides a framework to change the focus of political debates to "rights talk" across societies. Twining, *General Jurisprudence*, 174–175.

[16] Charles Taylor, *A Secular Age* (Cambridge, MA: Harvard University Press), 2007.

[17] The modern understanding has existed since the late eighteenth century in the West. Before that, there was primarily the acknowledgment and protection of certain liberties. See Daniel Elazar, "How Present Conceptions of Human Rights Shape the Protection of Rights in the United States," in Robert Licht (ed.), *Old Rights and New* (Washington, DC: The AEI Press, 1993), 39.

[18] Elazar, "How Present Conceptions of Human Rights Shape the Protection of Rights in the United States," 38–50.

[19] Jack Donnelly, "Cultural Relativism and Universal Human Rights," *Human Rights Quarterly* 6, no. 4 (November 1984): 411 and 414.

[20] Elazar, "How Present Conceptions of Human Rights Shape the Protection of Rights in the United States," 38–50.

had to be kept intact, even at the expense of individual liberties and rights," and from 1789 to the 1940s, "the maintenance of the social fabric was given equal billing with individual rights," starting in the late 1940s or so, "maintaining the social fabric became distinctively secondary if not incidental in the face of individual rights challenges."[21] Whereas once there was a fair amount of religiosity within public institutions and cooperation between religious authorities and governments, the increasing focus on individualism and secularism progressively pushed faith into the private domain. The Supreme Court started using Thomas Jefferson's metaphor of a "wall of separation between church and state" in 1947 as it restricted the relationship in case after case,[22] changing its meaning in the process from the protection of religious minorities from the state to the protection of the state from religion.[23] While modern constitutional thought sought to secure rights through strengthening institutions and balancing forces within society, postmodern constitutional thought looks to the "guaranteeing of rights through judicial fiat, almost without regard to the other institutional arrangements and relationships."[24]

This evolution has left the thin society West with a "very particular and context-bound theory of rights"[25] that is different in a number of ways from the rights-based morality that preceded it. This theory has particular definitions of who has rights, what rights are covered, how rights can be exercised, and what qualifies as violations against rights – and it pushes for adult autonomy in ways that a different vision of how society works would not.[26] For instance, whereas approval of any right to kill or harm oneself was once unthinkable, now ever widening forms of physician-assisted suicide are becoming acceptable. While the amputation or reshaping of the body was formerly seen as unethical and dangerous, now sex reassignment surgery is accepted and encouraged. Marriage used to emphasize the needs of children; now it is centered on the rights of adults. Instead of developing a concept of children's rights that constrains the freedom of parents, the West has developed a concept of adult rights that

[21] Ibid., 45.
[22] Mary Ann Glendon, "Religious Freedom: Yesterday, Today, and Tomorrow," The 2015 Cardinal Egan Lecture, New York University Catholic Center, May 16, 2015, www.magnificat.com/foundation/pdf/M_A_Glendon_2015.pdf.
[23] Jefferson used this phrase in 1802 in a letter to assure the Danbury Baptist Association that they didn't need to fear government restrictions on their religious practices and organization. The Bill of Rights guaranteed this.
[24] Elazar, "How Present Conceptions of Human Rights Shape the Protection of Rights in the United States," 47.
[25] Ross Douthat, "The Liberalism of Adult Autonomy," *The New York Times*, June 4, 2015, http://douthat.blogs.nytimes.com/2015/06/04/the-liberalism-of-adult-autonomy/?_r=0.
[26] Ibid.

often deprives children of much needed social support.[27] "The idea that the child might ... have been deprived of something, might have a right that's been traduced or a claim of harm to make, is regarded as strange, irrelevant, offensive, antique."[28] In all these cases, what is at issue is not the importance of mores and rights, but which rights and harms to emphasize, and who is permitted to make choices. "The current definitions advanced by social liberalism ... treat adult autonomy as a morally-elevated good, and rate other possible rights and harm claims considerably lower as a consequence."[29]

The massive growth and transformation[30] of the middle class in the United States and Europe in the decades following World War II fueled the dramatic expansion of the region's human rights organizations (through donations) and contributed to the topic becoming an important part of political discourse. Such organizations used astute marketing to leverage three social changes – (1) growth of mass media, particularly television; (2) expansion of foundation money for new groups; and (3) more money and a greater orientation toward civic causes and progressive ideals among young people – to develop a "humanitarian marketplace," which could fuel their rapid development.[31] The United States government's direct international intervention on the side of human rights, which started under President Carter in the late 1970s, gave the movement's actors greater influence, further spurring the organizations' growth.[32]

The end of the Cold War dramatically accelerated the movement's expansion. As Stephen Hopgood describes,

> The two decades from Carter to Clinton were an exciting but uncertain time for global human rights advocates ... A combination of post–Cold War atrocity, human rights entrepreneurialism, growing UN self-confidence, and the "peace dividend" created a window of opportunity to build human rights infrastructure in the 1990s. Most important of all was unipolarity: the power of the United States as the sole global superpower could be yoked to the project ...[33]

---

[27] There is a children's rights movement, but it has never attempted to limit adult autonomy in the way described here. Instead, it has looked upon the state as the mechanism to reduce child labor, hunger, illness, mistreatment, etc.

[28] Douthat, "The Liberalism of Adult Autonomy."

[29] Ibid.

[30] Stephen Hopgood, *The Endtimes of Human Rights* (Ithaca, NY: Cornell University Press, 2013), xi.

[31] Ibid., 95–118.

[32] Ibid., 95–118.

[33] Ibid., 102.

Congress established the human rights bureau within the US State Department in 1976, with a mandate to report annually on the human rights conditions in every country. The head of the bureau was changed in 1994 from Assistant Secretary of State for Human Rights and Humanitarian Affairs to Assistant Secretary of State for Democracy, Human Rights, and Labor in 1994, reflecting the agency's enhanced ambitions in a new era. The promotion of human rights was henceforth to be tied to the promotion of democracy and free markets.[34] "There is now a vast human rights 'industry,' with an increasing body of specialists, activists, NGOs, agencies for monitoring and enforcement, and a booming literature."[35]

The changes in ambition and focus are reflected in the nature of leading human rights organizations. Whereas from the nineteenth century to the later parts of the twentieth century, neutrality, reciprocity, and noninterference in the affairs of sovereign states were considered core human rights values (as exemplified by the International Committee of the Red Cross, or ICRC), since the late 1970s an interventionist approach, backed by Western (especially American) power, has been dominant.[36]

Human Rights Watch (HRW), founded in 1978 in New York City, has typified the latter. Small and law-focused, it is both steeped in American ideas – especially with regard to the desirability of exporting neoliberal democracy – and oriented toward influencing and leveraging American power to achieve its aims.[37] The contrast with Amnesty International (AI), which was born in a different human rights era (1961), reflected a more European sensibility, with a less strong position on the desirability of democracy; was more skeptical about working with any power; and was built more on solidarity – with over a million members – than confrontation, was noticeable. Whereas AI's "staff had been trained to prune their reports to the bare minimum, HRW gave journalists and political scientists license to put their storytelling skills to use."[38] Today, AI is dispersing its centralized research and management from London to the South in order to become more locally owned and locally accountable. HRW, which has no membership and is accountable only to its donors, is

---

[34] Makau Mutua, "Savages, Victims, and Saviors: The Metaphor of Human Rights," *Harvard International Law Journal* 42, no. 1 (Winter 2001): 239.

[35] Twining, *General Jurisprudence*, 179.

[36] Hopgood, *The Endtimes of Human Rights*, 95–118.

[37] Ibid., xi–xii, 100, and 109–14.

[38] Alex de Waal, "Writing Human Rights and Getting It Wrong," *Boston Review*, June 6, 2016, https://bostonreview.net/world/alex-de-waal-writing-human-rights.

	Classicists ←→ Minimalists ←→ Maximalists ←→ Solidarists

Engagement with political authorities	Eschew public confrontations	←————————→	Advocate controversial public policy
Neutrality	Avoid taking sides	←————————→	Take the side of selected victims
Impartiality	Deliver aid using proportionality and non-discrimination	←————————→	Skew the balance of resource allocation
Consent	Pursue as sine qua non	←————————→	Override sovereignty as necessary

FIGURE 5.1 The political spectrum of humanitarians
Source: Thomas Weiss, "Principles, Politics, and Humanitarian Action," *Ethics and International Affairs* 13, no. 1 (1999): 4

ramping up its global capacity to produce reports that can name and shame governments[39] – including democratic ones that don't meet its standards[40] – and its lobbying capacity to influence the US Congress and other important political actors.[41] The contrast between classical humanitarian organizations (such as the ICRC) and the more political entities are laid out in Figure 5.1.

Western human rights organizations have worked to enlarge the international legal infrastructure that supports their efforts, creating state-like institutions such as the International Criminal Court, and doctrines such as the "Responsibility to Protect," over which they have significant influence.[42] These have increased their ability to set global standards – and have seen

---

[39] Hopgood, *The Endtimes of Human Rights*, xi–xii, 100, and 109–14.
[40] Human Rights Watch is also increasingly criticizing open societies – such as Israel – that don't meet its moral worldview, something that led its chairman from 1978 to 1998, Robert Bernstein, to break with the organization in a *New York Times* opinion article in 2009. Bernstein, "Rights Watchdog, Lost in the Mideast," *The New York Times*, October 19, 2009, www.nytimes.com/2009/10/20/opinion/20bernstein.html.
[41] Hopgood, *The Endtimes of Human Rights*, xi–xii, 100, and 109–14.
[42] Ibid., xi–xii, 100, and 109–114.

increased pushback from China, Africa, and other parts of the world that don't feel the resulting agenda is representative.[43] In the gay rights movement, for instance, Western pressure has tapped into deep-rooted resentment about how the West treats Africa; the results are tougher laws, stronger rhetoric, more funding of anti-gay rights organizations, and even greater harassment of activists. "More Africans came to believe that gay rights were a Western imposition."[44]

The move to a more interventionist approach infused with a liberal modernist conception of human rights has also been reflected in the rhetoric of politicians, the discourse of public policy forums and academia, and in the priorities of governments throughout the thin society West. Despite differences between the expansionist liberalism of those on the right, such as American neoconservatives, and the liberal internationalists of those on the left, such as Human Rights Watch,[45] American government policy has consistently reflected this firm, universalist perspective since the late 1970s. Consider (Republican) US President George W. Bush's 2012 State of the Union address, the first after the terrorist attacks of September 11, 2001:

> America will lead by defending liberty and justice because they are right and true and unchanging for all people everywhere. No nation owns these aspirations and no nation is exempt from them. We have no intention of imposing our culture, but America will always stand firm for the non-negotiable demands of human dignity, the rule of law, limits on the power of the state, respect for women, private property, free speech, equal justice and religious tolerance.[46]

Or (Democrat) US President Barack Obama's 2011 crucial speech on American policy in the Middle East in the aftermath of the Arab Spring uprisings:

---

[43] See, for instance, Thomas Carothers and Saskia Brechenmacher, "Closing Space: Democracy and Human Rights Support Under Fire," *Carnegie Endowment for International Peace*, February 2014, http://carnegieendowment.org/2014/02/20/closing-space-democracy-and-human-rights-support-under-fire/h1by.

[44] Onishi, "Obama Kenya Trip Sets Off Gay Rights Debate in Africa."

[45] Hopgood, *The Endtimes of Human Rights*, xii.

[46] George W. Bush, "State of the Union Address," United States Capitol, January 29, 2002, http://georgewbush-whitehouse.archives.gov/news/releases/2002/01/20020129–11.html. Richard Shweder used a similar analogy and quoted the same speech in Shweder, "Relativism and Universalism," 91.

We support a set of universal rights. Those rights include free speech; the freedom of peaceful assembly; freedom of religion; equality for men and women under the rule of law; and the right to choose your own leaders.[47]

This "incontestable universal framework for promoting moral development and social progress on a global scale"[48] has repeatedly played a major role in American (and to a lesser extent European) policymaking, from the founding of the National Endowment of Democracy in the early 1980s to the emphasis on the Washington Consensus – which ignored the role of institutions – in the late 1980s and "good governance" – which ignored local context – in more recent 1990s and 2000s development discourse.[49]

Although the election of Donald Trump suggests a turn away from a universalist approach, history suggests he will steer back toward it. The ideological underpinning of American society remains unchanged despite the latent isolationism that the 2016 campaign exposed. In fact, criticism at the lack of focus on human rights in foreign policy intensified during the first few months of the new administration. As Representative Randy Hultgren, a Republican from Illinois, who is chairman of the Tom Lantos Human Rights Commission, argued, "We remain strong when our values are upheld around the world, and when leaders understand we are serious when it comes to defending human rights across any border."[50] After the Syrian government deployed chemical weapons against its citizens in April 2017, Trump declared, "America stands for justice," suggesting that human rights abuses may require the United States to act, a view consistent with that of previous US presidents.[51]

In Western contexts, thick community religious groups and persons feel increasingly constrained by the policies of their governments.[52] States that used to actively support religion now limit its influence in multiple ways.

---

[47] Barack Obama, "Remarks by the President on the Middle East and North Africa," The White House, May 19, 2011, www.whitehouse.gov/the-press-office/2011/05/19/remarks-president-middle-east-and-north-africa. Melissa Thomas used this quote in a book launch presentation at Johns Hopkins University in April 2015.

[48] Shweder, "Relativism and Universalism," 91.

[49] There are many critiques. See, among others, Kavaljit Singh, *Questioning Globalization* (London: ZED, 2013); Ha-Joon Chang, *Kicking Away the Ladder: Development Strategy in Historical Perspective* (London: Anthem Press, 2003).

[50] Peter Baker, "For Trump, a Focus on U.S. Interests and a Disdain for Moralizing," *New York Times*, April 5, 2017, www.nytimes.com/2017/04/04/us/politics/syria-bashar-al-assad-trump.html.

[51] Peter Baker, "The Emerging Trump Doctrine: Don't Follow Doctrine," *New York Times*, April 8, 2017, www.nytimes.com/2017/04/08/us/politics/trump-doctrine-foreign-policy.html.

[52] See, among others, Roger Trigg, "Threats to Religious Freedom in Europe," *Public Discourse*, June 28, 2013, www.thepublicdiscourse.com/2013/06/10439/.

Freedom of religion is being redefined as the freedom of conscience, with limitations on what individuals and groups may or may not do.[53] Those who disagree with the values embodied in liberal, secular modernity are seen as mistaken and misdirected. As such, those who differ with the new consensus face the risk that they will have to switch careers or close their organizations due to fines, procedural harassment, the loss of public funds, and social media feeding frenzies.[54] Such changes in the direction of human rights would certainly puzzle those, such as John Locke, who first developed the theory of human rights using theocratic foundations.[55] We will examine this issue in detail in the next chapter.

HUMAN RIGHTS BECOMES MONOCULTURAL

The human rights movement has become monocultural, representing one particular moral matrix, set of values, and way of living the good life. It prefers to downplay the role of culture as a factor in how people act and think and is thus less likely to recognize its own culture and how that might differ from cultures in other communities.[56]

Within the discourse of human rights, culture is often used as a synonym for tradition, something that must evolve from a primitive, earlier stage of evolution to become modern, and civilized.[57] It is used to describe rural, poor, religious, thick society, and Southern places, not more developed, secular, thin society, or Western areas. As Merry explains,

---

[53] Trigg, "Threats to Religious Freedom in Europe"; Wesley Smith, "Freedom of Worship's Assault on Freedom of Religion," *First Things*, July 13, 2012, www.firstthings.com/web-exclusives/2012/07/freedom-of-worships-assault-on-freedom-of-religion. For instance, as we will learn in Chapter 6, a German judge recently decided that the circumcision of children is wrong because the "fundamental right of the child to bodily integrity outweighed the fundamental rights of the parents" to carry out their religious beliefs. Circumcision is not protected under freedom of conscience, only freedom of religion. "Jewish Groups Condemn Court's Definition of Circumcision as Grievous Bodily Harm," *The Telegraph*, June 27, 2012, www.telegraph.co.uk/news/worldnews/europe/germany/9358636/Jewish-groups-condemn-courts-definition-of-circumcision-as-grievous-bodily-harm.html.

[54] Douthat, "The Terms of Our Surrender," *The New York Times*, March 1, 2014, www.nytimes.com/2014/03/02/opinion/sunday/the-terms-of-our-surrender.html.

[55] See John Locke, "Second Treatise on Government," in *Two Treaties of Government* (Cambridge: Cambridge University Press, 1963).

[56] Merry, *Human Rights and Gender Violence*, 10–11 and 16. This is to be expected given the findings of cultural psychology. See, among others, Jonathan Haidt, *The Righteous Mind: Why Good People Are Divided by Politics and Religion* (New York, NY: Pantheon Books, 2012), 110.

[57] Merry, *Human Rights and Gender Violence*, 10–11 and 16.

> Culture was often juxtaposed to civilization during the civilizing mission of imperialism, and this history has left a legacy in contemporary thinking ... UN meetings [and other human rights fora] are deeply shaped by a culture of transnational modernity, one that specifies procedures for collaborative decision-making, conceptions of global social justice, and definitions of gender roles. Human rights law is itself primarily a cultural system.[58]

If culture is a synonym for tradition, then modernization is equated with Westernization. This is something few outside the West would agree with (see Chapter 4). Modernization is assumed to have, in the words of Donnelly, "reached into, and transformed, [most] traditional communities, [making] traditional approaches ... seem objectively inappropriate."[59] According to this logic, the changes wrought by modernization, globalization, and their accompanying forces have been so great that there is no alternative to a human rights system focused on protecting individuals. While society once played an important role in people's lives, it has now been replaced by "the modern state, the modern economy, and the modern city, as an alien power that assaults his dignity."[60]

Anyone appealing to culture or tradition is seen as either "dangerously paternalistic" or as using these as "a mere cloak for self-interest or arbitrary rule."[61] Arguments that there are other means of promoting and ensuring human dignity are dismissed as unrealistic.[62] Non-Western cultures (including subcultures with religious impulses) are seen as too weak to play a significant role improving lives in the modern world.

The global–local divide is usually conceptualized as that between rights and culture or even civilization and culture.[63] There is a significant gap between the global settings where Western universalist human right actors prepare standards, evaluations, and strategies and the specific situations where they

---

[58] Merry, *Human Rights and Gender Violence*, 10–11 and 16.

[59] Jack Donnelly, "Cultural Relativism and Universal Human Rights," *Human Rights Quarterly* 6, no. 4 (November 1984): 406. Most of the quotes used in this paragraph come from Donnelly's earlier essays. His thinking has evolved over the years and become closer to the framework articulated in this book, albeit still significantly Western universalist.

[60] Donnelly, "Human Rights and Human Dignity: An Analytic Critique of Non-Western Conceptions of Human Rights," in Frederick Snyder and Surakiart Sathirathai (eds.), *Third World Attitudes toward International Law: An Introduction* (Dordrecht, The Netherlands: Martinus Nijhoff Publishers, 1987), 351–352.

[61] Donnelly, "Cultural Relativism and Universal Human Rights," 412.

[62] "... alternative mechanisms for protecting or realizing human dignity in the contemporary world ... usually refer to an allegedly possible world that no one has had the good fortune to experience." Jack Donnelly, "The Relative Universality of Human Rights," *Human Rights Quarterly* 29, no. 2 (May 2007): 288.

[63] Merry, *Human Rights and Gender Violence*, 6 and 12.

are deployed. Ideas mostly travel in one direction; transnational actors and some national elites generally do not consider complicated local social practices and contexts.[64] African, Asian, and other non-Western human rights institutions and laws are marginalized on the assumption that the West is the leader in the field and everyone else just a follower – even when this is not true.[65] As we'll see later, academic literature and major institutions across the field rarely cite non-Western case law or activities as examples of best practice or as indicators of progress in the human rights field.[66]

Merry notes, "Instead of viewing human rights as a form of global law that imposes rules, it is better imagined as a cultural practice, as a means of producing new cultural understandings and actions" in societies targeted for change.[67] And, as a cultural practice, Upendra Baxi argues that human rights have become, "in this era of the end of ideology, as the only universal ideology in the making," legitimizing the power and practices of organizations and activists promoting a particular, thin society way of living.[68] This particular cultural framework becomes universalized through various means, including a key element of any culture: the narrative. As Alex de Waal writes, "Unlike an academic writer, who is obliged to be clear about methods and analytical frameworks, a human rights writer can simply tell a story. This story then gains uncommon gravitas thanks to its validation by a human rights organization. . . . This choice, no matter how principled, is not neutral."[69]

The human rights field is a "black-and-white construction that pits good against evil."[70] This requires, as Makau Mutua argues, the re-engineering of the state and society because freedom "from the tyrannies of the state, tradition, and culture" depends on

> the freedom to create a better society based on particular values. In the human rights story, the savior is the human rights corpus itself, with the United Nations, Western governments, INGOs, and Western charities as the rescuers, redeemers of a benighted world. In reality, however, these institutions are

---

[64] Ibid., 2–3; Rachel Murray, "International Human Rights: Neglect of Perspectives from African Institutions," *The International and Comparative Law Quarterly* 55, no. 1 (Jan. 2006): 193–204.
[65] Chelsea Purvis, "Emerging Voices: Engaging with African Human Rights Law," *Opinio Juris*, July 19, 2013, http://opiniojuris.org/2013/07/19/emerging-voices-engaging-with-african-human-rights-law/.
[66] Murray, "International Human Rights," 196.
[67] Merry, *Human Rights and Gender Violence*, 229.
[68] Upendra Baxi, *The Future of Human Rights* (Oxford: Oxford University Press, 2006), 1–2.
[69] de Waal, "Writing Human Rights and Getting It Wrong."
[70] Mutua, "Savages, Victims, and Saviors," 202–205.

merely fronts. The savior is ultimately a set of culturally based norms and practices that inhere in liberal thought and philosophy.[71]

Even though many human rights agreements explicitly call for respecting and protecting diversity, the movement operates as if these are only possible within a liberal modern framework. It paradoxically seeks to promote diversity in a nonnegotiable manner that limits it. "The doors of difference appear open while in reality they are shut."[72]

There are wide-ranging implications for the discourse and workings of the whole human rights system. In this "Age of Human Rights," in the words of Baxi, the language of human rights has, at least for Western and transnational secular elites, come to supplant all other ethical languages.[73] It has become, as Suzanne Last Stone argues, "the dominant mode of public moral discourse, replacing such discourses as distributive justice, the common good, and solidarity. Indeed, it has become something of a faith of its own."[74]

This "sacralization of human rights" is detrimental to developing a consensus, especially one that must encompass non-Christian, nonreformed religions and value systems. "The incontrovertible or absolute character of human rights blurs the division between secular morality based on unaided reason and the realm of the sacrosanct, inviolable, or the sacred occupied by religion." By trying to create "a common language of sanctity," Western universalists have instead created more distrust and division, as religious believers feel that the human rights discourse is being elevated above their own faith.[75]

A few distinctions regarding religious groups will help us see why this is the case. Whereas Protestant Christianity and other reformed religions are "primarily concerned with belief rather than law or public practice," and see faith as a private matter of conscience depending on individual action, Catholics, Mormons, Orthodox Jews, Muslims, and those steeped in Confucian, African, and other Southern value systems emphasize group cohesion, institutional authority, rules of conduct, and public behavior.[76] Indeed, the Protestant

---

[71] Ibid., 202–205.
[72] Makau Mutua, *Human Rights: A Political and Cultural Critique* (Philadelphia, PA: University of Pennsylvania Press, 2002), 3–4.
[73] Baxi, *The Future of Human Rights*, 1–2.
[74] Suzanne Last Stone, "Religion and Human Rights: Babel or Translation, Conflict or Convergence," paper presented at *Role of Religion in Human Rights Discourse* conference, Israel Democracy Institute, May 16–17, 2012, 7.
[75] Stone, "Religion and Human Rights," 4–5.
[76] Stone makes this contrast, but for a much smaller group of cases. Stone, "Religion and Human Rights," 3–4.

worldview is not only most congenial to the human rights worldview and discourse, but also its historic source.[77] With these roots in "right belief," human rights actors view alternative approaches to improving the human condition, based on different moral languages and seeking to take into account local cultural, social, and political contexts, as being "culturally relativist."[78] Of course, the Protestant worldview's influence on the Western universalist framework does not mean that Protestant religious minorities support all of those framework's contemporary secular commitments.[79]

By assuming a particular evolution of society – by predicting the future of countries – the human rights field has become very historicist.[80] However, as Karl Popper writes in *The Poverty of Historicism*, this would require the remaking of people such that they thought and acted differently.[81] Human action can never be predicted with certainty and therefore neither can the future.[82] Knowledge about how one part of the world developed does not necessarily help one understand how another part will.[83] Any analysis of a society will come up short because the number of elements within it is infinite.[84] It is possible to exclude certain events or paths for a society, but

[77] Ibid., 3–4.

[78] Tom Zwart, "Balancing Yin and Yang in the International Human Rights Debate," Paper for the Sixth Beijing Human Rights Forum, Beijing, China, September 12–13, 2013, 2; Jack Donnelly, "Human Rights and Human Dignity: An Analytic Critique of Non-Western Conceptions of Human Rights," The *American Political Science Review* 76, no. 2 (June 1982): 303–316.

[79] Many evangelicals and other more orthodox Protestants support human rights in some form. There are, for instance, groups calling for everything from a stop to torture, environmental protection, and efforts to stamp out sex trafficking. There are divisions of course, with different groups taking different stands on issues. Instead of using the language of the human rights field, however, these groups typically ground their arguments in the language of *imago Dei* (image of God), which captures thick society concepts of inherent dignity but is also akin to natural rights. See, for instance, Joel Nichols, "Evangelicals and Human Rights: The Continuing Ambivalence of Evangelical Christians' Support for Human Rights," *Journal of Law and Religion* 24, no. 2 (2008–09): 629–662; and Ethna Regan, *Theology and the Boundary Discourse of Human Rights* (Washington, DC: Georgetown University Press, 2010), 66–67.

[80] Historicism has sometimes been used to dispute the validity of human rights across cultures. Relativists argue that only history can be a source of values and standards. See, for instance, Sarhan Dhouib, "Limits of the Culturally Relative View of Human Right," in Wilhelm Gräb and Lars Charbonnier (eds.), *Religion and Human Rights: Global Challenges from Intercultural Perspectives* (Berlin: Walter de Gruyter, 2015), 60–62. I am more interested in liberal historicism here. For an example of its use, see Jan-Werner Müller, "Rawls, Historian: Remarks on Political Liberalism's 'Historicism,'" *Revue Internationale de Philosophie* 237 (3/2006): 327–339.

[81] Karl Popper, *The Poverty of Historicism* (New York, NY: Routledge, 2002), 58–65.

[82] Ibid., 141–148.

[83] Popper, *The Poverty of Historicism*, 96–110.

[84] Ibid., 70–76.

it is impossible to narrow down the range of possibilities to just one.[85] Implementing historicist programs such as Marxism – which shares many "end of history" qualities with the modern human rights movement – risks producing lots of unintended consequences due to the complexity of the relationships and institutions that make up a society.[86]

All of this raises the question of whether the imperialistic legacy has habituated Westerners to "a status of hegemony – including a hegemony of truth – vis-à-vis persons in the South." Westerners (or at least Western elites), some argue, tend to presume that their own experiences and outlook are ideal and ought to be universal. This presumption is partly due to centuries of technological and military superiority, colonial domination, and the strong influence of a faith (Christianity) that assumed universality.[87] Accordingly, while Islam and Confucianism represent cultural areas just as large and significant, their values are considered particular while Western mores are considered the de facto standard.[88] And, while Western cultures were once strongly religious – and sought to convert the world to their faith – an increasing number of Westerners now consider any particularity associated with religion (or tradition) to be "backward, irrational and opposed to science."[89]

Thick society Southerners and religious actors within the West feel forced to act defensively, invoking – with greater success, at least recently – sovereignty and noninterference internationally and – with less success – the legal right to religious freedom domestically, as they respond to what they perceive as efforts to change their values and ways of life.[90] Suspicion of human rights universalism among many of these actors runs deep:[91] It risks

---

[85] Ibid., 120–132.

[86] Ibid., 58–65. Popper suggests an approach to change that focuses on "piecemeal social engineering" whereby only small and reversible reforms are introduced, tested, assessed, and evaluated one-by-one. Ibid., 53–65.

[87] See, for instance, Michael Freeman, "Human Rights," in Peter Burnell, Vicky Randall, and Lise Rakner (eds.), *Politics in the Developing World* (Oxford: Oxford University Press, 2014), 281–82.

[88] Yasuaki Onuma "Towards an Intercivilizational Approach to Human Rights," in Joanne Bauer and Daniel Bell (eds.), *The East Asian Challenge for Human Rights* (Cambridge: Cambridge University Press, 1999), 112.

[89] Melissa Eddy, "In Germany, Ruling over Circumcision Sows Anxiety and Confusion," *The New York Times*, July 14, 2012, www.nytimes.com/2012/07/14/world/europe/in-germany-ruling-over-circumcision-sows-anxiety-and-confusion.html.

[90] Zwart, "Balancing Yin and Yang in the International Human Rights Debate," 3; Jack Donnelly, "The Relative Universality of Human Rights," 304–305.

[91] Yuchao Zhu, "China and International 'Human Rights Diplomacy,'" *China: An International Journal* 9, no. 2 (September 2011): 221–222.

being seen as a "Trojan horse"[92] that continues the long, negative experiences Southern countries had with Western colonialism and imperialism and religious groups had with the secular state since its establishment. Indeed, some may argue that Western governments and interest groups have at times employed the language of human rights in the service of their own political, economic, and military objectives.[93]

The colonial experience has prompted Southerners to see at least some of the actions undertaken by Western human rights actors as a continuation of that earlier era's imperialism.[94] In this context, the positive slogans that often emanate from human rights actors can sound eerily like the *mission civilisatrice* that was used to rationalize intervention or colonization in the past, and which mostly amounted to the Westernization of indigenous peoples in the name of civilization. As such, "grudges and animosities against colonial rule, external intervention, economic exploitation, racial discrimination, and religious prejudices" affect peoples' perspective, even when criticisms are legitimate.[95] Similarly, for people of faith in the West, domestic human rights campaigns can often seem like a continuation of antireligious attacks that have occurred throughout history.[96] The Western universalist approach can also seem self-interested, as individual liberty, public speech, and pluralism are pursued according to narrow definitions.[97]

LIBERAL MONISM

Narrow interpretations of human rights assume that there is a supreme good, definitive ranking of goods, or common measure of goods. This liberal monism contrasts with the liberal pluralism explored in Chapter 4, and it reflects a desire for a more complete theory of how life ought to be lived.

---

[92] R. Panikkar and R. Panikkar, "Is the Notion of Human Rights a Western Concept?," *Diogenes* 30, no. 120 (1982): 90.

[93] Mary Ann Glendon, *A World Made New: Eleanor Roosevelt and the Universal Declaration of Human Rights* (New York, NY: Random House, 2001), 229.

[94] See, for instance, Michael Freeman, "Human Rights," in Peter Burnell, Vicky Randall, and Lise Rakner (eds.), *Politics in the Developing World* (Oxford: Oxford University Press, 2014), 281–282.

[95] "The idea of *mission civilisatrice* was used to rationalize imperialistic policies by the Western powers from the late nineteenth to the early twentieth century. The idea of 'humanitarian intervention' was frequently resorted to by Western powers when they intervened militarily in Turkey and other Afro-Asian states in the same period." Onuma, "Towards an Intercivilizational Approach to Human Rights," 105–106.

[96] See, for instance, Lynn Hunt (ed.), *The French Revolution and Human Rights* (New York, NY: Bedford/St. Martin's, 1996).

[97] Douthat, "Diversity and Dishonesty."

For Western universalists – including most Western human rights actors – the good life is progressive secular liberalism. This liberal monist outlook proclaims that all aspects of social life – including all social institutions – ought to be ruled by autonomy, individualism, and equality, and a particular ordering of values.[98]

Although it may work relatively well in theory, liberal monism is challenging to put into practice given the realities of how human life is actually lived. There is not, for instance, agreement among proponents what the general principle for ranking choices should be – some think it ought to be the equal right to be free; others the general right of liberty; others the right to fair treatment, not to be treated cruelly, not to be subject to degradation or exploitation; and others the right to participate in procedures by which deep conflicts are adjudicated. The preferred general principles are often mutually incompatible.[99] And, as Walzer writes, "There will be different interpretations and, absent Hercules, no final and definitive interpretation."[100]

Shweder calls this worldview "imperial liberalism" because it promotes an attitude of moral superiority (as cultural psychology suggests it should) and intervention in communities and countries that have different moral matrices.[101] It uses language to rank relative progress, employing "a developmental scale from savage to civilized or backward to advanced."[102] Imperial liberals believe that the "liberal ways of life are superior or more valuable than illiberal ways of life," and that the "defining liberal value of autonomy ... trumps all other values."[103]

There are implications of this worldview worth noting. "In a world of belief pluralism, and in multi-cultural and multi-ethnic societies, one cannot expect

---

[98] For a supportive perspective on liberal monism, see Ronald Dworkin, *Sovereign Virtue: The Theory and Practice of Equality* (Cambridge, MA: Harvard University Press, 2000).

[99] Licht, "Introduction," in Licht (ed.), *Old Rights and New* (Washington, DC: The AEI Press, 1993), 14; William Galston, "Between Philosophy and History: The Evolution of Rights in American Thought," in Licht (ed.), *Old Rights and New*, 67–68.

[100] Michael Walzer, "'Spheres of Justice': An Exchange," *The New York Review of Books*, July 21, 1983, www.nybooks.com/articles/1983/07/21/spheres-of-justice-an-exchange/.

[101] Shweder, "'What about Female Genital Mutilation?' And Why Understanding Culture Matters in the First Place," in Shweder, Martha Minow, and Hazel Rose Markus (eds.), *Engaging Cultural Differences: The Multicultural Challenge in Liberal Democracies* (New York, NY: Russell Sage Foundation, 2002), 234–236. Gil Gott uses the phrase "imperial humanitarianism" to describe a similar attitude. See Gott, "Imperial Humanitarianism: History of an Arrested Dialectic," in Berta Esperanza Hernández-Truyol (ed.), *Moral Imperialism: A Critical Anthology* (New York, NY: New York University Press, 2002), 19–38.

[102] Shweder, "Relativism and Universalism," 87.

[103] Shweder, "Shouting at the Hebrews: Imperial Liberalism v Liberal Pluralism and the Practice of Male Circumcision," *Law, Culture and the Humanities* 5, no. 2 (June 2009): 260.

to find much scope for a universal ideology or moral system – unless through domination and imposition."[104] It may, for instance, only be possible to enforce a particular view on gender identity and sexuality – whether domestically or internationally – by force or financial or legal sanction. That such tools could be used over issues as difficult to understand as circumcision should give human rights actors pause, especially given how powerfully culture influences perspectives on all sides. Similarly, enforcing a particular view of family life, work, the role of social institutions, political liberalization in ethnically divided societies, or the need to balance justice and reconciliation after a war – all areas where there are legitimate areas of disagreement – ought to be approached cautiously. Galston warns, "[T]he decision to throw state power behind the promotion of individual autonomy can undermine the lives of individuals and groups that do not and cannot organize their affairs in accordance with that principle without undermining the deepest sources of their identity."[105]

Although most liberals assume that "autonomy and diversity fit together and complement one another," as Galston argues, "these principles do not always, or usually, cohere." Galston posits that many disagreements in areas such as education and the free exercise of religion actually show autonomy and diversity in direct conflict.[106]

Ross Douthat argues that "If we take pluralism seriously, the whole point of the concept is to enable groups to 'throw up a shield' against the pressure of consensus, and develop and promote alternatives that are rejected by the powerful, or by society as a whole."[107] This is true whether the consensus is based on old, traditional ideas (such as those rooted in religion) or on new ideas represented as progressive, enlightened, or modern – and even if claimed by majorities in national assemblies believing themselves to be sovereign – for the simple reason that both can be equally wrong, misguided, cruel, or immoral. The nineteenth and twentieth centuries were filled with "modern," "advanced" ideas that turned out badly – ideas that Western universalists would today find quite repugnant. Seen in this context, tolerance and pluralism are, beyond their intrinsic and practical values, a kind of hedge against the possibility that we are wrong or that we might change our minds later. As Douthat notes,

[104] Twining, *General Jurisprudence*, 180.
[105] Galston, *Liberal Pluralism: The Implications of Value Pluralism for Political Theory and Practice* (Cambridge: Cambridge University Press, 2002), 21.
[106] Ibid., 21.
[107] Douthat, "The Challenge of Pluralism," *The New York Times*, March 19, 2014, http://douthat.blogs.nytimes.com/2014/03/19/the-challenge-of-pluralism/.

It's when a consensus is at its most self-confident, in other words – and therefore most vulnerable to the errors of overconfidence – that the kind of pluralism that might serve as a corrective becomes hardest for that consensus's exponents to accept.[108]

Limitations on religious groups and individuals do not always involve state-sponsored persecution. Various forms of legal and social pressure by themselves can reduce the scope and variety of services offered by churches, ministers, hospitals, adoption agencies, charities, businesses, and persons. This reduces some important public goods, which may result in a harsher, more self-centered society and economy. "Beliefs can be pressured without being persecuted; disfavored without being explicitly discriminated against; challenged without being subjugated."[109] We will see evidence of this in the next chapter.

WESTERN INFLUENCE ON ACADEMIC DISCOURSE

Due to the influence Western universalists have on major human rights journals, conferences, funding mechanisms, and so on, alternative perspectives and research often find it difficult to get a fair hearing and wide audience.

As Zwart argues,

> ... the Northern view [of human rights] has almost become the exclusive perspective in academia, while pushing alternative approaches and critiques to the margins. As a result, the human rights discourse has been narrowed, to make it fit within the perimeters of legalism and modernity.[110]

Alongside a narrow discourse in scholarly fora, international human rights organizations are rarely "the subject of probing critiques." Even academia has been slow to critique what are considered the "good guys." As Mutua argues,

> INGOs and their supporters see those who question them as naive at best and apologists for repressive governments and cultures, at worst. This climate of intolerance has a chilling effect on human rights speech, particularly of young and probing scholars and activists. It also encourages a "herd" mentality and mafia-like compliance with official or knee jerk human rights

[108] Ibid.
[109] Douthat, "On Persecution," *The New York Times*, March 6, 2014, http://douthat.blogs.nytimes .com/2014/03/06/on-persecution/.
[110] Zwart, "Balancing Yin and Yang in the International Human Rights Debate," 6.

strategies, positions, or responses. It certainly does not encourage innovation on the part of the movement.[111]

A belief in the "rightness" of Western universalist ideas and mores extends beyond the human rights field. The majority of scholarly literature in the social sciences – particularly in economics and psychology – relies on an implicit assumption that all humans think and all societies are organized the same way, the WEIRD way.[112] As mentioned in Chapter 3, even though 96 percent of the subjects used in behavioral science research published between 2003 and 2007 in six top academic journals were from Western industrialized democracies (and 68 percent were American), the conclusions drawn were assumed to reveal traits common to all humans. Even within the West, the typical sampling method is far from representative – two-thirds of the American and four-fifths of the other samples were comprised of undergraduates in psychology courses.[113]

Literature in the social sciences often looks at phenomena as if the mind is stripped of culture and as if humans are hardwired for behavior; perception and cognition are assumed to be universal.[114] In many fields, such as economics and political science, the emphasis on quantitative research has become so pervasive that students often do not learn, journals do not publish, and academics do not debate many of the qualitative differences that exist across societies and countries.[115] As a result, the biggest questions facing many fields remain unaddressed. As Robert Zoellick, who was president of the World Bank (but not an economist) said in 2011,

> Too often research economists seem not to start with the key knowledge gaps facing development practitioners, but rather search for questions they can

---

[111] Mutua, "Savages, Victims, and Saviors," 241. Also see Mutua, "The Ideology of Human Rights," 589 and 591.

[112] Watters, "We Aren't the World."

[113] Joseph Henrich, Steven Heine, and Ara Norenzayan, "The Weirdest People in the World?," *Behavioral and Brain Sciences* 33, no. 2–3 (June 2010): 63.

[114] Watters, "We Aren't the World."

[115] Albert Hirschman made this point half a century ago, when the emphasis on quantitative research started taking over his field. Jeremy Adelman, *Worldly Philosopher: The Odyssey of Albert O. Hirschman* (Princeton, NJ: Princeton University Press, 2013). It has appeared and reappeared in different guises over the years. For a recent critique, see Dani Rodrik, *Economics Rules: The Rights and Wrongs of the Dismal Science* (New York, NY: W. W. Norton & Company, 2015). The decline of university area studies is a related phenomenon. See Charles King, "The Decline of International Studies: Why Flying Blind Is Dangerous," *Foreign Affairs* 94, no. 4 (July/August 2015): 88–98.

answer with the industry's currently favorite tools ... We need to know what works: we need a research agenda that focuses on results.[116]

Research conducted by Syed Farid Alatas[117] and Raewyn Connell[118] shows that "social theory is still very much determined by Eurocentric concepts, insights and methodologies" even though the "validity of such approaches for Southern parts of the world has only rarely been tested."[119] For instance, most "social psychological theorizing begins with an autonomous individual whose relationships are a means to certain asocial ends." American researchers "tend to discuss forms of social influence with pejorative labels," such as obedience, groupthink, and conformity.[120]

Observers note that secular elites, the thinnest part of a thin society, produces most of the people doing social science research and human rights work, and neither of these fields have many religious or socially conservative Westerners among their ranks.[121] What Jonathan Haidt admits with regard to

---

[116] Bob Davis, "World Bank Chief Ignites a Debate," *Wall Street Journal*, September 30, 2010, www.wsj.com/articles/SB10001424052748703431604575521940492730342.

[117] Syed Farid Alatas, *Alternative Discourses in Asian Social Science: Responses to Eurocentrism* (New Delhi: Sage, 2006).

[118] Raewyn Connell, *Southern Theory: The Global Dynamics of Knowledge in Social Science* (Cambridge: Polity Press, 2007).

[119] Zwart, "Balancing Yin and Yang in the International Human Rights Debate," 6.

[120] Alan Page Fiske, Shinobu Kitayama, Hazel Rose Markus, and Richard Nisbett, "The Cultural Matrix of Social Psychology," in Susan Fiske, Daniel Gilbert, and Gardner Lindzey (eds.), *The Handbook of Social Psychology*, Volume 2, 4th ed. (New York, NY: McGraw-Hill, 1998), 919.

[121] Jonathan Haidt, "A New Science of Morality, Part 1," Edge.org, September 17, 2010, http:// edge.org/conversation/a-new-science-of-morality-part-1. For an overview of Haidt's work and other research on liberal bias in academia, see John Tierney, "Social Scientist Sees Bias Within," *The New York Times*, February 8, 2011, www.nytimes.com/2011/02/08/science/08tier .html. The lack of diversity in academia extends to political diversity. There is, for instance, a 10 ½ to 1 ratio of liberals to conservatives in academic psychology, undermining the validity of much research by "the embedding of liberal values into research questions and methods, steering researchers away from important but politically unpalatable research topics, and producing" unjustified conclusions. Such biases are paralleled across the social sciences and humanities, which have similar imbalances. In contrast, in the United States as a whole the ratio of liberals to conservatives is roughly 1 to 2. See, for instance, Christopher Cardiff and Daniel Klein, "Faculty Partisan Affiliations in All Disciplines: A Voter-Registration Study," *Critical Review* 17, nos. 3–4 (2005): 237–255. Ross Douthat, a columnist for *The New York Times*, observes "the assumptions of social liberalism are so ingrained in the intelligentsia that it would simply never occur to many highly-intelligent people to question them... Even when well-educated people pick up some socially-conservative impulses – which time, experience, and parenthood often instill – they remain instinctively horrified and/or baffled by the idea of being associated with social conservatism *as an ideology*, which they associate with fundamentalists, bigots, hypocrites, and all those culturally-alien folks out in Jesusland. ... [This] creates a very striking intellectual blind spot: The kind of obvious issues [that social conservatives would consider important] don't get much airing in elite circles, large numbers of

the field of moral psychology can be said about almost every other social science as well as the human rights field:

> We've got to be very, very cautious about bias ... Nearly all of us doing this work are secular Liberals. And that means that we're at very high risk of misunderstanding those moralities that are not our own. If we were judges working on a case, we'd pretty much all have to recuse ourselves. But we're not going to do that, so we've got to just be extra careful to seek out critical views, to study moralities that aren't our own, to consider, to empathize, to think about them as possibly coherent systems of beliefs and values that could be related to coherent, and even humane, human ways of living and flourishing.[122]

The development field is, as David Booth and Frederick Golooba-Mutebi argue, dominated by naïve liberalism: the belief that progress depends on introducing the "right" set of policies, state institutions, and liberal democratic norms.

> Naïve liberalism infuses both the academic literature and the global journalistic discourse. ... The global influence of naïve liberalism creates an ideological climate in which non-standard approaches to constitution-making are seldom countenanced. ... The lack of any robust and influential alternative to naïve liberal concepts of governance for development is what emerges as the principal international constraint [to alternative approaches].[123]

In some cases and fields, "nonstandard approaches" may be exactly what local people prefer or need. As Kwang-Kuo Hwang, a Chinese pioneer scholar in cultural psychology, argues,

> [T]he reliance on Western psychologies to understand the behavior of non-Western people constitutes an egregious error that frames the behavior of non-Western people within a template that is not only limited in its validity, but also potentially dangerous in terms of the conclusions that are reached, and the decisions too often made under the guise of Western scientific hegemony.[124]

---

educated people labor in ignorance of the range of social science findings that complicate (note that I didn't say disprove) socially-liberal beliefs, and many of our best and brightest end up taking as a given public-policy assumptions ... that don't actually have that much empirical support." Douthat, "Social Conservatives and Social Science," *The New York Times*, December 18, 2013, http://douthat.blogs.nytimes.com/2013/12/18/social-conservatives-and-social-science/.

[122] Jonathan Haidt, "A New Science of Morality, Part 1."

[123] David Booth and Frederick Golooba-Mutebi, "Developmental Regimes and the International System," Developmental Regimes in Africa, Policy Brief 5, January 2014, 2–4.

[124] Anthony Marsella and Wade Pickren, "Foreword," in Kwang-Kuo Hwang, *Foundations of Chinese Psychology: Confucian Social Relations* (New York, NY: Springer, 2012), viii.

On the whole, North American and European researchers "share a set of implicit and unexamined cultural values and practices that emphasize individual rights, independence, self-determination, and freedom." These values and practices infuse their analysis and interpretation of various phenomena, and they inform academic discourse. This discourse is perceived to be "objective," but many parts of the world – indeed, most – do not share the same cultural values and practices.[125] As a result, with the possible exception of historians and philosophers of science,[126] "[S]outhern approaches do not get through to the mainstream academic discourse and science is the poorer for it."[127]

This "academic imperialism" has led to a social science indigenization movement in some non-Western countries, most notably China and Taiwan. Local academics and practitioners have pushed for this because they believe that when Western models and research results are "transplanted blindly to non-Western countries, [they are] usually irrelevant, inappropriate, or incompatible."[128] These scholars and observers claim Western social science findings are at times merely "a cultural creation … neither universal nor scientific."[129]

The heavy influence of the WEIRD discourse on human rights scholarly work is complemented by Western universalist dominance of most of the field's funding sources and institutions.[130] Despite equality in sovereignty, there is vast inequality in financial resources between richer and poorer countries; this influences international negotiations, participation at international conferences and events (poor countries often have no representation), and funding for NGOs. NGOs are almost always funded by Western universalist donors – increasing the suspicion that they have ulterior motives.[131] These donors not only have far more resources than any thick society Southern counterparts, they also place a higher priority on funding

[125] Fiske, Kitayama, et al., "The Cultural Matrix of Social Psychology," 919.
[126] Historians and philosophers of science have raised the possibilities that at least ancient Greek and Chinese scientists and philosophers were different. See Richard Nisbett and Takahiko Masuda, "Culture and Point of View," *Proceedings of the National Academy of Sciences* 100, no. 19 (September 16, 2003): 11163.
[127] Zwart, "Balancing Yin and Yang in the International Human Rights Debate," 6.
[128] Kwang-Kuo Hwang, *Foundations of Chinese Psychology: Confucian Social Relations* (New York, NY: Springer, 2012), 8.
[129] Marsella and Pickren, "Foreword," viii.
[130] Merry, *Human Rights and Gender Violence*, 20–21 and 223–226; Alex de Waal, *Advocacy in Conflict: Critical Perspectives on Transnational Activism* (London: Zed Books, 2015).
[131] Merry, *Human Rights and Gender Violence*, 20–21 and 223–226.

human rights organizations.[132] As a result, most Southern NGOs depend heavily on Western funding, influencing their programming, hiring, advocacy work, and so on.[133] This limits resources for innovative programs, research, and new initiatives that offer a contrarian perspective – ensuring that those who attend international meetings and events will share the Western liberal modernist perspective.[134] As de Waal argues,

> These Western NGOs wield enormous influence in choosing topics for advocacy efforts, selecting a southern NGO or activist as a junior partner or client, and determining the nature of advocacy . . . Unfortunately, this transfer of "ownership" and political bias in advocacy efforts can lead to an unhealthy failure to get to grips with the problems of people who are ostensibly being represented![135]

There are few academically grounded studies of alternative approaches to human rights. Because policymakers generally do not consider other options, international organizations rarely stray from standard formulas on how to stabilize countries, promote development, and improve well-being. Officials and workers on the ground are usually beholden to Western universalist norms or funds and are either unwilling or unable to challenge the status quo.[136] Thick society countries are greatly limited in their policy choices to deal with problems that are often of a much greater scale and difficulty than anything experienced in the recent history of the West, as the discussion in Chapter 7 will show. The human rights field – and, more broadly, the international development field – runs the risk of ignoring potentially useful ideas.

SOCIAL PRESSURE AND PARADIGM MAINTENANCE

The Western universalist ideology can be limiting in a way that adherents generally do not appreciate. Take, for instance, the example of gay marriage. As discussed earlier, promoting the rights of the individual as supreme impacts understandings of institutions like marriage. Marriage in a WEIRD context is an institution worth upholding primarily for the benefits it grants

---

[132] Ibid., 20–21 and 224–225.
[133] Ibid., 222–226.
[134] Ibid., 222–226; de Waal, *Advocacy in Conflict*.
[135] Aditya Sarkar, "Event Summary: Advocacy in Conflict Book Launch," World Peace Foundation *Reinventing Peace Blog*, November 13, 2015, https://sites.tufts.edu/reinventingpeace/2015/11/13/event-summary-advocacy-in-conflict-book-launch/.
[136] Merry, *Human Rights and Gender Violence*, 222–226.

to individuals as such – not for the broader benefits it provides to children and society. Not surprisingly, it is difficult to defend or champion perspectives that restrict the rights of individuals.

During the debate over gay marriage in the United States, no major law firm was willing to represent the side opposing gay marriage at the Supreme Court.[137] The medium-sized firm where the main lawyer arguing the case (*Obergefell v. Hodges*), John Bursch, is a partner refused to stand behind him because the case was too controversial. Paul D. Clement, a former solicitor general who has argued more than 75 cases before the Supreme Court, was forced to quit his firm in 2011 defending a similar position because the firm withdrew support.[138] He wrote at the time that he resigned "out of the firmly held belief that a representation should not be abandoned because the client's legal position is extremely unpopular in certain quarters."[139]

Of course, the convictions of their partners is only one reason law firms may not want to oppose gay marriage. Outside social pressure plays a very important role and there are consequently significant economic concerns.[140] Law firms worry about losing clients and potential recruits.[141] Unlike the majority of controversial social issues, opposing gay marriage has an enormous cost. The social and economic activism of gay marriage's supporters has left some lawyers and scholars feeling "bullied into silence." This is notable because there is a long history of representing unpopular clients in the United States, a tradition that is central to maintaining the strength of the judicial system. As Adam Liptak of *The New York Times* reports, major firms

> are willing to represent tobacco companies accused of lying about their deadly products, factories that spew pollution, and corporations said to be complicit in torture and murder abroad. But standing up for traditional marriage has turned out to be too much for the elite bar.[142]

---

[137] The court decided the case in 2015.

[138] He defended the federal Defense of Marriage Act, which reached the Supreme Court in 2013.

[139] Adam Liptak, "The Case against Gay Marriage: Top Law Firms Won't Touch It," *The New York Times*, April 11, 2015, www.nytimes.com/2015/04/12/us/the-case-against-gay-marriage-top-law-firms-wont-touch-it.html; Sophia Pearson, "Clement Quits King & Spalding over Marriage Act Decision," *Bloomberg*, April 25, 2011, www.bloomberg.com/news/articles/2011-04-25/clement-quits-king-spalding-over-marriage-act-decision-2-; Andrew Cohen, "In DOMA Dispute, Paul Clement Leaves with a Bang," *The Atlantic*, April 25, 2011, www.theatlantic.com/national/archive/2011/04/in-doma-dispute-paul-clement-leaves-with-a-bang/237829/.

[140] Liptak, "The Case against Gay Marriage"; Cohen, "In DOMA Dispute, Paul Clement Leaves with a Bang."

[141] Liptak, "The Case against Gay Marriage."

[142] Ibid.

The social pressure to conform also impacts employees in other industries. In April 2014, for instance, Brendan Eich, the recently appointed CEO of Mozilla, which produces the popular Firefox web browser, was forced to resign under pressure because of his opposition to same-sex marriage. Some employees discovered that he had donated $1000 in support of a 2008 California ballot initiative (known as Proposition 8) that would have limited marriage to heterosexual couples, and they attacked him on social media. They picked up support inside and outside the nonprofit organization, leading to a boycott of the company's web browser. When Eich did not repudiate his support for traditional marriage, he was pressured to resign.[143] Although Eich stressed the importance of inclusiveness at Mozilla and was never accused of treating anyone unfairly, it appears, as a *Wall Street Journal* opinion article summarized,

> that simply holding a private belief that was shared by a majority of Californians in 2008 and by President Obama until May of 2012 is no longer tolerated by the extreme wing of the movement to redefine marriage – or by the Silicon Valley technology community. Has a culture that once prided itself on its openness and inclusiveness become so bigoted that it cannot accept anyone who holds traditional Christian, Jewish or Muslim beliefs?[144]

Andrew Sullivan, a well-known gay writer and influential supporter of same-sex marriage, disagreed with how the Eich matter was handled, writing on his widely read blog that Mr. Eich had been "scalped by some gay activists."[145] The Western universalist view of marriage has international implications as well. Gay rights is now a foreign policy priority for both the United States and the European Union. Donors look increasingly askance at countries that criminalize homosexuality, reducing or suspending their foreign aid in some cases (such as Uganda and Gambia) in order to force changes in government policy. In 2011, the US Secretary of State passionately argued in a speech to the

[143] There was ample coverage of the controversy in the newspaper and on news websites. See, for instance, Seth Rosenblatt, "Mozilla CEO Eich Resigns After Gay-Marriage Controversy," CNET, April 3, 2014, www.cnet.com/news/mozilla-ceo-eich-resigns-after-controversy/ and Brian Fung, "Mozilla's CEO Steps Down Amid Gay Marriage Furor," *Washington Post*, April 3, 2014, www.washingtonpost.com/news/the-switch/wp/2014/04/03/mozillas-ceo-steps-down-amid-gay-marriage-furor/.
[144] James Freeman, "Mozilla's Intolerance," *Wall Street Journal*, April 4, 2014, http://online.wsj.com/news/articles/SB10001424052702303532704579481031176656974.
[145] Nick Bilton and Noam Cohen, "Mozilla's Chief Felled by View on Gay Unions," *The New York Times*, April 4, 2014, http://bits.blogs.nytimes.com/2014/04/03/eich-steps-down-as-mozilla-chief/.

UN Human Rights Commission that "Gay rights are human rights, and human rights are gay rights." Shortly afterwards, she directed American embassies around the world to prioritize the promotion of gay rights.[146] The Obama administration expanded the funding of overseas gay rights organizations (spending more than $700 million on gay rights groups and causes between 2012 and 2015), tied foreign aid to the protection of gay rights, and created a new special envoy to promote the human rights of lesbian, gay, bisexual, and transgender people.[147] While Trump may not prioritize this kind of support, it is unlikely he will completely end it; certainly, many in the State Department will continue to press for such rights. In 2013, UK Prime Minister David Cameron announced that he wanted the ministers and officials working on legalizing gay marriage in the country to "now work on exporting same-sex marriage around the world."[148] In the same year, ministers from ten European countries and the EU at the UN General Assembly endorsed the statement "Those who are lesbian, gay, bisexual and transgender (LGBT) must enjoy the same human rights as everyone else."[149] To date, however, there is no treaty that upholds gay rights, which means that sovereign states are currently under no obligation to implement laws to that effect.[150] Seventy-eight countries ban homosexuality, showing that there is no global consensus

---

[146] Omar Encarnación, "Gay Rights: Why Democracy Matters," *Journal of Democracy* 25, no. 3 (July 2014): 101–102.

[147] Norimitsu Onishi, "Obama Kenya Trip Sets Off Gay Rights Debate in Africa," *The New York Times*, July 21, 2015, www.nytimes.com/2015/07/22/world/africa/africans-to-welcome-obama-but-not-a-scolding-on-gay-rights.html?_r=0. Onishi, "American Support for Gay Rights May Leave Africans Vulnerable," *The New York Times*, December 21, 2015, www.nytimes.com/2015/12/21/world/africa/us-support-of-gay-rights-in-africa-may-have-done-more-harm-than-good.html.

[148] Encarnación, "Gay Rights," 101–102.

[149] Somini Sengupta, "Antigay Laws Gain Global Attention; Countering Them Remains Challenge," *The New York Times*, March 1, 2014, www.nytimes.com/2014/03/02/world/africa/antigay-laws-gain-global-attention-countering-them-remains-challenge.html.

[150] I agree with Jack Donnelly, who argues that "International human rights law does not prohibit discrimination on the basis of sexual orientation. Sexual orientation is not mentioned in the Universal Declaration or the Covenants, and arguments that it falls within the category of 'other status' in Article 2 of each of these documents are widely accepted, at least at the level of law, only in Europe and a few other countries. Nonetheless, everyone is entitled to security of the person. If the state refuses to protect some people against private violence, on the grounds that they are immoral, the state violates their basic human rights ... And the idea that the state should be permitted to imprison or even execute people solely on the basis of private voluntary acts between consenting adults, however much that behavior or 'lifestyle' offends community conceptions of morality, is inconsistent with any plausible conception of personal autonomy and individual human rights." Jack Donnelly, "The Relative Universality of Human Rights," *Human Rights Quarterly* 29, no. 2 (May 2007): 304.

on how to handle the issue.[151] Western support may actually be generating a backlash by "trigger[ing] people's defense mechanism," as one gay person in Nigeria commented, making LGBTs in Africa and elsewhere less safe.[152] Moreover, as *The Economist* noted after the president of the World Bank (another Western-dominated institution) declared that the promotion of gay rights was an "urgent task" that the organization should undertake,

> Of the many forms of bigotry . . . it is not clear that anti-gay laws are the most harmful to the poor. The bank lends to plenty of places that discriminate against women under Islamic law. It also lends to countries with laws that discriminate against minorities. The economic impact of these forms of bigotry is far bigger.[153]

The gay rights example is included here because it is emblematic of "paradigm maintenance"[154]; that is, how discourses are strengthened and preserved once they get established.[155] It shows how difficult it is to change organizations, social networks, and professions once they have become dominated by a particular set of ideas, norms, or incentives. These become path dependent (see Chapter 3) because they have their own elaborate mechanisms for creating, maintaining, and propagating their value systems, rules, and institutions – even if evidence emerges that challenge their assumptions. Of course, this is more likely in the humanities, social sciences, and human rights fields than in the hard sciences, where data refuting an idea speaks much louder.[156] Paradigm maintenance works through numerous channels, including hiring; promotion; funding decisions; selective enforcement of rules – for example, dissident research is not just rejected more often, and

---

[151] "Human Rights: The Gay Divide," *The Economist*, October 11, 2014, www.economist.com/news/leaders/21623668-victories-gay-rights-some-parts-world-have-provoked-backlash-elsewhere-gay.

[152] Onishi, "American Support for Gay Rights May Leave Africans Vulnerable."

[153] "The World Bank: Right Cause, Wrong Battle," *The Economist*, April 12, 2014, www.economist.com/news/leaders/21600684-why-world-banks-focus-gay-rights-misguided-right-cause-wrong-battle.

[154] Robert Wade first articulated this concept. See Wade, "Japan, the World Bank, and the Art of Paradigm Maintenance: The East Asian Miracle in Perspective," *New Left Review* 217 (May/June 1996): 3–36.

[155] Of course, unlike most issues, the ideological paradigm surrounding gay marriage changed very rapidly in the 2000s. See, for instance, Chris Cillizza, "How Unbelievably Quickly Public Opinion Changed on Gay Marriage, in 5 Charts," *Washington Post*, June 26, 2015, www.washingtonpost.com/news/the-fix/wp/2015/06/26/how-unbelievably-quickly-public-opinion-changed-on-gay-marriage-in-6-charts/.

[156] It is much easier for a wrong economics theory to maintain widespread support in the face of contrary information than a wrong physics theory.

forced to undergo stricter reviews, but is also delayed in ways that wear down authors; the discouragement of dissonant discourse – dissidents are deemed to be eccentric, disgruntled, or even a misfit; criticism is repeatedly disparaged to ensure it gains no traction; the alteration of results, as when summaries or reports of dissident papers may not reflect content; the management of images internally and externally, for example organizations support those with the right positions and ignore troublemakers; ostracization, which can be very public via social media; social pressure as in the gay marriage case discussed earlier; and how the media focuses or frames issues.[157]

The pressure within many Western countries to uphold and advance a particular position or paradigm on gay rights in many ways mirrors what the situation was a few decades ago with regard to the issue – but in reverse. Gays were routinely discriminated against in the West until early in the twenty-first century; few institutions or individuals would openly question their prejudice and evident discomfort toward LGBT individuals. Challenging that consensus left one vulnerable professionally, sometimes left one vulnerable personally depending on what company you kept, and occasionally left one vulnerable legally depending on what you did where. Just like today, few major law firms or businesses or major public figures would risk the opprobrium – and financial loss – from taking a public stand in favor of gay rights. The prevailing view, at least among elites and popular culture, has changed dramatically in recent years on the issue,[158] but society's need to rigidly uphold a single moral position has not – just as cultural psychology suggests. The anger that this sudden paradigm shift prompted among religious communities and the working class – both of which are thicker than elite culture – was arguably a significant reason for the Republican victory in 2016, but because the paradigm maintenance mechanisms are so strong, it is likely overall support for LGBT rights will continue.

---

[157] Many of these ideas originate in a study of paradigm maintenance at the World Bank. See Robin Broad, "Research, Knowledge and the Art of 'Paradigm Maintenance,'" Bretton Woods Update 53 (November/December 2006), www.brettonwoodsproject.org/2006/11/art-546206/; Wade, "Japan, the World Bank, and the Art of Paradigm Maintenance," 3–36. In many ways, paradigm maintenance is simply one way a society's or group's values and moral matrices are reproduced, as explained in Chapter 3.

[158] Cillizza, "How Unbelievably Quickly Public Opinion Changed on Gay Marriage, in 5 Charts." Michael Walzer notes, "Boundaries ... are vulnerable to shifts in social meaning, and we have no choice but to live with the continual probes and incursions through which these shifts are worked out. Commonly, the shifts are like sea changes, very slow. ... But the actual boundary revision, when it comes, is likely to come suddenly." Walzer, *Spheres of Justice: A Defense of Pluralism and Equality* (New York, NY: Basic Books, 1983), 319.

Understanding paradigm maintenance should matter to Western human rights actors because the language and approach they use may actually make their ability to improve lives – their ostensible goal – harder to achieve at times. By presenting a stark choice between culture or religion and rights – as opposed to considering ways that these can be reconciled – they encourage many moderate people and groups to develop hostile attitudes to human rights positions.[159] By working in a proselytizing manner, Western universalists are regarded as "arrogant, uncivilized, and counterproductive."[160] By framing so many issues in terms of rights, they impede compromise and limit the ability of different groups and countries to discover common ground and repair the overlapping consensus of an earlier era. They make it difficult for societies to find the appropriate balance between various trade-offs and come to agreements over priorities, a process for which the UDHR carved out space. And by undervaluing public goods that cannot be expressed in terms of rights, they often end up promoting short-term concerns at the expense of long-term welfare. All of this heightens social conflict, especially as it promotes unrealistic expectations that a society may find hard to fulfill without making compromises in other areas that may be equally, or even more, important.[161]

This book's two case studies illustrate these challenges in the contemporary context. In thin society Europe, as we shall see in the next chapter, controversy has erupted over circumcision, a thick society custom that Jews and Muslims have practiced for thousands of years. This controversy is part of a general movement to limit religious institutions. Some have felt forced to emigrate to protect their freedom to practice religion. Others have protested, and vowed to carry on even if the state declares their practices illegal. Legal battles in the United States have occurred over the right of a photographer, a florist, and a baker to refuse to provide service for a same-sex wedding; over the position of hospitals and charities vis-à-vis adoption, assisted reproduction, and sex changes; and over the stances of religious groups on college campuses and religious college and universities that currently receive public funds and/or access to university facilities.[162]

In thick society Africa, anger against Western universalist judicial practices and foreign aid policies promoted by human rights activists has risen in recent

---

[159] Daniel Bell, "East Asian Challenge to Human Rights: Reflections on an East West Dialogue," *Human Rights Quarterly* 18, no. 3 (August 1996): 652.

[160] Ibid., 658.

[161] Glendon, *Rights Talk: The Impoverishment of Political Discourse* (New York, NY: The Free Press, 1991), x–xi and 14.

[162] Douthat, "As Goes Andrew Sullivan, So Goes Pluralism," *The New York Times*, March 11, 2014, http://douthat.blogs.nytimes.com/2014/03/11/as-goes-andrew-sullivan-so-goes-pluralism/.

years, with many feeling these practices and policies are both inappropriate for local needs and unfairly aimed at the continent because of its weak international position.[163] Whereas restorative justice has traditionally played an important role on the continent, human rights actors have focused almost exclusively on retributive justice, which generally prevails in the West.[164] In Rwanda, as we shall see in Chapter 7, the government put into place an elaborate hybrid legal regime – over the objections of the human rights establishment – to handle the cases of hundreds of thousands that participated in the country's genocide in order to achieve a broader set of goals beyond retribution, with reasonably effective results.

The Rwandan example hints at a better approach – which the book unpacks in Chapter 8 – that would seek to draw upon the resources of local culture to promote human rights. Indeed, there are many reasons to think that this approach – flexible universalism – would be more effective. As Daniel Bell argues, it would more likely embed human rights within local cultures, producing a stronger commitment to its ideas and practices; highlight which groups within society are most likely to favor and work toward bringing about social and political change; enable practitioners to draw upon the most persuasive justifications to advance human rights goals; encourage the adoption of the most appropriate attitude when promoting human rights; and encourage the exploration of alternatives to legal mechanisms "for the protection of the vital human interests normally secured by a rights regime in a Western context."[165] For some rights – such as the right of the elderly to be cared for by their children; the right of children to be brought up in a stable, loving family; and the right of a woman to be treated with dignity by her spouse and his family – it is hard to imagine anything but the resources of a local culture being effective.

[163] See, for instance, Karen Alter, James Thuo Gathii, and Laurence Helfer, "Backlash against International Courts in West, East and Southern Africa: Causes and Consequences," iCourts Working Paper Series, No. 21; Duke Law School Public Law & Legal Theory Series, May 12, 2015, http://papers.ssrn.com/sol3/papers.cfm?abstract_id=2591837. As an example, see: Onishi, "American Support for Gay Rights May Leave Africans Vulnerable."

[164] See, for instance, Phil Clark, *The Gacaca Courts, Post-Genocide Justice and Reconciliation in Rwanda: Justice without Lawyers* (Cambridge: Cambridge University Press, 2010); Clark and Zachary Kaufman (eds.), *After Genocide: Transitional Justice, Post-Conflict Reconstruction and Reconciliation in Rwanda and Beyond* (New York, NY: Columbia University Press, 2009).

[165] Daniel Bell, "East Asian Challenge to Human Rights: Reflections on an East West Dialogue," *Human Rights Quarterly* 18, no. 3 (August 1996): 656–659.

6

Case Study: Male Circumcision in Europe

On June 26, 2012, a Cologne court ruled that the circumcision of boys should be considered a prosecutable physical assault.[1] In a judgment stemming from the case of a four-year-old Muslim boy, judges declared that permanent physical alteration of any part of the body infringes on the child's right to decide his beliefs for himself. The verdict against the doctor who had performed the procedure stated that neither the rights of parents nor the right to religious freedom could justify "serious and irreversible interference with physical integrity."[2]

Human rights advocates, medical associations, and many legal experts in Germany supported the decision. Holm Putzke, a legal expert at the University of Passau, who has long argued for a ban on nonmedical circumcision, praised the result, stating, "This decision could not only affect future cases, but, in the best case, lead the religions concerned to change their mentality when it comes to respecting children's fundamental rights."[3] Georg Ehrmann, the chairman of Deutsche Kinderhilfe, a child rights organization, told a news conference that "In the clear opinion of experts, the amputation of the foreskin is a grave interference in the bodily integrity of a child."[4] Meanwhile,

---

[1] Michael Bohlander "Amtsgericht Kön (County Court of Cologne) Judgment no 528 Ds 30/11 and Landgericht Köln (District Court of Cologne) Judgment no 151 Ns 169/11," *Oxford Journal of Law and Religion*, first published online December 29, 2012, http://ojlr.oxfordjournals.org/content/early/2012/12/28/ojlr.rws053.full.

[2] Jessica Phelan, "German Court Rules Religious Circumcision of Minors is 'Assault,'" *Global Post*, June 26, 2012, www.globalpost.com/dispatch/news/regions/europe/germany/120626/cologne-religious-circumcision-assault.

[3] Von Matthias Ruch, "Gericht stellt religiöse Beschneidung unter Strafe," *Stern*, June 26, 2012, www.ftd.de/politik/deutschland/:koerperverletzung-gericht-stellt-religioese-beschneidung-unter-strafe/70054618.html.

[4] Reuters, "Germany Resumes Ritual Circumcisions after Dispute," *Jerusalem Post*, October 1, 2012, www.jpost.com/LandedPages/PrintArticle.aspx?id=286236.

a leading criminal-law expert called for a national discussion about "how much religiously motivated violence against children a society is ready to tolerate."[5] A survey taken in 2012 showed that 60 percent of Germans consider child circumcision to be genital mutilation.[6] Most medical groups, including the German Academy for Pediatric and Adolescent Medicine, the German Association for Pediatric Surgery, and the Professional Association of Pediatric and Adolescent Physicians have condemned the practice as causing bodily harm.[7]

Supporters of the decision did not see it as impinging on the rights of parents or religious groups. As the court stated, "The religious freedom of the parents and their right to educate their child would not be unacceptably compromised, if they were obliged to wait until the child could himself decide to be circumcised."[8]

Jews, Muslims, and Christians jointly protested the ruling.[9] The Council of the Coordination of Muslims in Germany, which has some four million

[5] William Galston, "Mark of Belonging: Why Circumcision Is No Crime," *Commonweal*, May 5, 2014, www.commonwealmagazine.org/mark-belonging.

[6] Joshua Hammer, "Anti-Semitism and Germany's Movement against Circumcision," *The Atlantic*, January 7, 2013, www.theatlantic.com/health/archive/2013/01/anti-semitism-and-germanys-movement-against-circumcision/266794/.

[7] See, for instance, the German Academy for Pediatric and Adolescent Medicine (Deutsche Akademie für Kinder- und Jugendmedizin e.V., DAKJ), "Stellungnahme zur Beschneidung von minderjährigen Jungen," July 25, 2012.

[8] Michelle Castillo, "German Court Rules Circumcision Goes Against 'fundamental right of the child to bodily integrity,'" *CBS News*, July 13, 2012, www.cbsnews.com/news/german-court-rules-circumcision-goes-against-fundamental-right-of-the-child-to-bodily-integrity/. In August of the same year, criminal charges were lodged against Rabbi David Goldberg for performing circumcisions in northern Bavaria. They were later dismissed. Raphael Ahren, "Criminal Charges Filed against German Rabbi for Performing Circumcisions," *The Times of Israel*, August 21, 2012, www.timesofisrael.com/criminal-charges-filed-against-german-rabbi-for-performing-circumcisions/.

[9] Benjamin Weinthal, "Jews, Muslims, Christians Protest Circumcision Ban," *Jerusalem Post*, September 9, 2012, www.jpost.com/Jewish-World/Jewish-News/Jews-Muslims-Christians-protest-circumcision-ban. In the United States, a bipartisan group of twenty members of Congress sent a protest letter to the German ambassador arguing that the Cologne decision is "an affront to religious freedom" because, for Jewish and Muslims communities, circumcision is "a fundamental rite of passage and affirmation of faith." Office of Representative Henry Waxman Press Release, "Members of Congress Urge Germany to Safeguard Religious Freedom and Undo Circumcision Ban," *Legistorm*, August 8, 2012, www.legistorm.com/stormfeed/view_rss/29435/member/525.html. Abraham Foxman, the New York-based national director of the Anti-Defamation League, said that the decision by the court, "places an intolerable burden on the free exercise of religion by Jews and also by Muslims who practice male circumcision as part of their religious faith ... While the ruling by the court in Cologne does not appear to have anti-Semitic intent, its effect is to say 'Jews are not welcome.'" Abraham Foxman, "German Parliament Should Act to Protect Circumcision as

members, condemned the ruling, stating that it was "a serious attack on religious freedom." Ali Kizilkaya, a spokesman for the council, said that "The ruling does not take everything into account, religious practice concerning circumcision of young Muslims and Jews has been carried out over the millennia on a global level."[10] Dieter Graumann, the president of the Central Council of Jews in Germany, which represents about 120,000 people, condemned the decision as "outrageous and insensitive" and called it "an unprecedented and dramatic intrusion on the self-determination of religious communities."[11] Muslim and Jewish leaders issued a joint statement declaring the ruling to be "an affront on our basic religious and human rights. Circumcision is an ancient ritual that is fundamental to our individual faiths and we protest in the strongest possible terms this court ruling."[12]

Top Christian clerics responded as well. The German Bishops Conference called the ruling "extremely disconcerting." Heinrich Mussinghoff, the Roman Catholic archbishop of Aachen, said "To ban circumcision is a serious attack on religious freedom."[13] The head of the Protestant Church in

Religious Practice," *Anti-Defamation League*, June 26, 2012, http://archive.adl.org/PresRele/RelChStSep_90/6339_90.htm.

[10] Gavan Reilly, "German Court: 'Circumcising Young Boys is Grievous Bodily Harm,'" *TheJournal*.ie, June 28, 2012, www.thejournal.ie/germany-circumcision-young-boys-gbh-islam-judaism-503045-Jun2012/.

[11] Nicholas Kulish, "German Ruling against Circumcising Boys Draws Criticism," *The New York Times*, June 26, 2012, www.nytimes.com/2012/06/27/world/europe/german-court-rules-against-circumcising-boys.html?_r=0.

[12] Representatives of Jewish and Islamic communities, "International Appeal against the Judgment of the Cologne District Court on Circumcision: Common Statement," July 11, 2012, www.ditib.de/detail1.php?id=307&lang=de. The decision caused a minor diplomatic incident. Numerous Israeli politicians denounced the ruling as anti-Semitic. An Israeli parliamentary committee said the decision infringes upon religious freedom and evokes memories of the Holocaust. Blake Sobczak, "Germany Circumcision Ban: Israeli Parliament Slams Decision by Cologne Court," *Huffington Post*, July 9, 2012, www.huffingtonpost.com/2012/07/09/germany-circumcision-ban-_n_1659423.html.

It summoned the German ambassador to explain the ruling. The country's Interior Minister wrote to the German chancellor: "Don't force the Jews living in your country to choose between following the law and obeying a divine command that we have observed over the years according to our tradition." Philip Podolsky, "Israeli Cabinet Minister Pleads with Merkel to Prevent Prosecutions for Circumcision," *The Times of Israel*, August 22, 2012, www.timesofisrael.com/israeli-cabinet-minister-pleads-with-merkel-to-step-in-and-prevent-prosecutions-for-circumcision/.

[13] Martin Barillas, "German Christians Join Jews against Circumcision Ruling," *Spero News*, July 9, 2012, www.speroforum.com/a/CQKJMBWHDZ14/72957-German-Christians-join-Jews-against-circumcision-ruling#.UhE3prx1G00.

Germany, Hans Ulrich Anke, said the ruling should be appealed, as it did not take "sufficiently" into account the religious significance of the rite.[14]

Jewish leaders reported a strong backlash against their stance supporting circumcision. Stephan Kramer, secretary general of the Jewish Community in Berlin, said that "We've gotten thousands of emails, 95 percent against us. People are saying things like 'Jews are torturing their own children, living in caves, performing ancient rituals for nothing.' It has made us strangers in our country."[15]

Egemen Bağış, Turkey's EU Minister, wrote in the German newspaper Süddeutsche Zeitung that the judgment is an

> explicit violation of the one of the areas of the fundamental rights and freedoms of Muslims and Jews in Germany... The boundaries of faith should not be drawn by courts. This ruling is completely in contradiction with the freedom to practice religion guaranteed by law. Criminalising circumcision as injury is an indicator of a lack of knowledge of culture and history.[16]

For Jews and Muslims, circumcision is not just an integral part of their identity and an ancient custom that strengthens communal bonds; it is a holy commandment issued by God.[17] As Genesis 17 of the Torah (the Hebrew Bible) states, the Jewish patriarch Abraham received detailed instructions about circumcision directly from God:

> This is My covenant, which you shall observe between Me and between you and between your seed after you, that every male among you be circumcised.

---

[14] Reinhard Mawick, Evangelical Church in Germany (EKD) Press Office, "EKD Critical of Cologne Circumcision Decision," EKD, June 27, 2012, www.ekd.de/english/ekd_press_releases-4792.html.

[15] Hammer, "Anti-Semitism and Germany's Movement against Circumcision."

[16] Egemen Bağış, "The German Ruling on Circumcision Is a Mistake," egemenbagis.com, August 28, 2012, http://egemenbagis.com/en/5460.

[17] Roughly three out of ten of all males in the world are circumcised. Islam accounts for roughly 70 percent of these. World Health Organization (WHO), *Male Circumcision: Global Trends and Determinants of Prevalence, Safety and Acceptability* (Geneva: WHO, 2007); WHO, *Neonatal and Child Male Circumcision: A Global Review* (Geneva: WHO, 2010). Most of these circumcisions are, in fact, not performed on newly born children. That is a custom unique to Jews, Americans, and a few other groups. Most other societies perform the procedure on youths. Muslims typically circumcise before the age of 10; many do it when they are seven; some as early as the seventh day. In South Korea, the overwhelming majority does it between age six and the late teenage years as part of a kind of customary rite of passage into adulthood. Richard Shweder, "Shouting at the Hebrews: Imperial Liberalism v Liberal Pluralism and the Practice of Male Circumcision," *Law, Culture and the Humanities* 5, no. 2 (June 2009): 248 and 256–257.

> And you shall circumcise the flesh of your foreskin, and it shall be as the sign
> of a covenant between Me and between you. And at the age of eight days,
> every male shall be circumcised to you throughout your generations ... And
> an uncircumcised male, who will not circumcise the flesh of his foreskin –
> that soul will be cut off from its people; he has broken My covenant.[18]

Jews have practiced the custom on German soil for some 1,700 years –
Cologne had a synagogue at least as early as AD 321, when Constantine the
Great ruled the city as part of the Roman Empire – well before the majority of
the current inhabitants' ancestors had moved there.[19]

Although there are variations in the timing depending on family, region,
and country – some do it as early as the seventh day after birth, others as late as
puberty – circumcision has been a religious norm from the beginning of
Islam. Many of Muhammad's early disciples were circumcised to symbolize
their inclusion within the emerging Islamic community, as recited by many
hadith (sayings or acts of Muhammad). It continues to be a sign of belonging
to the wider Muslim community as well as a sign of purity.

As a result, any ban on the practice would be hard to implement. If a
government or human rights organization made a serious effort, religious
believers would have no choice but to emigrate.[20] As Stephan Kramer said,
"the bris [circumcision] is fundamental for our religion. If this is put into a
legal jeopardy, then we have to reconsider whether we can stay in Germany or
not."[21] Gonca Sapci, a first-generation immigrant from Turkey, said, "To call
circumcision into question is idiotic. Just as washing your face, your hands
and behind your ears is a ritual in Islam, so is circumcision."[22]

For these believers, failing to circumcise their male infants would lead to
expulsion from their communities and cause serious spiritual harm to both
parents and children. After all, "circumcision is a God-given obligation, the
key to and symbol of membership in an ancient and worthy community.
Rearing their children in that community, they believe, is the greatest gift they

---

[18] Genesis 17: 10–14, www.chabad.org/library/bible_cdo/aid/8212/jewish/Chapter-17.htm.
[19] Maimon and Ellis, "The Circumcision Crisis," 6.
[20] Joel Fetzer, "Immigration, Segregation, and Religious Freedom in Europe: Responding to The
      EU Immigration Crisis and Its Relationship to Religious Freedom," *Cornerstone Blog*,
      Religious Freedom Project, Berkley Center for Religion, Peace, and World Affairs,
      Georgetown University, June 9, 2015, http://berkleycenter.georgetown.edu/cornerstone/the-eu-
      immigration-crisis-and-its-relationship-to-religious-freedom/responses/immigration-segregation-
      and-religious-freedom-in-europe.
[21] Hammer, "Anti-Semitism and Germany's Movement against Circumcision."
[22] Melissa Eddy, "In Germany, Ruling over Circumcision Sows Anxiety and Confusion," *The
      New York Times*, July 14, 2012, www.nytimes.com/2012/07/14/world/europe/in-germany-ruling-
      over-circumcision-sows-anxiety-and-confusion.html.

can give them."[23] If a government bans circumcision, it is, in essence, banning religion as understood by Jews and Muslims.

EUROPEAN ATTITUDES TOWARD CIRCUMCISION

The consequences of the German ruling echoed elsewhere in the German-speaking world. Two hospitals in Switzerland announced that they would temporarily stop performing circumcisions in light of the German ruling.[24] In Austria, the governor of Vorarlberg province, seeing the decision in Germany as a "precedence-setting judgment," ordered state-run hospitals to stop circumcisions except for health reasons until the legal situation was clarified.[25]

The controversy exemplified a growing trend across Northern Europe, a particularly thin society context, where an "intactivist" movement pushing for a ban is gaining momentum.[26] A number of countries have debated whether to require medical supervision for all circumcisions (something Sweden and Norway have done since 2001 and 2014, respectively) or even to ban the practice outright.[27] Sweden's Pediatric Society called circumcision the "mutilation of a child unable to decide for himself"[28] and advocated putting an end to the practice, as did the Royal Dutch Medical Association, the Danish College of General Practitioners, and Norway's association of nurses and children's welfare adviser.[29] The Danish and Swedish medical

[23] Galston, "Mark of Belonging."
[24] Ofer Aderet, "Following German Court Ruling, Switzerland Hospitals Suspend Circumcisions," *Haaretz*, July 23, 2012, www.haaretz.com/jewish-world/jewish-world-news/following-german-court-ruling-switzerland-hospitals-suspend-circumcisions-1.453077.
[25] "Hospitals in Austria and Switzerland Suspend Circumcision," *The Telegraph*, July 25, 2012, www.telegraph.co.uk/news/worldnews/europe/austria/9427592/Hospitals-in-Austria-and-Switzerland-suspend-circumcision.html.
[26] Hammer, "Anti-Semitism and Germany's Movement against Circumcision."
[27] The Social Liberal Party, a member of Denmark's ruling coalition; Norway's Center Party; Finland's third largest party, the populist True Finns; and Sweden's Democrats Party have all announced that they favor prohibition of the practice. Galston, "Mark of Belonging."
[28] Galston, "Mark of Belonging."
[29] "Health Bosses in Denmark, Norway Resist Calls to Ban Circumcision," *Jewish Telegraphic Agency*, April 11, 2014, www.jta.org/2014/04/11/news-opinion/world/health-bosses-in-denmark-norway-resist-calls-to-ban-milah. The Royal Dutch Medical Association (KNMG) released a report in 2010 that called circumcision a "violation of children's rights to autonomy and physical integrity," something that "can cause complications – bleeding, infection, urethral stricture and panic attacks are particularly common." It asked "doctors to actively and insistently inform parents ... of the absence of medical benefits and the danger of complications." Royal Dutch Medical Association (KNMG), "KNMG Viewpoint: Non-therapeutic Circumcision of Male Minors," KNMG, 2010, http://knmg.artsennet.nl/Publicaties/KNMGpublicatie/77942/Nontherapeutic-circumcision-of-male-minors-2010.htm.

associations similarly recommended waiting until a child is old enough to give his informed consent.[30]

The five Nordic children's ombudspersons released a joint resolution in September 2013 calling for a ban on nontherapeutic circumcision for underage boys.[31] Anne Lindboe, the Norwegian children's ombudswoman, declared in November 2013 that "With good information about risk, pain and lack of health benefits of the intervention, I think parents from minorities would voluntarily abstain from circumcising children." In 2012, she proposed that Jews and Muslims perform a symbolic, nonsurgical ritual in its place.[32]

One of Denmark's most prestigious newspapers published an article calling circumcision a custom involving "black-clad men" who torture and mutilate babies.[33] Similarly, a Norwegian newspaper published a cartoon in which law enforcement officers question a rabbi who holds a religious book while he stabs a baby in the head with a devil's pitchfork and a woman with a bloodied religious book cuts off the child's toe. The woman asserts, "Mistreating? No, this is tradition, an important part of our belief!"[34] A poll in the United Kingdom showed that almost two-fifths of the population favored banning nonmedical circumcision.[35]

Widespread sentiments such as these led the Parliamentary Assembly of the Council of Europe (PACE) – which cannot pass binding legislation but is highly influential – to pass Resolution 1952 on "Children's Right to Physical Integrity" in October 2013 with a resounding vote of 78 in favor, 13 against, and

---

In 2011, KNMG denounced the practice as a "painful and harmful ritual" and called on ministers, MPs, and human rights organizations to speak out against the practice. "Doctors Campaign against 'Risky and Painful' Circumcision of Boys," *DutchNews*.nl, September 14, 2011, www.dutchnews.nl/news/archives/2011/09/doctors_campaign_against_risky.php.

[30] "Circumcision Divide between Denmark and Israel," Denmark's *Online Post*, January 24, 2014, http://cphpost.dk/news/circumcision-divide-between-denmark-and-israel.8440.html; Michael Schulson, "Do Circumcision Bans Protect Kids' Rights, or Infringe upon Parents'?," *The Daily Beast*, February 2, 2014, www.thedailybeast.com/articles/2014/02/02/do-circumcision-bans-protect-kids-rights-or-infringe-upon-parents.html.

[31] Galston, "Mark of Belonging."

[32] "Norwegian Official: Jews, Muslims Circumcise out of Ignorance," *Jewish Telegraphic Agency*, November 25, 2013, www.jta.org/2013/11/25/news-opinion/world/norwegian-official-jews-muslims-circumcise-out-of-ignorance.

[33] Galston, "Mark of Belonging."

[34] Pale Vale, "Circumcision Cartoon in Norwegian Newspaper Angers Jewish Groups," *The Huffington Post UK*, May 31, 2013, www.huffingtonpost.co.uk/2013/05/31/circumcision-cartoon-in-norwegian-newspaper_n_3364643.html.

[35] Cnaan Liphshiz, "Poll: 45 Percent of Britons Favor Banning Kosher Slaughter," *Jewish Telegraphic Agency*, March 29, 2013, www.jta.org/2013/03/29/news-opinion/world/poll-45-percent-of-britons-favor-banning-kosher-slaughter.

15 abstentions.[36] It states in Article 2 that it is "particularly worried about a category of violation of the physical integrity of children, which supporters of the procedures tend to present as beneficial to the children themselves despite clear evidence to the contrary. This includes ... the circumcision of young boys for religious reasons." An amendment removing a reference to the "religious rights of parents and families" passed with a large majority.[37]

This resolution was based on a report prepared by PACE's Committee on Social Affairs, Health, and Sustainable Development, which argued that "circumcision applied to young boys is clearly a human rights violation" because it permanently changes a child's physical integrity at an age when he is clearly unable to give a well-informed consent.[38] As a result, "male circumcision should ... be strongly questioned today, both in the medical and the religious context." The rapporteur of the report commented that "as a children's-rights activist," arguments in favor of the practice are "purely serving the adults who wish to avoid a confrontation with the 'dark side' of their own religion, traditions and, finally, identity."[39]

Although German lawmakers overrode the judicial ruling – in December 2012 they passed legislation explicitly permitting parents the right to have their boys circumcised[40] – the issue is unlikely to disappear given the growing opposition among Germany's general population, which holds a thin society framework and understanding of rights. The same is true in many parts of the West, especially the Protestant countries of Northern Europe, which have a narrower understanding of religion than Catholic countries, with Catholicism's greater emphasis on ritual and community, and the United States, with its history as a refuge from religious persecution.[41]

---

[36] Jewish Telegraphic Agency, "Europe Council: Circumcision a 'Violation of the Physical Integrity of Children,'" *Jerusalem Post*, October 2, 2013, www.jpost.com/Jewish-World/Jewish-News/European-council-Circumcision-a-violation-of-the-physical-integrity-of-children-327692.

[37] Ibid.

[38] Jonathan Fisher, "Circumcision Could Be Banned," *The Jewish Chronicle*, November 8, 2013, www.thejc.com/comment-and-debate/comment/113074/circumcision-could-be-banned.

[39] Fisher, "Circumcision Could Be Banned"; Marlene Rupprecht, "Children's Right to Physical Integrity," Parliamentary Assembly of the Council of Europe, September 6, 2013, http://assembly.coe.int/nw/xml/XRef/X2H-DW-extr.asp?FileID=20057&Lang=en.

[40] Melissa Eddy, "German Lawmakers Vote to Protect Right to Circumcision," *The New York Times*, December 12, 2012, www.nytimes.com/2012/12/13/world/europe/german-lawmakers-vote-to-protect-right-to-circumcision.html.

[41] In the United States, a group tried to get a ban on what it called Male Genital Mutilation put to a vote in San Francisco, but after collecting enough signatures in 2011 for the citizen initiative to take effect, a judge struck it down, on the grounds that such regulations were the responsibility of the state, not a city. Lisa Leff, "Circumcision Ban to Be Stricken from San Francisco Ballot, Judge Says," *Huffington Post*, July 27, 2011, www.huffingtonpost.com/2011/07/

A HIERARCHY OF RIGHTS

This circumcision case study exemplifies how human rights are interpreted differently by various groups, cultures, and societies. As cultural psychology suggests is likely, there is a stark difference of opinion about what rights ought to be prioritized. And, much like intersociety disputes between countries in the West and those in the South, the intrasociety argument in this case is between those who emphasize individual rights – the proponents of the ban on neonatal circumcision – and those who believe that religious law or the needs of the community ought to matter more.

Both sides claim that they are backed both by the law and by human rights conventions. For instance, many Western universalists can point to Article 5 of the UDHR, which states that "no one shall be subjected to torture or to cruel, inhuman, or degrading treatment or punishment,"[42] and argue that circumcision qualifies as "cruel, inhuman, or degrading treatment." It is "contrary to modern ethics," as one Danish doctor wrote in a Danish newspaper, and therefore "religious arguments must never trump the protection of children's basic human rights."[43] Deutsche Kinderhilfe, the German child rights organization, argues that religious circumcision may contravene the Convention on the Rights of the Child, which has been ratified, accepted, or acceded to by 193 countries (including Germany, but not including the United States).[44] J. Steven Svoboda, founder of the California-based Attorneys for the Rights of the Child, similarly argues that "Male circumcision also violates four core human rights documents – the Universal Declaration of Human Rights, the Convention on the Rights of the Child, the International

---

27/circumcision-ban-stripped-from-san-francisco-ballot_n_911590.html. US activists are trying to put such measures to a vote across the country. One of the movement's leaders says "the end goal for us is making cutting boys' foreskin a federal crime." Melissa Eddy, "German Lawmakers Vote to Protect Right to Circumcision," *The New York Times*, December 12, 2012, www.nytimes.com/2012/12/13/world/europe/german-lawmakers-vote-to-protect-right-to-circumcision.html.

[42] UN General Assembly, *Universal Declaration of Human Rights*, December 10, 1948, 217 A (III), available at: www.un.org/en/documents/udhr/index.shtml.

[43] "Circumcision Divide between Denmark and Israel," Denmark's *Online Post*.

[44] UN General Assembly, *Convention on the Rights of the Child*, November 20, 1989, United Nations, Treaty Series, vol. 1577, p. 3, available at: www.ohchr.org/en/professionalinterest/pages/crc.aspx. Article 24.3 states that "States Parties shall take all effective and appropriate measures with a view to abolishing traditional practices prejudicial to the health of children." While it does state in article 14.3 that "Freedom to manifest one's religion or beliefs may be subject only to such limitations as are prescribed by law and are necessary to protect public safety, order, health or morals, or the fundamental rights and freedoms of others," it also makes it clear that it is up to governments to define and protect these.

Covenant on Civil and Political Rights, and the Convention against Torture."[45] The Charter of Fundamental Rights of the European Union somewhat unusually states in Article 3 that "everyone has the right to respect for his physical and mental integrity."[46]

On the other side, supporters of circumcision also point to the UDHR, which – as discussed in Chapter 2 – gives strong backing to religious freedom and the right of families to decide how to raise their children. It states (Article 18) that "everyone has the right to freedom of thought, conscience and religion; this right includes . . . freedom, either alone and in community with others and in public or private, to manifest his religion or belief in teaching, practice, worship, and observance."[47] The Charter of Fundamental Rights of the European Union states (Article 10) that "Everyone has the right to freedom of thought, conscience and religion. This right includes the freedom . . . to manifest religion or belief, in worship, teaching, practice and observance."[48] In both documents, "practice" would seem to include circumcision. The United Nations Declaration on the Elimination of All Forms of Intolerance and of Discrimination Based on Religion or Belief guarantees (Article 5.1) parents "the right to organize the life within the family in accordance with their religion or belief."[49]

Rabbi Aryeh Goldberg, vice president of the Rabbinical Center of Europe, said the German ruling was a violation of religious freedom. "The decision is contrary to human rights charter of the European Union, to which the German legal system is committed, and undermines the basic right to worship in the German constitution."[50] Avichai Apel, the chief rabbi of Dortmund, said: "Circumcision is for us a duty, and the basis for a Jewish child to be a part

---

[45] J. Steven Svoboda, "Circumcision of Male Infants as a Human Rights Violation," *Journal of Medical Ethics* 39, no. 7 (July 2013): 469–474.
[46] European Union, *Charter of Fundamental Rights of the European Union*, October 26, 2012, 2012/C 326/02, available at: http://eur-lex.europa.eu/legal-content/EN/TXT/?uri= CELEX:12012P/TXT.
[47] UN General Assembly, *Universal Declaration of Human Rights*.
[48] European Union, *Charter of Fundamental Rights of the European Union*.
[49] UN General Assembly, *Declaration on the Elimination of All Forms of Intolerance and of Discrimination Based on Religion or Belief*, November 25, 1981, A/RES/36/55, available at: www.un.org/documents/ga/res/36/a36r055.htm.
[50] Jacob Edelist, "German Court Criminalizes Religious Circumcision," *The Jewish Press*, June 26, 2012, www.jewishpress.com/news/breaking-news/german-court-criminalizes-religious-circumcision/2012/06/26/.

of the Jewish people. Religious freedom is being curtailed, and that is something we cannot accept here in Germany."[51]

Philippe Boillat, director general of human rights and legal affairs of the
Council of Europe, said that PACE's resolution "ran totally contrary to all the
European laws on religious freedom." Several other officials from the organization also distanced themselves from the resolution.[52] Heiner Bielefeldt,
the United Nations Human Rights Council's special rapporteur on freedom
of religion, supported the Jewish and Muslim position, stating, "Freedom of
religion and belief in its application goes far beyond any pre-defined lists of
classical religions. It protects human beings in their broad variety of convictions, and also conviction-based practices. So issues like male circumcision are
part of that."[53]

These differing viewpoints reflect the need to consider context and seek to
balance the various rights and needs of increasingly diverse societies. In the
circumcision case, there are obvious tensions between the freedom of religion
and the physical integrity of individuals; the role of state responsibility versus
that of parental rights; the values of multiculturalism versus that of
nationalism; and the differing perspectives of religious morality versus that
of secular morality.[54]

It also reflects differing attitudes between thick and thin societies –
or between a thin society and a minority thick community, as is the case
here – toward the role of human rights in determining how people ought to

---

[51] David Rising, "Rabbis Urge German Jews to Continue Circumcisions," *Huffington Post*,
July 12, 2012, www.huffingtonpost.com/2012/07/12/rabbis-urge-german-jews-to-continue-
circumcisions_n_1667916.html.

[52] "Council of Europe Official Raps Group's Resolution against Ritual Circumcision," *Jewish
Telegraphic Agency*, April 30, 2014, www.jta.org/2014/04/30/news-opinion/world/council-of-
europe-official-criticizes-groups-resolution-against-circumcision. In September 2015, PACE
passed Resolution 2076 recommending (clause 9) that "member States provide for ritual
circumcision of children not to be allowed unless practised by a person with the requisite
training and skill, in appropriate medical and health conditions." In addition, it states that "the
parents must be duly informed of any potential medical risk or possible contraindications and
take these into account when deciding what is best for their child, bearing in mind that the
child's interest must be considered the first priority." Although it does mention (clause 13) the
need to ensure that "religious communities and their members are able to exercise the right to
freedom of religion without impediment and without discrimination," the new resolution
arguably repeats its previous anticircumcision stance.

[53] Tovah Lazaroff, "UN Official Says Circumcision Protected by Freedom of Religion,"
Jerusalem Post, March 14, 2014, www.jpost.com/Diplomacy-and-Politics/UN-official-says-
circumcision-protected-by-freedom-of-religion-345359.

[54] Dov Maimon and Nadia Ellis, "The Circumcision Crisis: Challenges for European and World
Jewry," The Jewish People Policy Institute, Jerusalem, Israel, 2012, 7–10, http://jppi.org.il/news/
117/58/The-Circumcision-Crisis/.

behave. Whereas many Western universalists see human rights as their sole moral framework, flexible universalists believe that "the language of human rights hardly exhausts the realm of moral and spiritual goods."[55] For the latter, entering into unchosen relationships – family, community, religion, nation – is a natural part of human existence and brings obligations as well as rights.[56]

Tensions result from an expansion of what Western public authorities consider "child abuse" – situations where authorities will intervene to protect a child's rights. Although there are situations when such interventions will find broad support across all groups, like sexual abuse, when a government substitutes its own standards for those of the parent in areas such as levels of supervision, sex education, and religious practice, there are likely to be many cases of disagreement between what some may see as a parent's prerogative or community right and others may see as legitimate action to protect a child's rights. This may be true even when both the family and government broadly share similar values, but is likely to be especially true when they do not, as is the case of a thin society government and a thick community in its jurisdiction.

In Germany, the court recognized that there were different rights involved before deciding that the child's right to physical integrity was more important than the others. As Dr. Angelika Günzel of the University of Trier summarized in the *Oxford Journal of Law and Religion*:

> The court held that there are three conflicting fundamental rights involved: the parents' right to religious freedom (Article 4(1, 2) German Basic Law, BL), the parents' right to the care and upbringing of their children (Article 6(2) BL), and the child's right to physical integrity (Article 2(2) BL). Ascribing the right to physical integrity a very high value and ranking amongst the fundamental rights, at the same time reducing the concept of the best interests of the child to purely physical well-being, the court came to the conclusion that a religiously motivated circumcision would not be in the best interests of the child.[57]

Different priorities reflect different societal values and norms. In Germany, much of Europe, and parts of the United States – all Millian, thin societies – particular familial and communal thick society traditions such as circumcision

55 Galston, "Mark of Belonging."
56 Ibid.
57 Angelika Günzel, "Nationalization of Religious Parental Education? The German Circumcision Case," *Oxford Journal of Law and Religion* 2, no. 1 (2013): 206–209, http://ojlr .oxfordjournals.org/content/early/2013/01/15/ojlr.rws066.full.

are increasingly viewed, as John Stuart Mill put it in *On Liberty*, as "the despotism of custom ... standing hindrance to human advancement."[58]

Such sentiment is linked to a particular concept of the body and sexual relations.[59] According to this understanding, control over one's body is a primary right, and any unusual damage or physical alteration requires an individual's consent. Michael Schmidt-Salomon, the founder of Giordano Bruno Foundation, a German humanist organization, represents the concerns of many when he calls circumcision "high-risk, painful, sometimes even traumatizing" and claims that it can lead to "secondary hemorrhage, infections, boils ... even amputations of the penis."[60] Some argue that circumcision reduces a man's ability to fully experience sexual pleasure.[61]

To many, there is no substantial difference between female genital surgery[62] – which has stirred an international campaign, mainly based in the West, to stamp out the practice – and male circumcision.[63] As Astrid Grydeland Ersvik, director of the Norwegian Nurses Organization argues, "If we get a law that allows this in boys while it is illegal in girls, then this is discriminatory."[64]

Ersvik's statement ignores significant diversity in the procedures and health conditions that both encompass – some types and environments are relatively mild and safe, others more invasive and dangerous. If opponents pushed for

---

[58] John Stuart Mill, *On Liberty and Other Writings* (Cambridge: Cambridge University Press, 2003), 70.

[59] Richard Shweder, "'What about Female Genital Mutilation?' And Why Understanding Culture Matters in the First Place," in Shweder, Martha Minow, and Hazel Rose Markus (eds.), *Engaging Cultural Differences: The Multicultural Challenge in Liberal Democracies* (New York, NY: Russell Sage Foundation, 2002), 233.

[60] Hammer, "Anti-Semitism and Germany's Movement against Circumcision."

[61] One study appearing in the *British Journal of Urology* in 2007, for instance, stated that "circumcised males have a significant penile sensory deficit as compared with non-circumcised intact men" and that "the most sensitive regions in the uncircumcised penis are those removed by circumcision." Morris Sorrells, James Snyder, et al., "Fine-touch Pressure Thresholds in the Adult Penis," *British Journal of Urology* 99, no. 4 (April 2007): 864–869.

[62] Female genital surgery is a more neutral expression than the term widely used in the West: female genital mutilation. Public Policy Advisory Network on Female Genital Surgeries in Africa, "Seven Things to Know About Female Genital Surgeries in Africa," *Hastings Center Report* 42, no. 6 (November/December 2012): 19.

[63] Generally speaking, Europeans are against both male and female circumcision, Africans are in favor of both male and female circumcision, and Americans are in favor of male but against female circumcision. Shweder, "The Goose and the Gander: The Genital Wars," *Global Discourse: An Interdisciplinary Journal of Current Affairs and Applied Contemporary Thought* 3, no. 2 (2013): 348.

[64] "Norwegian Nurses Seek Brit Milah Ban," *Jewish Telegraphic Agency*, March 21, 2014, www.jta .org/2014/03/21/news-opinion/world/norwegian-nurses-seek-brith-milah-ban.

safe practices that respected traditions instead of eradication, they would likely find partners within communities that would help them have a bigger impact on those affected instead of sparking a backlash (see later).[65]

Michael Bongardt, a professor of ethics from Berlin's Free University, said the ruling reflected a profound lack of understanding of religion in modern Germany: "The often very aggressive prejudice against religion as backward, irrational and opposed to science is increasingly defining popular opinion."[66] For most people in the country, Jews and Muslims are outsiders clinging to backward, unsavory rituals and beliefs.[67] Rabbi Pinchas Goldschmidt, the president of the Conference of European Rabbis, said that the court's decision was part of a growing infringement of religious freedom across Europe that encompassed France's ban on face-covering Muslim veils and Switzerland's ban on the construction of new minarets for mosques.[68]

The World Health Organization (WHO) takes no definitive position on circumcision, but does recommend the practice in the parts of Africa where AIDS is especially prevalent because it has been shown to reduce HIV infection risk by about 60 percent.[69]

Supporters say that circumcision helps prevent urinary tract infections in babies and sexual transmitted infections, such as HIV, in adults. A group of researchers in 2012 from Johns Hopkins University estimated that a two-decade decline in circumcision rates within the United States had led to $2 billion in extra healthcare costs.[70] A survey of some 3,000 studies published in April 2014

---

[65] Brian Earp, who opposes male and female circumcision, argues convincingly that male and female circumcision are more alike than different, that neither is monolithic, and that what matters most is the type of procedure and environment in which it is implemented. See Earp, "Female Genital Mutilation (FGM) and Male Circumcision: Should There Be a Separate Ethical Discourse?," *Practical Ethics Blog*, University of Oxford, February 18, 2014, http://blog .practicalethics.ox.ac.uk/2014/02/female-genital-mutilation-and-male-circumcision-time-to-confront-the-double-standard/.

[66] Melissa Eddy, "In Germany, Ruling over Circumcision Sows Anxiety and Confusion," *The New York Times*, July 14, 2012, www.nytimes.com/2012/07/14/world/europe/in-germany-ruling-over-circumcision-sows-anxiety-and-confusion.html.

[67] Hammer, "Anti-Semitism and Germany's Movement against Circumcision."

[68] Blake Sobczak, "Germany Circumcision Ban: Israeli Parliament Slams Decision by Cologne Court," *Huffington Post*, July 9, 2012, www.huffingtonpost.com/2012/07/09/germany-circumcision-ban-_n_1659423.html.

[69] Castillo, "German Court Rules Circumcision Goes against 'Fundamental Right of the Child to Bodily Integrity.'"

[70] Arian Campo-Flores, "Circumcision Coverage Comes into Focus," *Wall Street Journal*, January 20, 2014, http://online.wsj.com/news/articles/SB10001424052702 304419104579327013566659736; Johns Hopkins Medicine News Release, "Declining Rates of U.S. Infant Male Circumcision Could Add Billions to Health Care Costs, Experts Warn," *Johns Hopkins Medicine*, August 20, 2012, www.hopkinsmedicine.org/news/media/

in the medical journal *Mayo Clinic Proceedings* found that the procedure significantly reduced the risk of getting urinary tract infections, human papillomavirus, and HIV. "When considered together with ethical and human rights arguments, neonatal circumcision should logically be strongly supported and encouraged as an important evidence-based intervention akin to childhood vaccination," wrote the three authors.[71] Moreover, complications are rare and generally quite minor.

As for concerns about sexual function, many studies show that they have no scientific basis. Some men actually report an increase in sensitivity, while many report no significant change.[72] While a systematic review of the highest quality studies concluded that circumcision "has no adverse effect on sexual function, sensitivity, sexual sensation, or satisfaction,"[73] the WHO declared that it "has not been systematically reviewed, and remains unclear due to substantial biases in many studies."[74]

Although there are a few survivors groups pushing for action to curtail circumcision, their membership is small relative to the number of people who have received the procedure, especially when compared to groups that exist for, say, child sexual abuse and violence against women.

All of these factors make opposition to circumcision hard to understand outside a cultural or political framework.[75] Indeed, for Muslims, the attacks are viewed as part of a continent-wide backlash against their increasing

---

releases/declining_rates_of_us_infant_male_circumcision_could_add_billions_to_health_care_costs_experts_warn.

[71] Anthony Weiss, "Latest Salvo in Circumcision War, Study Cuts against 'Intactivist' Arguments," *Jewish Telegraphic Agency*, April 10, 2014, www.jta.org/2014/04/10/news-opinion/united-states/latest-salvo-in-circumcision-wars-study-cuts-against-intactivist-arguments; Brian Morris, Stefan Bailis, et al., "Circumcision Rates in the United States: Rising or Falling? What Effect Might the New Affirmative Pediatric Policy Statement Have?," *Mayo Clinic Proceedings* 89, no. 5 (May 2014): 677–686.

[72] Mark Joseph Stern, "How Circumcision Broke the Internet, *Slate*, September 18, 2013, www.slate.com/articles/health_and_science/medical_examiner/2013/09/intactivists_online_a_fringe_group_turned_the_internet_against_circumcision.html. The article refers to a number of academic studies, such as Brian Morris and John Krieger, "Does Male Circumcision Affect Sexual Function, Sensitivity, or Satisfaction? – A Systematic Review," *The Journal of Sexual Medicine* 10, no. 11 (November 2013): 2644–2657.

[73] Morris and Krieger, "Does Male Circumcision Affect Sexual Function, Sensitivity, or Satisfaction? – A Systematic Review," 2644–2657.

[74] Lane, "The Stink of Cologne"; WHO, *Male Circumcision: Global Trends and Determinants of Prevalence, Safety and Acceptability*.

[75] Ben Cohen, "Norway Moves against Circumcision," *Commentary*, November 15, 2013, www.commentarymagazine.com/2013/11/15/norway-moves-against-circumcision/.

numbers.[76] For Jews, they are a continuation of long-standing attacks against their presence in Europe going back at least to the Middle Ages.[77]

CULTURAL ATTITUDES TOWARD CIRCUMCISION

The German judge who ruled against circumcision in the aforementioned case believed he was upholding rights, but cultural psychology suggests that human rights practitioners should be very wary of such certitude. Opposition to circumcision has deep cultural roots, and it is dependent on the culturally specific cognitive processes that have produced the particular moral outlook of any lawmaker, judge, or activist. Opponents may think they are simply basing their judgment on a purely rational thought process and set of laws, but both the legal system itself as well as their interpretation of it are partly a product of a millennia-old value system.

Indeed, circumcision has long been an article of conflict between Europeans and Middle Easterners.[78] In the ancient world, Semitic groups such as Jews, Arabs, and Phoenicians widely practiced the custom, while the Greeks and Romans found it repulsive and tried to eliminate it.

The second century BCE Jewish revolt against Greek rule, known as the Maccabees Revolt and commemorated by Jews worldwide as a heroic defense of religious freedom known as Hanukkah, was caused in part by the banning, under penalty of execution, of circumcision.[79] Early Christians criticized the

---

[76] On the rise of Europe's far right parties, see, among others, Humayun Ansari and Farid Hafez, *From the Far Right to the Mainstream: Islamophobia in Party Politics and the Media* (Frankfurt, Germany: Campus Verlag, 2012); Peter Walker and Matthew Taylor, "Far Right on Rise in Europe, Says Report," *The Guardian*, November 6, 2011. For the Muslim reaction, see Robert Leiken, *Europe's Angry Muslims: The Revolt of The Second Generation* (Oxford: Oxford University Press, 2011).

[77] Dov Maimon, "European Jewry – Signals and Noise," The Jewish People Policy Institute, Jerusalem, Israel, 2013, http://jppi.org.il/news/132/76/European-Jewry-%EF%BF%BD-Signals-and-Noise/; Maimon and Ellis, "The Circumcision Crisis."

[78] Shweder, "The Goose and the Gander: The Genital Wars," *Global Discourse: An Interdisciplinary Journal of Current Affairs and Applied Contemporary Thought* 3, no. 2 (2013): 348–366.

[79] The Seleucid Greeks also desecrated the Jewish Temple and ordered Jews to eat unkosher animals such as pork and break Shabbat, their day of rest. See Maccabees 1. Shweder, "Shouting at the Hebrews," 254. As the first book of Maccabees records, the Greek ruler, Seleucid king Antiochus IV Epiphanes (175–165 BCE), ordered the Jews "to leave their sons uncircumcised, and to defile themselves with every kind of impurity and abomination; so that they might forget the law and change all its ordinances. Whoever refused to act according to the command of the king was to be put to death." Maccabees 1: 48–50, www.usccb.org/bible/1mc/1; Peter Charles Remondino, *History of Circumcision from the Earliest Times to the Present* (Philadelphia: F. A. Davis, 1891), 65–69. According to Tacitus, one of the greatest Roman

practice as being morally inferior to baptism because it was exclusionary of women and gender biased (baptism is ecumenical).[80] In the Middle Ages, attacks on Jews often identified circumcision as a problem. Anti-Semitic literature slammed the "barbaric and cruel" Jews for being "merciless ... forsekinne-clippers."[81] In the nineteenth century, the impression that circumcision was a form of "barbaric bloodletting" led to accusations of ritual murder against Jews. "The argument ran: if the Jews will do this to their own children, imagine what they will do to ours!"[82]

Doctors are also shaped by their cultures in how they view circumcision. Whereas most German medical groups, such as the German Academy for Pediatric and Adolescent Medicine, are strongly opposed to the practice (as are many medical groups in northern Europe, as noted earlier), both the American Academy of Pediatrics and the American Urological Association take the position that parents should decide.[83] The American Academy of Pediatrics most recent statement concludes:

> Evaluation of current evidence indicates that the health benefits of newborn male circumcision outweigh the risks and that the procedure's benefits justify access to this procedure for families who choose it.[84]

That two Western, thin societies have such differences of opinion demonstrates the futility of trying to create a universal ranking of the importance of

historians, Antiochus did this because he "endeavored to abolish Jewish superstition and to introduce Greek civilization." Frederick Hodges, "The Ideal Prepuce in Ancient Greece and Rome: Male Genital Aesthetics and Their Relation to *Lipodermos*, Circumcision, Foreskin Restoration, and the *Kynodesme*, " *The Bulletin of the History of Medicine* 75, no. 3 (Fall 2001): 375–405.

[80] Shaye Cohen, *Why Aren't Jewish Women Circumcised?* (Berkeley, CA: University of California Press, 2005).

[81] The quotes appear in Brendan O'Neill, "Circumcision Ruling: European Bureaucrats are Effectively Banning Jewish Boys," *The Telegraph*, October 3, 2013, http://blogs.telegraph.co.uk/news/brendanoneill2/100239551/circumcision-ruling-european-bureaucrats-are-effectively-banning-jewish-boys/. For more information, see Elizabeth Wyner Mark, *The Covenant of Circumcision: New Perspectives on an Ancient Jewish Rite* (Lebanon, NH: Brandeis University Press, 2003).

[82] Sander Gilman, *Making the Body Beautiful: A Cultural History of Aesthetic Surgery* (Princeton, NJ: Princeton University Press, 1999), 291.

[83] Charles Lane, "The Stink of Cologne," *Washington Post*, June 27, 2012, www.washingtonpost.com/blogs/post-partisan/post/the-stink-of-cologne/2012/06/27/gJQAqeod7V_blog.html; American Academy of Pediatrics Task Force on Circumcision, "Circumcision Policy Statement," *Pediatrics* 103, no. 3 (March 1999): 686–693; American Urological Association, "Policy Statement: Circumcision," updated May 2012, www.auanet.org/about/policy-statements/circumcision.cfm.

[84] American Academy of Pediatrics Task Force on Circumcision, "Circumcision Policy Statement," *Pediatrics* 130, no. 3 (September 2012): 585–586.

the various human rights. Different societies often have very different opinions about which issues matter more – even when both are thin or thick. Americans, as discussed in Chapter 2, have very different opinions than Europeans when it comes to gun rights, religious freedom, property rights, freedom of speech, the death penalty, and social and economic rights. Of course, when one society is thin and the other is thick – or a thick community lives in a thin society, as is the case here – the differences are likely to be much greater.

PARALLELS WITH FEMALE GENITAL SURGERY

Concerns regarding female genital surgery parallel the circumcision debate to some extent. Although there is enormous variation in the style and degree of surgery – of the three distinct types, approximately 90 percent of surgeries in Africa are categorized as one of the two less-intrusive types[85] – and age of when it is carried out (from birth up to the late teenage years)[86], and it is in "the vast majority" of cases "safe, even with current procedures and under current conditions,"[87] female genital surgery is condemned in the West as "dark, brutal, primitive, barbaric, and unquestionably beyond the pale."[88] As a report published by the Hastings Center, a well-known bioethics research institute, indicates, "advocacy organizations often make claims about female genital surgeries in Africa that are inaccurate or overgeneralized or that don't apply to most cases."[89] The studies on which activist campaigns and media reports are based are "data-free" or dependent on "sensational testimonials, second-hand reports, or inadequate samples."[90]

---

[85] Public Policy Advisory Network on Female Genital Surgeries in Africa, "Seven Things to Know about Female Genital Surgeries in Africa," 22.

[86] Public Policy Advisory Network on Female Genital Surgeries in Africa, "Seven Things to Know about Female Genital Surgeries in Africa," 22; Shweder, "'What about Female Genital Mutilation?' And Why Understanding Culture Matters in the First Place," 223–224.

[87] Public Policy Advisory Network on Female Genital Surgeries in Africa, "Seven Things to Know about Female Genital Surgeries in Africa," 22.

[88] Shweder, "'What about Female Genital Mutilation?' And Why Understanding Culture Matters in the First Place," 219.

[89] Public Policy Advisory Network on Female Genital Surgeries in Africa, "Seven Things to Know about Female Genital Surgeries in Africa," 19.

[90] Shweder, "'What about Female Genital Mutilation?' And Why Understanding Culture Matters in the First Place," 219 and 227–228; Public Policy Advisory Network on Female Genital Surgeries in Africa, "Seven Things to Know about Female Genital Surgeries in Africa," 19–27. Carla Obermeyer, a medical anthropologist and epidemiologist at Harvard University, published a comprehensive review of the literature in 1999, concluding that the anti-FGM movement's claims were highly exaggerated. Carla Obermeyer, "Female Genital Surgeries: The Known, the Unknown, and the Unknowable," *Medical Anthropology Quarterly* 13, no. 1 (March 1999): 79.

Instead of seeking to understand the history, the culture, and the possible benefits of this widespread ritual – and seeking ways to ameliorate its unsafe or objectionable elements by, for instance, making the operation more sanitary and professional – Western human rights actors have long sought to abolish it. This is true even when the practice is, as in large parts of Indonesia, "mostly symbolic (no cutting at all)."[91] This stance is similar to that of an earlier era's religious missionaries, who found the practice offensive to their own (Christian) morality and sought to end it.[92]

Approval ratings for the custom in the cultures that practice it are generally high.[93] Some women say they feel incomplete without it.[94] For them, bodily integrity is actually increased, not limited, by the practice; many may actually feel disgusted, ugly, and undignified without it. "Where the practice of female circumcision is popular ... it is widely believed by women that these genital alterations improve their bodies and make them more beautiful, more feminine, more civilized, and more honorable."[95] The procedure is typically controlled by women and paralleled by male genital surgery, meaning that an "empirical association between patriarchy and genital surgeries is not well established."[96] The importance of such operations to local people explains why female genital surgery has persisted as widely as it has, including among the most educated, in so many societies despite generations of attempts by Westerners to end the practice.

[91] The quote comes from Jurnalis Uddin, the chairman of the Center for Population and Gender Studies at Yarsi University in Jakarta. Pam Belluck and Joe Cochrane, "Unicef Report Finds Female Genital Cutting to Be Common in Indonesia," *New York Times*, February 5, 2016, www.nytimes.com/2016/02/05/health/indonesia-female-genital-cutting-circumcision-unicef.html?_r=0.

[92] Shweder, "'What about Female Genital Mutilation?' And Why Understanding Culture Matters in the First Place," 228–229.

[93] Female genital surgery mainly occurs in communities in East and West Africa, with some particular groups also in other parts of Africa, Southeast Asia, and the Middle East. Shweder, "'What about Female Genital Mutilation?' And Why Understanding Culture Matters in the First Place," 223; Public Policy Advisory Network on Female Genital Surgeries in Africa, "Seven Things to Know about Female Genital Surgeries in Africa," 19–27.

[94] Public Policy Advisory Network on Female Genital Surgeries in Africa, "Seven Things to Know about Female Genital Surgeries in Africa," 19–27; Shweder, "'What about Female Genital Mutilation?' And Why Understanding Culture Matters in the First Place," 224.

[95] Shweder, "'What about Female Genital Mutilation?' And Why Understanding Culture Matters in the First Place," 224; also see Public Policy Advisory Network on Female Genital Surgeries in Africa, "Seven Things to Know about Female Genital Surgeries in Africa," 19–27.

[96] Public Policy Advisory Network on Female Genital Surgeries in Africa, "Seven Things to Know about Female Genital Surgeries in Africa," 23.

INTOLERANCE TOWARD RELIGIOUS MINORITIES IN THE WEST

Opposition to a broad set of longstanding religious practices is building in Western countries,[97] making some among the faithful consider that, at least in Europe, religious life may become impossible there, forcing migration to other parts of the world.[98] As one Jewish think tank concluded in a report, "European Jewish life has quite possibly reached a negative inflexion point . . . we follow, however cautiously, the pessimistic observers that fear . . . a rejection of Jewishness and its subtle political and legal ejection from the public sphere."[99]

Besides efforts to ban circumcision on account of children's rights, there have been efforts to ban the ritual slaughter of meat – already successful in Sweden, Switzerland, Norway, Poland, Denmark, and Iceland, with efforts continuing in Holland and France – on account of animal rights;[100] the abolition of eternal cemeteries in Belgium and Switzerland on account of environmental concerns;[101] and increasing interference in the operation of religious schools in the United Kingdom and Belgium on account of ethnic nondiscrimination concerns.[102]

European courts forced a Belgian Jewish girls' school to admit boys;[103] ruled against a nurse who wanted to wear a cross because hospital managers claimed health and safety risks;[104] and accepted the dismissal of a government employee who refused to perform same-sex civil partnerships.[105] The Council of Europe has declared that all states ought to "require religious

---

[97] Dov Maimon, "European Jewry – Signals and Noise;" Roger Trigg, "Threats to Religious Freedom in Europe," *Public Discourse*, June 28, 2013, www.thepublicdiscourse.com/2013/06/10439/.
[98] Dov Maimon, "European Jewry – Signals and Noise;" Fetzer, "Immigration, Segregation, and Religious Freedom in Europe."
[99] Dov Maimon, "European Jewry – Signals and Noise."
[100] Shmuel Rosner, "Nip and Tuck?," *The New York Times*, August 27, 2012, http://latitude.blogs.nytimes.com/2012/08/27/when-german-judges-ban-circumcision/; Sam Sokol, "Polish Parliament Upholds Kosher Slaughter Ban," *Jerusalem* Post, July 12, 2013, www.jpost.com/Jewish-World/Jewish-News/Polish-Parliament-votes-to-uphold-Kosher-slaughter-ban-319660; Maimon, "European Jewry – Signals and Noise," 3.
[101] Rosner, "Nip and Tuck?"; Maimon, "European Jewry – Signals and Noise," 3.
[102] Maimon, "European Jewry – Signals and Noise," 3.
[103] Cnaan Liphshiz, "Antwerp Jewish Girls School Forced to Admit Boys," *Jewish Telegraphic Agency*, December 28, 2012, www.jta.org/2012/12/28/news-opinion/world/antwerp-jewish-girls-school-forced-to-admit-boys.
[104] The hospital managers claimed health and safety risks. Trigg, "Threats to Religious Freedom in Europe."
[105] Ibid.

leaders to take an unambiguous stand in favour of the precedence of human rights ... over any religious principle."[106]

In the United States, generally considered a more hospitable home to religion, the state also increasingly seeks to enforce ideological conformity in a broad range of areas. Whereas once religion was protected on the grounds that the constitution forbade the establishment of any law that infringed on religious duties if they were a matter of conscience that could be traced to sincerely held beliefs (such as the *Wisconsin v. Yoder Court* case of 1972), in recent years the courts have only protected religion from discrimination that directly targeted it.[107] The Supreme Court, for instance, started in the 1980s allowing the government to forbid religious activities as long as the prohibition was applicable to all citizens.[108] In 1988 it ruled that the US Forest Service could build a road on lands deemed sacred by Native Americans even though an environment assessment recognized that the damage would be severe and irreparable and suggested alternative routes.[109] In 1990, it ruled that Oregon could block unemployment benefits for a person fired for using peyote (which was prohibited in the state), even though its ingestion was part of a religious ceremony in the Native American Church and was used by the tribes for centuries.[110] The 2010 healthcare law originally did not allow religious organizations to opt out of its provisions to arrange and pay for insurance coverage of abortion-causing drugs.[111] Legal challenges ensued. In one prominent case, the US Supreme Court overturned lower court rulings against Little Sisters of the Poor, saying a reasonable accommodation could be made. Although the Trump administration issued an interim final rule that allowed for voluntary accommodations in October 2017, the issue is still being resolved in the courts at the time of writing.[112]

[106] Ibid.

[107] Shweder, "The Moral Challenges in Cultural Migration," in Nancy Foner (ed.), *American Arrivals: Anthropology Engages the New Immigration* (Santa Fe, NM: School of American Research Press, 2003), 271 and 280–281.

[108] "Religion," in Kermit Hall, James Ely, and Joel Grossman (eds.), *The Oxford Companion to the Supreme Court of the United States*, 2nd ed. (Oxford: Oxford University Press, 2005), 837–845.

[109] *Lyng v. Northwest Indian Cemetery Protective Association*, 485 U.S. 439 (1988).

[110] *Employment Division, Department of Human Resources of Oregon v. Smith*, 494 U.S. 872 (1990).

[111] Mary Ann Glendon, "Religious Freedom Is Not a 'Second-Class Right,'" *Washington Post on Faith Blog*, June 21, 2013, www.washingtonpost.com/blogs/on-faith/wp/2013/06/21/religious-freedom-is-not-a-second-class-right/.

[112] Becket Fund for Religious Liberty, "Case Summary: *Little Sisters of the Poor v. Price*," web page, www.becketlaw.org/case/littlesisters/.

One could argue that the cooking of live seafood, the force-feeding of animals, and hunting for sport are comparable to ritual slaughter, but these do not raise similar objections. In the same vein, opposition to circumcision does not translate into banning piercings, tattooing, orthodontic interventions (performed primarily for aesthetic reasons), facial normalizations of Down syndrome children, alterations of irregular lips or cleft palate, and the extraction of wisdom teeth for preventive purposes.[113] And activists do not seek to force children to speak a particular language at home, eat a particular set of foods, live in a particular neighborhood, or receive a particular type of education at home. It is hard to be human without being significantly shaped by the "cultural womb" into which one is born, and by the numerous decisions made by one's parents, community, and country long before we can begin to take part in deciding our own destiny.[114] As we learned in the chapter on cultural psychology, such influences shape moral matrices, beliefs, how we perceive the motivations of others, categorization, moral reasoning, and the boundaries between the self and others from birth. "Parents have no choice but to do the best they can, relying on their own understanding of what is right and good, in full knowledge that they will make mistakes, some of which will have lasting impact."[115]

Yet, "today we are witnessing an increasing number of government actions that seek to condemn and ban these religious practices . . . [even though] these practices are forms of religious expression, [and should not be] trumped by other values," said Lisa Rahmani, speaking on behalf of the World Jewish Congress.[116] European Muslim and Jewish leaders, for instance, have accused governments who outlaw ritual slaughter of putting animal rights before religious rights.[117]

Of course, not all religious practices should be condoned. For instance, no society or community should be able to prevent women from being educated or protected from violent treatment in the name of religion. But different societies will naturally have different standards that they will wish to uphold: Some societies will accept polygamy, while others will ban it. Religious practices (and long-standing traditional customs that have taken

---

[113] The PACE resolution mentions the first two, but no government has moved against them. See PACE, "Children's Right to Physical Integrity."
[114] Galston, "Mark of Belonging."
[115] Ibid.
[116] Lazaroff, "UN Official Says Circumcision Protected by Freedom of Religion."
[117] Sam Sokol, "Jewish, Muslim Leaders: Danish Minister 'Put[s] Animal Rights before Religious Rights,'" *Jerusalem Post*, March 22, 2014, www.jpost.com/Jewish-World/Jewish-News/Jewish-Muslim-leaders-Danish-minister-puts-animal-rights-before-religious-rights-346165.

on a religious flavor) are one of the hardest issues to address within a human rights framework because of the large number of potential conflicts with nonbelievers and necessary trade-offs with other rights.[118]

RELIGION AND THE ROOTS OF LIBERALISM

The turn against religious expression within the West is ironic given that democracy and liberalism were born from and nurtured by religion and the social institutions it produces. As Alexis de Tocqueville observed, democracy was not just founded on religious principles, democracy required it to "teach its citizens how to act in the wider interest, as well as for own good."[119] De Tocqueville writes in *Democracy in America* that

> Religion in America takes no direct part in the government of society, but it must nevertheless be regarded as the foremost of the political institutions of that country; for if it does not impart a taste for freedom, it facilitates the use of free institutions. Indeed, it is in this same point of view that the inhabitants of the United States themselves look upon religious belief. I do not know whether all the Americans have a sincere faith in their religion; for who can search the human heart? but I am certain that they hold it to be indispensable to the maintenance of republican institutions. This opinion is not peculiar to a class of citizens or a party, but it belongs to the whole nation, and to every rank of society.[120]

Although modern political theory is often assumed to be the product of secularization and fights against religion, this is a late Enlightenment interpretation; in reality Christian scholars, energized by their religious fervor, transformed political theory in the sixteenth and seventeenth centuries, during the early Enlightenment. Seeking to understand the institutions and practices of the perfect republic in the Hebrew Bible, they developed ideas such as toleration for diversity and the legitimacy of democracy, influencing the revolutionary politics of people such as John Milton, James Harrington, and Thomas Hobbes in the process.[121] Later on, religious pluralism – based on the recognition that religious beliefs held an essential place in each person's

---

[118] See, for instance, "Religious Rights and Human Rights: The Meaning of Freedom," *The Economist Erasmus Blog*, March 22, 2014, www.economist.com/blogs/erasmus/2014/03/religious-rights-and-human-rights.

[119] Trigg, *Equality, Freedom, and Religion* (Oxford: Oxford University Press, 2012), 141.

[120] Alexis de Tocqueville, *Democracy in America* (New York, NY: Pratt, Woodford, & Co., 1848), 334.

[121] Eric Nelson, *The Hebrew Republic: Jewish Sources and the Transformation of European Political Thought* (Cambridge, MA: Harvard University Press, 2011).

life, that religion itself was highly valuable, and that it was necessary to enable people of different beliefs to live together – became one of the building blocks of American and European democracy.[122]

Western universalism – also called imperial liberalism, as noted in Chapter 5, or liberal triumphalism[123] – conflicts with liberalism as originally conceived (classical liberalism), at least in the British tradition.[124] Its initial goal was to protect diversity. Classical liberalism sought to promote freedom, equal rights, and tolerance; government was to be restrained so as to not interfere in the choices individuals make.

John Locke, considered the "father of classical liberalism," supported religious toleration on the grounds that accepting diversity is crucial to maintaining peace and social order and avoiding "a narrowness of spirit on all sides."[125] The "part of the magistrate [government] is only to take care that the commonwealth receive no prejudice and that there be no injury done to any man."[126] Conflict and "miseries" are not caused by diverse political and religious opinions, but by the lack of tolerance for those with different opinions and the insatiable desire for domination.[127] As such, the word *liberal*, which traces its roots back to the Latin *liber*, meaning "free," was defined as "free from narrow prejudice" or "free from bigotry" during and right after the Enlightenment, when liberalism was first formulated as a political philosophy.[128]

Such thinking informed documents such as the Declaration of Independence, which is based on the idea that government is established by the people in order to secure their rights to life, liberty, and the pursuit of happiness.

---

[122] This was more the case in some countries (like the United States) and less so in other countries (like France). See Tomer Persico, "The Ban on Circumcision and How Europe Is Denying Its Past," *Tomer Persico – English Blog*, October 28, 2013, http://tomerpersicoenglish.wordpress.com/2013/10/28/the-ban-on-circumcision-and-how-europe-is-denying-its-past/.

[123] Galston, *The Practice of Liberal Pluralism* (Cambridge, UK: Cambridge University Press, 2004), 197.

[124] Friedrich Hayek identified two different traditions within classical liberalism: the "British tradition" and the "French tradition." The latter showed hostility to tradition and religion. Hayek, *The Constitution of Liberty* (London: Routledge, 1976), 55–56.

[125] John Locke originally published "A Letter Concerning Toleration" in 1689. Locke, "A Letter Concerning Toleration," in Locke, "The Works of John Locke Esq," Volume 2 (London: Printed for John Churchill at the Black Swan, 1714), 231.

[126] Ibid.

[127] Laure Principaud, "John Locke's 'Letter on Toleration,'" Book Review, *World Religion Watch*, The Observatory for Religious Phenomena, Institute of Political Studies at Aix-en-Provence, November 26, 2008, www.world-religion-watch.org/index.php/book-reviews-on-relevant-religious-and-cultural-issues/187-john-lockes-qletter-on-tolerationq.

[128] These definitions come from 1781 and 1823. Jonathan Gross, *Byron: The Erotic Liberal* (Oxford: Rowman & Littlefield, 2001), 5.

It works on the premise that, as Michael McConnell, the former director of the Stanford Constitutional Law Center writes, "In contrast to both ancient and modern neo-liberal regimes, government is not charged with the promotion of the good life for its citizens … Government must leave the definition of the good life to private institutions, of which family and church are the most conspicuous."[129]

This rationale continued to play a leading role in liberal thought into the twentieth century. Scholars such as Ludwig von Mises emphasized repeatedly that liberalism "demands toleration for doctrines and opinions that it deems detrimental and ruinous to society and even for movements that it indefatigably combats."[130] It protected dissenters, minorities, and unpopular points of view. Isaiah Berlin argued that liberalism meant a tolerant *modus vivendi* among competing value systems. As discussed in Chapter 4, he believed that liberal societies ought to allow for significant differences and guard against monism:

> If pluralism is a valid view, and respect between systems of values … is possible, then toleration and liberal consequences follow, as they do not either from monism (only one set of values is true, all the others are false) or from relativism (my values are mine, yours are yours, and if we clash, too bad, neither of us can claim to be right)… The enemy of pluralism is monism … monism is at the root of every extremism.[131]

Thus, as William Galston concludes,

> Properly understood, liberalism is about the protection of legitimate diversity… Liberalism that gives diversity its due … is expressed in public principles, institutions, and practices that afford maximum feasible space for the enactment of individual and group differences, constrained only by the ineliminable requirements of liberal society unity.[132]

In a genuinely liberal political order, there is a principled refusal to use the power of the state or international institutions to impose a particular way of life on others; instead, there is a commitment to "moral competition" through persuasion alone."[133]

---

[129] Michael McConnell, "The Origins and Historical Understanding of Free Exercise of Religion," *Harvard Law Review* 103, no. 7 (1990): 1465.

[130] Ludwig von Mises, *Liberalism* (Orange, CA: Important Books, 2012), 56.

[131] Isaiah Berlin, "My Intellectual Path," in Henry Hardy (ed.), *The Power of Ideas* (Princeton, NJ: Princeton University Press, 2002), 13–14.

[132] Galston, *Liberal Pluralism: The Implications of Value Pluralism for Political Theory and Practice* (Cambridge: Cambridge University Press, 2002), 23.

[133] Galston, *The Practice of Liberal Pluralism*, 4.

This echoes the view of John Rawls, who cautions, "It is unreasonable for us to use political power, should we possess it, or share with others, to repress comprehensive doctrines [particular value systems and worldviews] that are not unreasonable."[134] Rawls insisted that "liberalism was not a 'comprehensive' doctrine, that is, one which includes an overall theory of value, an ethical theory, an epistemology, or a controversial metaphysics of the person and society." Instead, he believed that political liberalism was not "yet another sectarian doctrine," but "a political framework that is neutral between such controversial comprehensive doctrines. If it is to serve as the basis for public reasoning in our diverse western societies, liberalism must be restricted to a core set of political principles that are, or can be, the subject of consensus among all reasonable citizens."[135] If "reasonable citizens" would include people from all major factions of a society (religious, secular, etc.) or parts of the world, a deep, wide, and lasting consensus could be forged on such political principles.

As such, it is worth asking whether liberalism has become illiberal over time. Today, liberalism is often equated with a particular lifestyle and set of values – based on the ideal of autonomous choice – and it appears intolerant of alternatives. Whereas it once focused on restraining the state, it now sees the state and international institutions (and social pressure) as legitimate tools to enforce its form of morality. As a result, instead of promoting "public principles, institutions, and practices" that protect difference, value diversity, and allow as much space as possible for distinctions across individuals and groups (constrained only by some very minimum standards and the need to ensure societal unity), it has become a homogenizing agent that reduces the scope of religious actors in the West and societies in the South to make their own choices on how they wish to live.[136] Whether because of the great social changes that have occurred in the West, or because it has become enmeshed with a particular ideology, or because of the activism that it engendered, liberalism risks becoming something quite different than what its originators intended.

FREEDOM OF RELIGION: MERELY FREEDOM OF CONSCIENCE?

Roger Trigg of Oxford University argues that Western thin society courts and governments are increasingly prioritizing almost any right over that of religious

[134] John Rawls, *Political Liberalism* (New York, NY: Columbia University Press, 2005), 61.
[135] Gerald Gaus and Shane Courtland, "Liberalism," in Edward Zalta (ed.), *The Stanford Encyclopedia of Philosophy* (Spring 2011 Edition), http://plato.stanford.edu/archives/spr2011/entries/liberalism/.
[136] Galston, *Liberal Pluralism*, 23.

freedom, even coming close to determining what is and is not central to a person's faith in some cases,[137] as we see with circumcision in Germany. The remarks of Lord Justice Laws of the English Court of Appeal are representative. Responding to a relationship counselor who had lost his job after raising objections to advising same-sex couples, he said: "In the eye of everyone save the believer, religious faith is necessarily subjective, being incommunicable by any kind of proof or evidence." Laws further argued that defending any position on purely religious grounds "is irrational, as preferring the subjective over the objective. But it is also divisive, capricious and arbitrary."[138]

As a result of Western universalist positions like Laws's, the freedom of religion is being reconfigured to simply mean the freedom of worship and association, on par with the freedom of conscience and political opinion.[139] This narrow understanding of faith does not reflect believers' daily realities.[140] It ignores the thick communal and institutional component of religion, both of which have little purchase in a thin society driven by an autonomy ethic.

"The extreme tension between resurgent religion and the liberal order seems," as Suzanne Last Stone writes,

> less over secularism per se, but, rather, over this re-enchantment of the secular state. Whereas before, under thinner conceptions of liberalism, political and public space was secular in the strict sense – profane, or not holy – and holiness resided in the private sphere, increasingly, universal human rights, for better or worse presents itself – and is certainly perceived – as a competing transnational, universal, sacred and transcendent realm.[141]

This intrasociety clash poses risks to the cohesion of the countries involved because it prevents the careful deliberation of the appropriate ways to govern liberal democratic societies increasingly defined by their diversity. Whereas once there was a widely accepted dominant ethos and worldview in relatively homogeneous countries such as the Netherlands, Norway, France, and, to a lesser extent, the United States (which was always more diverse), these

---

[137] Trigg, "Threats to Religious Freedom in Europe."

[138] Articles 23 and 24, Case No: A2/2009/2733, *McFarlane v Relate Avon Ltd* [2010] EWCA Civ 771, www.employmentcasesupdate.co.uk/site.aspx?i=ed5719.

[139] Roger Trigg, *Equality, Freedom, and Religion* (Oxford: Oxford University Press, 2012), 38, 93–96, and 105; David Koyzis, "Roger Trigg, Equality, Freedom, and Religion," *The Review of Faith & International Affairs* 10, no. 4 (Winter 2012): 75–76.

[140] Trigg, *Equality, Freedom, and Religion*, 96.

[141] Suzanne Last Stone, "Religion and Human Rights: Babel or Translation, Conflict or Convergence," paper presented at *Role of Religion in Human Rights Discourse* conference, Israel Democracy Institute, May 16–17, 2012, 13.

countries now find themselves with millions of recently arrived immigrants who do not share the same culture. In many cases, the new arrivals' thicker moral matrices emphasize the community and divinity pillars more than secular Westerners do. Moreover, secularization and individualization have splintered the previous consensus that existed around norms among original populations. Deciding what limits to set on thick subcultures at odds with the new exceedingly thin dominant ethos – with regard to marriage, divorce, female clothing, schooling, parent–child relationships, circumcision, and so on – requires a delicate touch. The Universal Declaration – and the way its drafters perceived how human rights should be implemented across cultures – might act as a bridge.

In the next chapter, we look at another case – an intersociety example – where a Western interpretation of human rights clashes with the needs and desires of a particular community when we turn to the challenge of reconciliation and justice in Rwanda following its genocide and civil war.

7

Case Study: Rwanda's *Gacaca* Courts

For about 100 days, between April and July 1994, Rwandans experienced a mass killing of unparalleled intensity and focus. Radicalized by an extremist Hutu government, the majority Hutu population slaughtered almost three-quarters of the minority Tutsi population and its perceived Hutu and Twa sympathizers, some 800,000 people in all.[1] The genocide only ended when the Tutsi Rwandan Patriotic Army (RPA) invaded from Uganda and forced out the government.

The killings were unusually brutal and labor intensive. Thirty-eight percent of the victims were killed with a machete, 17 percent with a club, and 15 percent with a firearm; others were killed by grenades, swords, knives, drowning, sticks, rocks, and physical assault. There were no death camps or advanced technologies to shield the massacre from view. Everything was very public.[2] There was widespread participation from the population: As many as one million Rwandans – one out of every three adults – was involved as a perpetrator, collaborator, profiteer, or beneficiary.[3]

In the months after the genocide, the new government rounded up about 120,000 suspects and placed them in jail. Most were never charged and were forced to live in appalling conditions, without adequate food, clean drinking

---

[1] The total is contested. The government puts the number at over one million. Independent estimates range from 500,000 to 800,000 killed out of a population of about eight million. Phil Clark puts the total at 800,000. Mark Drumbl thinks a wider range is more appropriate. Mark Drumbl, *Atrocity, Punishment, and International Law* (Cambridge: Cambridge University Press, 2007), 71 and footnote 9 on page 243. For Clark, see, among others, "Democracy in Rwanda, 20 Years after Genocide," *Huffington Post*, January 4, 2014, www.huffingtonpost.co .uk/dr-phil-clark/rwanda-democracy_b_5068013.html.

[2] Drumbl, *Atrocity, Punishment, and International Law*, 71.

[3] Ibid., 92.

water, or space.[4] As the country struggled to recover, dealing with the detainees was not a priority.

Rwanda's challenges included limited administrative and financial resources and enormous economic and social problems. The judicial system, which functioned poorly before the genocide, was devastated; many judges and lawyers had been killed or fled the country.[5] Although a 1996 law provided a mechanism to try suspects domestically and an international criminal court (the UN International Criminal Tribunal for Rwanda or ICTR) had been established in Arusha, Tanzania, little changed for most detainees in the years that followed.

By 2001, more than 10,000 detainees had died, and the government was paying $20 million a year to keep the remaining people in jail.[6] Many who participated in or benefitted from the genocide remained at large.

None of the options looked good. Rwanda needed to both decrease its prison population faster than was possible through conventional courts and the ICTR and to address a wide range of complex communal, societal, and economic legacies that the genocide had produced.[7] At the rate trials were going, it could take over 100 years to try everyone. The country needed a legal process that advanced reconciliation, reintegration, and reconstitution alongside retribution; involved the public as much as possible; and offered a way for the truth about the genocide to be learned and discussed.[8]

The country's social geography complicated matters. Victims and perpetrators were culturally very similar and lived together in the same villages and towns; they were economically and socially interdependent. Only a fraction of the perpetrators had been imprisoned. As there was massive participation in the killings and large numbers of victims, reconciliation and reintegration was a prerequisite for basic societal and economic relations.[9]

---

[4] Phil Clark, "The Legacy of Rwanda's Gacaca Courts," *Think Africa Press*, March 23, 2012.
[5] The domestic courts did improve substantially over time, becoming more efficient and even gaining some degree of praise from abroad for their performance.
[6] Clark, "How Rwanda Judged its Genocide," *Counterpoints*, Africa Research Institute, April 2012, 3.
[7] Clark, "The Rules (and Politics) of Engagement: The Gacaca Courts and Post-Genocide Justice, Healing and Reconciliation in Rwanda," in Clark and Zachary D. Kaufman (eds.), *After Genocide: Transitional Justice, Post-Conflict Reconstruction and Reconciliation in Rwanda and Beyond* (New York, NY: Columbia University Press, 2009), 299.
[8] Drumbl also mentions that the state wanted to develop by itself, and a homegrown solution would allow this better than any alternative. Drumbl, *Atrocity, Punishment, and International Law*, 86.
[9] Ibid., 98–99.

The strong communal, thick society characteristics of Rwandan culture made the need for restoration that much greater.

A LOCAL SOLUTION FOR RWANDA'S COMPLEX CHALLENGES

Given this context, in 2002 the Rwandan government innovated and established a hybrid institution – the *gacaca*.[10] Although it was based on a traditional institution that had been used by communities across the country to resolve disputes, manage conflict, and reconcile individuals, the new *gacaca* also integrated a number of ideas from modern judicial systems.[11] It was codified in law (a dramatic break with tradition); created mechanisms for plea bargaining and appealing; and gave women a prominent place as judges and witnesses (something not possible in the past). Lawyers and professional judges were not allowed to participate, however, because of fears they would distort the process.[12] Public involvement was highly encouraged, and community service and compensation were used alongside jail sentences.[13]

Although it was organized by the state, *gacaca* was highly decentralized and organic, with the people who had experienced the genocide firsthand heavily involved.[14] After it was launched in 2002, 11,000 different communities had their own hearings. Each was unique, strongly influenced by the local sociopolitical context and by informal processes that ran parallel to the formal courts and legal statutes that underpinned them.[15] In a typical *gacaca*, 100–200 people from the local community would assemble with the accused perpetrators in front of nine locally elected "people of integrity" who acted as judges. These judges, who totaled more than 250,000, received training on general legal principles and the specific procedures of *gacaca*.[16] As the majority of Rwanda's people are Hutu, the majority of judges and participants were too, meaning that *gacaca* often resulted in Hutu judging Hutu. Almost 40 percent of judges were female.[17]

---

[10] Clark, *The Gacaca Courts, Post-Genocide Justice and Reconciliation in Rwanda: Justice without Lawyers* (Cambridge: Cambridge University Press, 2010), 47–80.
[11] Ibid., 47–80.
[12] Clark, "How Rwanda Judged its Genocide," 3, 4, and 10.
[13] The latter was not found in traditional *gacaca*. Clark, "The Rules (and Politics) of Engagement," 297–319.
[14] Clark, *The Gacaca Courts, Post-Genocide Justice and Reconciliation in Rwanda*, 47–80.
[15] Clark, "The Rules (and Politics) of Engagement," 297–319.
[16] Clark, "How Rwanda Judged its Genocide," 3–4.
[17] Ibid., 10.

Trials were unpredictable, often very messy affairs lasting a whole day or even multiple days. Judges mediated a series of exchanges or discussions between the accused and the general assembly with the aim of achieving both legal and extralegal aims. Defendants, victims, and observers all contributed. As most prisoners admitted to their crimes beforehand, confession and plea bargaining were integral to the hearings, with the nine judges making final decisions on cases.[18] Everything was conducted in the local language, and businesses were closed, by regulation, to encourage broad participation. The proceedings included opportunities for the public, as represented by those in the General Assembly, to seek answers on issues that mattered to them – such as those related to the discovery of facts – beyond the "microscopic truths" that would normally dominate a court case.[19]

By the time the *gacaca* concluded in 2012, some 400,000 suspects were prosecuted – "the most extensive attempt at judging mass crimes anywhere to date."[20] *Gacaca* helped identify many perpetrators and clarified the broad level of public participation in the genocide – something many did not or could not believe beforehand.[21] About one-quarter of the cases ended in acquittal; the rate was the same for high-level (category one), mid-level (category two), and low-level (category three) offenders.[22] About two-fifths of cases were appealed to a *gacaca* appeals court, and some of these cases were further appealed to ordinary national courts.[23] Combined with the extensive use of commutation and community service (see following), the acquittals meant that *gacaca* directly led to the release of many from jail.[24]

Nearly the entire Rwandan adult population participated in some manner in *gacaca*.[25] Extensive information was gathered about who committed what crimes, where bodies were buried, how specific murders and atrocities were committed, and so on.[26] Using the plea bargaining system in place, the great majority of those convicted had their sentences commuted to community service and time already served in jail (some had been there for over 10 years),

---

[18] Clark, "Gacaca's Legacy," interview with Steve Terrill, *The Independent* (Uganda), May 29, 2012, www.independent.co.ug/rwanda-ed/rwanda/5842-gacacas-legacy.
[19] Drumbl, *Atrocity, Punishment, and International Law*, 85.
[20] Clark, "All Justice Is Local," *International New York Times*, June 12, 2014, www.nytimes.com/2014/06/12/opinion/all-justice-is-local.html.
[21] Drumbl, *Atrocity, Punishment, and International Law*, 91–92.
[22] Clark, "Gacaca's Legacy."
[23] Ibid.
[24] A large number of the very young, elderly, and sick detainees were also released in 2003.
[25] Clark, "The Legacy of Rwanda's Gacaca Courts."
[26] Clark, "Gacaca's Legacy."

allowing immediate reintegration into their communities. As a result, most convicted *génocidaires* now live in the same neighborhoods as survivors and their kin.[27]

THE HUMAN RIGHTS CRITIQUE

International lawyers, Western governments, and human rights activists criticized and opposed *gacaca* from its inception because it "fell short of international legal standards of fairness,"[28] encouraged "corruption and government interference at the community level,"[29] and did not meet "dominant understandings of due process."[30] Some even feared it would lead to mob justice, greater insecurity, and violence.[31] In early 1999, before Rwanda had even decided to use *gacaca*, the United Nations Office of the High Commissioner for Human Rights (OHCHR) fervently argued that community-based courts would be incapable of handling difficult cases related to the genocide.[32]

These critics emphasized one primary concern postgenocide: the need to punish in order to deter potential criminals using methods that conform to international standards of judicial procedure.[33] According to the Western universalist framework, there is an obligation to prosecute genocide, war crimes, and human rights violations in this way. Western human rights organizations such as Human Rights Watch and Amnesty International have been the most outspoken and have repeatedly been backed by Western institutions.[34] As a result, "the international community consistently has urged *gacaca* to resemble liberal legalist process and sanction, in which guilt instead of responsibility is the goal."[35]

In 2002, the executive director and a senior advisor of Human Rights Watch (HRW) wrote, in response to an article critical of the human rights field's interpretations of *gacaca*, that

---

[27] Clark, "The Legacy of Rwanda's Gacaca Courts."
[28] Clark, "How Rwanda Judged Its Genocide," 1.
[29] Clark, "The Legacy of Rwanda's Gacaca Courts."
[30] Drumbl, *Atrocity, Punishment, and International Law*, 94.
[31] Clark, "The Rules (and Politics) of Engagement," 299.
[32] United Nations Office of the High Commissioner for Human Rights (OHCHR), "Report on the Situation of Human Rights in Rwanda," February 8 1999, UN Doc. E/CN.4/1999/33, 12.
[33] Clark, "The Rules (and Politics) of Engagement," 309.
[34] Clark, "How Rwanda Judged Its Genocide," 1 and 4–6; Clark, "The Rules (and Politics) of Engagement," 297–319.
[35] Drumbl, *Atrocity, Punishment, and International Law*, 94.

[I]t is precisely at a time of atrocities . . . that a policy of trial and punishment is essential. Justice reinforces social norms and deters some would-be perpetrators . . . [O]ne can only imagine the long line of perpetrators who would choose therapy instead of prison cells. Before we agree to counseling instead of punishment [through *gacaca*], we owe it to the victims of the Rwandan genocide – and to all future victims of genocide – to contemplate [idea of therapy at *gacaca*] from their perspective.[36]

In December 2002, Amnesty International (AI) declared in a report that

[G]acaca trials need to conform to international standards of fairness so that the government's efforts to end impunity . . . are effective. If justice is not seen to be done, public confidence in the judiciary will not be restored and the government will have lost an opportunity to show its determination to respect human rights.[37]

By 2009, HRW was equating "Rwanda's highly discredited *gacaca* courts" with the US military commissions in Guantanamo Bay, describing both as "criminal justice systems . . . in which hearsay is admitted before a jury of non-lawyers."[38]

Western universalist donors were "uninspired by, skeptical of, and in some cases hostile to *gacaca* " because it did not look familiar and did not correspond to their thin society expectations of what normative justice should be.[39]

---

[36] The original article was written by Kenneth Roth, Alison DesForges, and Helena Cobban. "Justice or Therapy?," *Boston Review*, June 1, 2002, http://new.bostonreview.net/BR27.3/rothdesForges.html. Clark discusses this article and the Amnesty International report cited below in Clark, "The Rules (and Politics) of Engagement," 308–310.

[37] Amnesty International, "Rwanda – Gacaca: A Question of Justice," December 17, 2002, AI Index AFR 47/007/2002, 2.

[38] Human Rights Watch, "US: Revival of Guantanamo Military Commissions a Blow to Justice," May 15, 2009, www.hrw.org/news/2009/05/15/us-revival-guantanamo-military-commissions-blow-justice. Clark mentions this report in Clark, "How Rwanda Judged Its Genocide," 4.

[39] Drumbl, *Atrocity, Punishment, and International Law*, 95. The negative perception that these reports caused in the West had significant consequences. Besides limiting the amount of financial and technical support to Rwanda in support of the *gacaca*, it led to Western governments believing that Rwanda's judicial processes were so flawed that it was better to release genocide suspects instead of turning them over to the country for trial. This happened in the United Kingdom in 2009. "Statements by HRW, drawing on a handful of highly selective cases in the Rwandan courts, have become the basis of key ICTR decisions, which in turn have shaped national judgements around the world. Crucial international and domestic legal decisions regarding genocide crimes are therefore being made on the basis of a distanced form of information-gathering that is filtered through the position of one dominant advocacy group. The UK decision is particularly egregious because – unlike other European countries – the UK lacks the domestic legislation to prosecute the genocide cases that it chooses not to transfer to Rwanda. Given the choice between returning suspects to Rwanda to face trial to determine their guilt or innocence and letting them walk free, the UK judges needed

Although they have been generous with regard to the ICTR – paying $1.7 billion for 83 trials – they only modestly funded *gacaca*, which cost about $40 million in total.[40]

There are a number of responses to the human rights organizations' critique. First, they assume that a formal judicial process focused on deterring future action is the best response to genocide, but there is little evidence to support this. Second, they elevate legal statutes, but in doing so they lose sight of how *gacaca* actually works in practice and how it contributes to the Rwandans' other goals. Third, they disregard context: the needs of the country, its thick society traditions and values, the best use of its capacities and resources, and what might help it advance. Fourth, they assume that *gacaca* provides prejudicial justice, while it offers important safeguards.[41] Fifth, the criticisms draw attention away from the numerous problems that the ICTR, the sole international court set up to try Rwandan genocide suspects, has had. It was unable to handle even the limited caseload it received due to the slowness of its operation (producing a backlog);[42] its location, in neighboring Tanzania, limited the number of Rwandans who could attend, making the whole process seem distant and irrelevant to most of the population;[43] and administrative weaknesses tarred its credibility at times.[44] Sixth, Western universalist organizations such as AI and HRW have had "a tendency" to "identify the worst cases of corrupt or traumatizing hearings and suggest that they are representative."[45] This reflects the fact that they put much more emphasis on advocating for a particular perspective – thin society liberal modernity – than genuinely analyzing in a methodically sound manner the complex and diverse reality on the ground.[46] It also suggests a bias against the

---

watertight evidence that the former would result in an unfair trial. The High Court ruling was based on no such evidence." Phil Clark and Nicola Palmer, "The International Community Fails Rwanda Again," Oxford University's Transitional Justice Research Group Blog, May 5, 2009, https://oxfordtransitionaljustice.wordpress.com/2011/10/10/the-international-community-fails-rwanda-again/.

[40] Owen Bowcott, "Rwanda Genocide: The Fight to Bring the Perpetrators to Justice," *The Guardian*, April 2, 2014, www.theguardian.com/world/2014/apr/02/rwanda-genocide-fight-justice.

[41] Clark, *The Gacaca Courts, Post-Genocide Justice and Reconciliation in Rwanda*, 347–348.

[42] Martin Ngoga, "The Institutionalisation of Impunity: A Judicial Perspective of the Rwandan Genocide," in Clark and Kaufman (eds.), *After Genocide: Transitional Justice, Post-Conflict Reconstruction and Reconciliation in Rwanda and Beyond* (New York, NY: Columbia University Press, 2009), 329–332.

[43] Ibid., 329–332.

[44] Ibid., 329–332.

[45] Clark, "How Rwanda Judged Its Genocide," 6.

[46] Ibid., 6.

capabilities of average people (versus lawyers and international experts) and against African approaches (versus Western).

Critics also failed to offer a better approach to the great challenges that Rwanda faced. There was no practical way to prosecute the huge number of perpetrators according to the standards suggested. There was little concern for the myriad nonlegal problems that had to be dealt with, most notably how to enable millions of people who had experienced great trauma and hardship to live their lives in a satisfying way.

Although Western human rights actors critiqued *gacaca*, they lost sight of the on-the-ground conditions and the complexity of the issues Rwanda must deal with seriously, while not offering either practical solutions or ways to realistically enhance the solution that local people formulated.[47]

DYNAMICS AND OUTCOMES OF *GACACA*

Gacaca was designed from the start to achieve a broad set of goals beyond the relatively narrow mandate of ordinary courts. The *Gacaca* Law states that *gacaca* was set up to "achieve justice and reconciliation in Rwanda" and is designed "not only with the aim of providing punishment, but also reconstituting the Rwandan Society that had been destroyed by bad leaders."[48] It is thus more akin to a hybrid institution combining more restorative (traditional) elements with more retributive (modern) elements than a purely retributive justice regime. Postgenocide *gacaca* is more like a liberal criminal court than traditional *gacaca*, with retributive elements, formal written rules, protections for suspects, and checks on abuse.[49] Yet it is the traditional elements – including its "sacred, transcendental, revivalist, and religious aspects" – that have given *gacaca* its transformative potential.[50]

Gacaca is best understood as a "dynamic, lived socio-legal institution"[51] with a wide range of legal, political, and social goals, including reconciliation, peace, justice, healing, forgiveness, and truth.[52] It succeeded in each of these

---

[47] Clark, "Gacaca's Legacy."
[48] Government of Rwanda, Organic Law N° 16/2004 of June 19, 2004, "Establishing the Organisation, Competence and Functioning of Gacaca Courts Charged with Prosecuting and Trying the Perpetrators of the Crime of Genocide and Other Crimes Against Humanity, Committed Between October 1, 1990 and December 31, 1994," Kigali, Rwanda, 2004.
[49] Drumbl, *Atrocity, Punishment, and International Law*, 92–93.
[50] Ibid., 93.
[51] Clark, *The Gacaca Courts, Post-Genocide Justice and Reconciliation in Rwanda*, 5.
[52] Clark, "Establishing a Conceptual Framework: Six Key Transitional Justice Themes," in Clark and Kaufman (eds.), *After Genocide: Transitional Justice, Post-Conflict Reconstruction and Reconciliation in Rwanda and Beyond* (New York, NY: Columbia University Press, 2009), 193.

with varying effectiveness, depending on the local context. Indeed, it is hard to fully assess the impact of *gacaca* given the great number of communities involved, each with its own unique local influences and micropolitics.[53] Every place was impacted differently.

But, at the least, bringing prosecutions and discussions about the genocide near to where Rwandans live and involving them deeply in both have transformed the society in a way that distant international trials could never have. As Phil Clark, the most knowledgeable scholar on *gacaca*, and Nicola Palmer explained in 2009,

> Millions of everyday Rwandans have participated in gacaca, which takes place each week in village courtyards across the country. During gacaca hearings, genocide suspects and survivors tell their stories face-to-face. People hear personal, emotional narratives about the genocide, alongside the legal facts necessary to prosecute suspects. The impact of gacaca has not always been easy to predict, particularly given the volatile and often traumatising narratives that participants tell and hear. However, by doing justice locally, gacaca has come to matter to those most affected by the genocide.[54]

Excluding lawyers played a crucial role in allowing the average Rwandan to participate fully.[55] Attorneys would have altered the tone and power dynamics of hearings and prevented the inclusion of many nonlegal issues that were important to participants. Human rights organizations, in contrast, would have put lawyers at the center of the process on the assumption that the chief goal is deterrence. They would also have separated perpetrators from victims in ways that would limit engagement, healing, negotiation, forgiveness, reconciliation, and the pursuit of positive peace.[56]

On a practical level, *gacaca* was extraordinarily successful at handling the huge genocide caseload. As many as one million cases were examined, and prosecutions did not exacerbate the overcrowding of jails that had, in part, prompted the establishment of *gacaca* initially. Hundreds of thousands of *génocidaires* (perpetrators) were held accountable, and tens of thousands were acquitted in just over a decade. By commuting the sentences of a significant portion of those found guilty, *gacaca* facilitated the reintegration of most prisoners back into everyday society. By clearing the backlog of cases,

---

[53] Clark, *The Gacaca Courts, Post-Genocide Justice and Reconciliation in Rwanda*, 11.
[54] Clark and Palmer, "The International Community Fails Rwanda Again."
[55] Clark, *The Gacaca Courts, Post-Genocide Justice and Reconciliation in Rwanda*, 47–80.
[56] Clark, Ibid., 351.

it allowed the reallocation of money and people to invest in economic and social development and reconstruction.[57]

Gacaca was also conducive to truth telling. The active participation of the population led to the discovery and documentation of an immense amount of information about the killings.[58] Individuals, for the most part, benefitted emotionally and psychologically from this process by hearing detailed stories about the incidents involving their relatives and neighbors. These benefits applied to perpetrators as well: "Many guilty suspects claim to have gained a sense of release from feelings of shame and social dislocation by confessing to, and apologising for, their crimes in front of their victims and the wider community at *gacaca*."[59]

Perhaps surprisingly given the authoritarian nature of Rwanda's government, *gacaca* also "opened new spaces for political debate and spawned new forms of democratic participation." The vigorous community discussions developed new leaders and gave women, who were often the most active participants, new opportunities to play prominent roles in society. Many *gacaca* ended up discussing "sensitive and contentious issues" that extended well beyond its original mandate.[60]

Surveys showed that the Rwandan population (including Hutu prisoners) was more supportive of *gacaca* than either ICTR trials, to which they remained "relatively ambivalent and uninformed," or national court trials. They also showed that Rwandans felt that *gacaca* would contribute to reunification and peace.[61]

HOW *GACACA* BUILDS ON LOCAL VALUE SYSTEMS

Gacaca worked because it reflected the moral matrix of thick society Rwandans – in particular, their communal identities and religious beliefs (in Shweder's terms, the community ethic and divinity ethic).[62] These influences encouraged participation and shaped the informal practices that evolved around hearings as well as the interpretations and responses that *gacaca* produced.

---

[57] Clark, "Gacaca's Legacy."
[58] Clark, "How Rwanda Judged Its Genocide," 7–8.
[59] Clark, "The Legacy of Rwanda's Gacaca Courts."
[60] Clark, "How Rwanda Judged Its Genocide," 6–10.
[61] Drumbl, *Atrocity, Punishment, and International Law*, 97 and footnote 130 on 250–251.
[62] Clark, "The Rules (and Politics) of Engagement," 297–320.

Because personal attachments to the community are so crucial in shaping Rwandans' sense of their own identity – as expressed in some sources' descriptions of engaging as a "family" at gacaca – overcoming feelings of estrangement resulting from trauma is crucial for participants' sense of restoring their own humanity and regaining the unity of the self.[63]

Religion played an important role in the tilt toward forgiveness and reconciliation, as it did in South Africa after its transition to majority rule and northern Uganda and Sierra Leone after their conflicts. Many people took part in unofficial church-led *gacaca*, which took place in parallel with official *gacaca*, and they strongly influenced how the latter worked. In the church hearings, spiritual leaders often told participants that they had a religious duty to forgive and reconcile with the people who had done them wrong. Prisoners and survivors appropriated Christian ideas of redemption and renewal when the former equated confessions in public with healing, and survivors felt released and cleansed by discovering the detailed fates of their kin.[64] "Christian conceptions of grace, mercy, redemption, and atonement in particular manifest in much of the population's connection of *gacaca* with the pursuit of reconciliation, healing, forgiveness, and truth."[65]

This parallels the South African experience in the 1990s. As Mahmood Mamdani argued in 1996,

> "Reconciliation ... requires an acknowledgement of wrongs committed and a reevaluation by their perpetrators of the morality which lay behind them." Then only "can reconciliation trigger real catharsis, a word which, in its original Greek, contains the ideas of purification and spiritual renewal." Reconciliation (forgiveness) is neither automatic, nor a foregone conclusion; forgiveness is premised on confession, repentance and conversion.[66]

---

[63] Clark, *The Gacaca Courts, Post-Genocide Justice and Reconciliation in Rwanda*, 349.
[64] Ibid., 350.
[65] Ibid., 349.
[66] The quotes come from a book he is reviewing: Kader Asmal, Louise Asmal, and Ronald Suresh Roberts, *Reconciliation Through Truth: A Reckoning of Apartheid's Criminal Governance* (New York, NY: St. Martin's Press, 1997). Mahmood Mamdani, "Reconciliation without Justice," *Southern African Review of Books* 46 (November/December 1996), http://web.uct.ac.za/depts/sarb/X0045_Mamdani.html. In the same article, he also says: "The Christian alternative is a combination of forgiveness and conversion, with forgiveness conditional on confession, repentance and conversion. It is this shift, from the notion of a Manichean battle of good against evil to that of the inevitability of living with evil that, I suspect, informs the shift from justice to truth as the foundation of reconciliation. In other words, you must see the light, and acknowledge it as such – to be forgiven."

The role of religion, community, and other sociocultural factors that influenced how Rwandans interpreted *gacaca* receives little mention in the Western assessments of its use. Indeed, the dominant discourse does not recognize the way Rwandans actually understood and experienced *gacaca*; it remains focused on deterrence and judicial solutions.

THE ROLE OF RESTORATIVE JUSTICE

The communal and religious aspects of many African societies point to the importance of restorative justice. As Desmond Tutu argues, Western (thin society) jurisprudence has many differences with the traditional African (thick society) approach. The latter aims at

> the healing of breaches, the redressing of imbalances, the restoration of broken relationships, a seeking to rehabilitate both the victim and the perpetrator, who should be given the opportunity to be reintegrated into the community he or she has injured by his offense.[67]

Whereas the West sees reconciliation as stemming from accountability, the South prefers to emphasize healing. William Zartman, one of the world's leading experts on conflict prevention, describes this difference as

> between those that look back, however correctly, and those that look ahead, above all constructively. The first is primarily a Western or Northern approach ... The second is the basis of the African, Middle Eastern, and Asian (but not Latin American) notion of restorative justice ... The two approaches start from different premises and there is no basis for judging between them, but the methods and consequences of the two are profoundly different.[68]

Influenced by local notions about justice and community, *gacaca* contained significant restorative justice components both in how it operated and in how it judged (see Table 7.1 for a comparison between retributive and restorative justice). Active participation, engagement, and face-to-face interaction between parties previously involved in conflict was built into the *gacaca* process with the hope that they would help restore relationships between individuals and groups that had previously failed. Of course, results were unpredictable. Immense dedication from both sides and effective mediation were essential to establish and maintain trust through what was inevitably a difficult process.

---

[67] Desmond Tutu, *No Future without Forgiveness* (New York: Doubleday), 54–55.
[68] William Zartman, *Preventing Deadly Conflict* (Malden, MA: Polity Press, 2015), 183.

TABLE 7.1 *Retributive versus restorative justice*[69]

Retributive justice	Restorative justice
Crime is an act against the state, a violation of a law, an abstract idea	Crime is an act against a person and the community
Led by judge	Led by civil society leader
Seeks to determine individual guilt	Searches for societal patterns
Offender accountability defined as taking punishment	Accountability defined as assuming responsibility and taking action to repair harm
Punishment is effective because it changes behavior and deters crime	Punishment alone is not effective in changing behavior and is disruptive to communal harmony and good relationships
Establishes blame or guilt, focuses on the past (did he/she do it?)	Pursues problem solving, examines liabilities/obligations, focuses on the future (what should be done?)
Emphasis on adversarial relationship	Emphasis on dialogue and negotiation
Imposition of pain to punish and deter/ prevent; legal retaliation	Restitution as a means of restoring relationships; ritual reconciliation
Formal and rational-legalistic; dependence upon proxy professionals (lawyers, etc.)	Informal and ritualistic-communal; direct involvement by participants
Attention focused on suspect	Attention focused on victim
Everything happens in a courtroom, often far from where actions took place	Everything happens in hearings held within the affected community
State controlled; driven by international norms	Community organized; driven by local context
Promoted by UN, HRW, AI, and Western governments	Preferred by many local leaders

The contrast with the judicial process promoted by human rights actors could not be greater. The latter rarely if ever allows victims and perpetrators to interact and almost always limits discussion to legal matters. As Clark writes: "[Human rights activists] not only ignor[e] the effects of popular involvement in *gacaca* ... but also view popular involvement as anathema to impartial justice."[70]

[69] Conflict Solutions Center, "Retributive vs. Restorative Justice," Santa Barbara, CA, 2014, www.cscsb.org/restorative_justice/retribution_vs_restoration.html; and Huyse, "Introduction," 5.
[70] Clark, *The Gacaca Courts, Post-Genocide Justice and Reconciliation in Rwanda*, 348.

Gacaca was, in fact, somewhat exceptional in the depth of interaction and reconciliation that it encouraged. Even truth commissions, such as South Africa's Truth and Reconciliation Commission, did not yield as many face-to-face discussions as occurred in Rwanda; instead, they generally provided people the opportunity to tell their stories in front of a commission without a lot of interaction.[71]

Gacaca judgments also had restorative elements. Community service and compensation were often used as punishment instead of jail time, especially for lesser criminals. These promoted meaningful engagement between perpetrators and victims, such as when the former provided labor or restitution directly for the latter.[72] Community service might involve tilling fields, donating produce, building roads, or renovating houses.[73] Compensation improved the living conditions of victims – something that international genocide trails and truth commissions such as South Africa's cannot do. Imprisonment may have been justified – and it was used for higher-level criminals – but it does little to reconcile or restore, and it may actually hurt efforts at both.

Jail times were lower in *gacaca* than for similar crimes committed in ordinary circumstances. And if a perpetrator confessed his or her crime and pleaded guilty, he or she received a reduction in sentencing that is normally unavailable.[74] For instance, while category two criminals (the middle of the three categories used) who killed or planned to kill would normally receive 25–30 years in jail, if they confessed after their names appeared on a list compiled by a *gacaca* court's investigative arm, they would only receive 12 to 15 years, half in custody and half in community service; if they confessed before the list was compiled, they would receive a sentence of only 7–12 years, half in custody and half in community service. A *gacaca*'s General Assembly could disallow a partial or insincere confession.[75]

Restorative justice not only better fits with the African thick society approach to justice than retributive justice, but it also better fits with the complex landscape that exists in postconflict or postrepression societies.[76]

---

[71] Clark, "The Rules (and Politics) of Engagement," 314–315.
[72] Clark, *The Gacaca Courts, Post-Genocide Justice and Reconciliation in Rwanda*, 346.
[73] Drumbl, *Atrocity, Punishment, and International Law*, 88.
[74] Ibid., 69.
[75] Ibid., 87–88.
[76] Luc Huyse, "Introduction: Tradition-Based Approaches in Peacemaking, Transitional Justice and Reconciliation Policies," in Huyse and Mark Salter (eds.), *Traditional Justice and Reconciliation after Violent Conflict: Learning from African Experiences* (Stockholm: International IDEA, 2008), 2–5.

Besides transitional justice concerns, these countries must also rebuild the civil service, maintain security, disarm rebels, reorganize military forces, rebuild infrastructure, reconstruct the economy, establish an independent judiciary, reintegrate populations, and help victims heal. It is impossible to do all these things; choices must be made. A focus on retributive justice alone can be destabilizing (e.g., it might encourage rebels to keep fighting or weaken security) as well as counterproductive (e.g., it might eliminate the best human resources from the civil service, or reduce the incentive for the largest enterprises in the economy to invest).[77]

Of course no judicial system is completely restorative or retributive. All include elements of both, with variations existing along a continuum. As such, *gacaca* represents something that is likely to be increasingly common in the East and South: a hybrid institution that combines both international (Western) and local (traditional) elements, developed in response to local needs and seeking to take advantage of the technological and institutional gains made elsewhere while building on the values and worldview of native people and society. It thus embodies what modernization will often look like outside the West.

THE LIMITATIONS OF GACACA

Gacaca was far from perfect and, like most institutions in Rwanda, had various problems. Inadequacies included corruption, bribery of judges, intimidation of witnesses, and the hiding of evidence.[78] In many places, low turnout or limited willingness to participate – partly because of the enormous amount of time required – held back the process.[79] Some victims complain that the sentences given to convicted *génocidaires* was too lenient, and that community service is a poor replacement for jail. Some Hutu contend that the *gacaca* should have addressed revenge killings committed by the Tutsi Rwandan Patriotic Front (RPF) after it invaded the country in 1994 and not just genocide crimes. Some genocide criminals falsely confessed to crimes less severe than they committed in order to minimize their punishments.[80] Yet, given the scale of *gacaca* – decade-long, involving 11,000 jurisdictions, and

---

[77] Huyse, "Introduction," 4.
[78] Clark, "How Rwanda Judged Its Genocide," 6.
[79] Clark, "The Rules (and Politics) of Engagement," 317–319.
[80] Clark, "The Legacy of Rwanda's Gacaca Courts."

encompassing as many as one million cases – these problems were relatively mild and far less widespread than critics often claim.[81]

Gacaca failed to live up to its full potential as a restorative mechanism at times. As Mark Drumbl noted in 2007, "A variety of pressures, some exogenous, have moved *gacaca* away from restorative and reconciliatory goals and structures and to something that is more punitive and retributive."[82] These included international pressure, especially from human rights actors and donors, to conform to international standards; government pressure to "centralize and bureaucratize" to meet its own objectives; and the fact that *gacaca* as originally designed, in its premodern form, was not meant to handle something as evil as a genocide, and rehabilitating murderers is anything but a simple matter.[83]

The central government's authoritarianism and strong emphasis on national unity and reconciliation according to its reading of history has hampered some aspects of how *gacaca* worked. It certainly limited the scope for discussion, at least formally, of many postgenocide issues – such as the RPF's crimes – and ensured that alternative ideas and narratives did not receive a wide hearing. The role of media and civil society were limited. The latter, for instance, played little role in the development and implementation of *gacaca*.[84] Churches, the most important nongovernmental institutions in the country, were asked to support *gacaca*, and, perhaps because of the role some of their members played in the genocide, were generally supportive and submissive.[85] No one outside the government was given an opportunity to challenge the purpose, structure, and methods of *gacaca*.

There has also been tension between the many objectives that *gacaca* sought to achieve, especially between truth and healing and between retribution and reconciliation. Recounting the facts of the genocide may be remedial in many ways, but it always risks hurting victims. Often it depends on the circumstances and individuals involved. Some may benefit while others may not. There is no easy way to balance the two objectives. Similarly, although *gacaca* deliberately tried to shift the judicial process toward restoration, it did contain retributive elements that may have damaged such efforts. In addition,

---

[81] Clark, "How Rwanda Judged Its Genocide," 6.
[82] Drumbl, *Atrocity, Punishment, and International Law*, 94.
[83] Ibid., 94.
[84] Victims associations have played a role supporting survivors, but never questioning the overall framework.
[85] Burt Ingelaere, "The Gacaca Courts in Rwanda," in Huyse and Salter (eds.), *Traditional Justice and Reconciliation after Violent Conflict: Learning from African Experiences* (Stockholm: International IDEA, 2008), 46–58.

what are perceived as restorative justice punishments – such as community service – may be perceived as too lenient or too severe depending on the circumstances and individuals involved. Some may demand too much; others may offer too little.[86]

But, as discussed earlier, Western universalist critiques focused on only one aspect of *gacaca*: its insufficiently retributive outcomes. This limited perspective significantly reduced the chance that human rights and development organizations' input could improve *gacaca*'s weaknesses.

A NARROW CONCEPT OF HOW SOCIETIES WORK

As was evident in the previous chapter, there is a striking difference between thin and thick societies. In the former, the role of the individual is paramount. Human rights should be interpreted the same everywhere, whatever the context. There is little room for compromise or adaptation. In thick societies, in contrast, communal ties and religious values play prominent roles. Context is paramount. Human rights are important but should be sought in a way that builds on and leverages local values and institutions, and takes into account the broader needs of a society.

Steeped in the values of thin societies, Western universalists have consistently argued that Rwanda should prioritize retributive justice over other goals, going as far as to claim that it was a prerequisite for peace and reconciliation.[87] This reflects the belief that a small number of individuals are responsible for evil and that by holding such people accountable, it can be eliminated. Prosecution will change behavior and deter potential criminals from acting similarly in the future. It will also instill confidence and trust in public authority, improving efforts to increase security and the workings of government.

Most international analysts have assessed *gacaca* through this narrow lens, ignoring the legal statutes and on-the-ground reality that clearly depict *gacaca* as having numerous objectives, and that make reconciliation and reconstruction as important as justice. Such issues have been

> glaringly absent from the orthodox interpretations of gacaca, even when they appear in the same documents on which proponents of this view base their analyses ... the dominant discourse is founded on a highly selective reading of gacaca's legal statutes and that, as a result, it provides an inadequate view of gacaca's aims.[88]

---

[86] Clark, *The Gacaca Courts, Post-Genocide Justice and Reconciliation in Rwanda*, 345–347.

[87] Clark, "Establishing a Conceptual Framework," 192.

[88] Clark, *The Gacaca Courts, Post-Genocide Justice and Reconciliation in Rwanda*, 348–349.

In fact, the dominant human rights perspective has so heavily influenced governance models that it has overturned some long-held beliefs without any evidence to support the change. The "legal paradigm has become dominant in the study of conflict and post-conflict societies, proffering procedural, academic, and institutional 'remedies' that too often fail to recognize other important perspectives." The "physical, psychological, and psycho-social needs of individuals and groups" are undervalued, or simply ignored.[89]

The relationship between order and justice has been reversed. As Dominik Zaum argues,

> Traditionally, the relationship between order and justice has been described as characterized by tensions, with justice seen to be realizable only within the context of order. In recent years, however, this relationship has often been reversed, and international organizations and liberal Western states have increasingly viewed justice issues as a condition for order, peace, and stability ... It is claimed, transitional justice is a condition not only for peace and security, but also for the establishment of functioning political institutions; it contributes not only to peace-building but also to state-building.[90]

Yet, even in the Balkans, the postconflict region most influenced by Western norms about justice (and much else), there is little evidence that this emphasis on justice has worked as advertised. Prosecutions in Bosnia-Herzegovina and elsewhere have exacerbated tensions between ethnic groups.[91] The emphasis on international justice has led to an underemphasis on the development of a functioning domestic legal system, which is more important to public order, democratization, and economic development.[92] Although the effort to bring war criminals to justice undoubtedly helped bring peace to the region, it has contributed much less to other goals.[93]

This broadened expectation for what legal justice can achieve reflects the changes in how human rights have been interpreted and promoted by the field since the 1990s, as discussed in Chapter 5. Leading actors actively sought

---

[89] Clark and Kaufman, "Introduction and Background: After Genocide," in Clark and Kaufman (eds.), *After Genocide: Transitional Justice, Post-Conflict Reconstruction and Reconciliation in Rwanda and Beyond* (New York, NY: Columbia University Press, 2009), 1.

[90] Dominik Zaum, "Balancing Justice and Order: State-building and the Prosecution of War Crimes in Rwanda and Kosovo," in Clark and Kaufman (eds.), *After Genocide: Transitional Justice, Post-Conflict Reconstruction and Reconciliation in Rwanda and Beyond* (New York, NY: Columbia University Press, 2009), 364–365.

[91] Zaum, "Balancing Justice and Order," 376–379.

[92] Ibid., 376–379.

[93] Ibid., 376–379.

to expand the domain where their ideas would matter. They sought to create vehicles for their ideals in the shape of global institutions such as the International Criminal Court that could mimic the state. This greater power led to a growing international aversion to amnesties and restorative justice, especially in places with weak influence such as Africa. Backed by the Rome Statute (the treaty that established the ICC in 1998) and a vastly expanded lobby of NGOs pushing for transitional justice that meets international standards – and is thus retributive in nature – the claims of global justice triumphed over the needs of local communities.[94]

In thick societies, in contrast, the assumption is that the healing of society is a prerequisite for progress on other fronts. This stems from a conviction that the interests of the individual and the group are inseparable; communal identity is permanent and must be built on continuity with the past; dialogue and negotiation, not confrontation, best solve problems; and spiritual concerns – such as repentance, forgiveness, harmony, and ritual – are crucial to the natural order.[95] Such assumptions underpin *gacaca* in both its traditional form and modern implementation.

Although Africa has been transformed over the past two centuries by colonialism, conflict, massive population growth, urbanization, and the many travails of state building, it retains many of its core values, beliefs, and traditions, which differ substantially from Western norms.[96] African cultures continue to value "the unity and solidarity of, and harmony among, members of the group."[97]

In South Africa, for instance, punishment was deemed to contradict reconciliation and thought too risky given the chance that it would lead to conflict. Instead, a political compromise was forged that exchanged amnesty for truth telling and laid the groundwork for reconciliation. This was more in keeping with the African concept of restorative justice and societal healing, but it was also much more practical given the circumstances.[98] The case is anything but unique. Indeed, many in Africa and elsewhere have argued that, as David Booth says, "pursuing judicial remedies in situations of political

---

[94] Stephen Hopgood, *The Endtimes of Human Rights* (Ithaca, NY: Cornell University Press, 2013), 119–141 and 178.

[95] Tutu, *No Future without Forgiveness*; Huyse, "Introduction," 1–7.

[96] Francis Deng, *Identity, Diversity, and Constitutionalism in Africa* (Washington, DC: United States Institute of Peace Press, 2008).

[97] Ibid., 78–79.

[98] Tutu, *No Future without Forgiveness*; Thabo Mbeki and Mahmood Mamdani, "Courts Can't End Civil Wars," *International New York Times*, February 6, 2014, www.nytimes.com/2014/02/06/opinion/courts-cant-end-civil-wars.html.

conflict bordering on civil war can be harmful to the maintenance of peace, as well as to the quality of policy generally."[99]

Indeed, in contrast to the situation following World War II, when the Nuremberg (and Tokyo) model of justice embodied in the ICTR (and the ICC) and favored by Western human rights organizations was developed, in many postconflict countries today the perpetrators and victims must live side by side and work together to build a new society after a war ends. South Africa's blacks and whites and Rwanda's Hutus and Tutsis had no choice but to cooperate in the aftermath of a change in the political order.[100] In such circumstances, retribution without restoration creates winners and losers, and it can easily block progress toward reconciliation and rebuilding. As Thabo Mbeki and Mahmood Mamdani argue in discussing South Sudan, South Africa, Uganda, Mozambique, and other African conflicts in "Courts Can't End Civil Wars,"

> Courts are ill-suited to inaugurating a new political order after civil wars; they can only come into the picture after such a new order is already in place. Because criminal trials are driven by a winner-takes-all logic – you are either innocent or guilty – those found guilty and punished as perpetrators are denied a life in the new political order. And this can be a dangerous outcome...[101]

In Rwanda's case, the emphasis on restoring and transforming society actually allowed the country to hold far more people accountable than would ever have been possible if justice was pursued the way international human rights organizations wanted to. By using a mixture of international, national, and especially *gacaca* courts – and a combination of reduced sentences, community service, and compensation – the state's response to genocide penetrated deeper into society and reached a much larger proportion of participants than anything undertaken elsewhere. The focus on community and society thus actually led to a much more determined effort to prosecute. As William Schabas argues, Rwanda represented

> one of the most principled manifestations of the commitment of international human rights law and policy. While many other post-conflict societies have

---

[99] David Booth and Frederick Golooba-Mutebi, "Developmental Regimes and the International System," Developmental Regimes in Africa, Policy Brief 5, January 2014.
[100] Mbeki and Mamdani, "Courts Can't End Civil Wars."
[101] Ibid.

delayed, postponed and even prevaricated ... Rwanda has insisted upon holding perpetrators accountable.[102]

In some ways, this should not be surprising. Thick societies with their strong emphasis on community and religion are more likely to recognize the manifold nature of violent conflict and crimes as great as genocide, and not to assume that only a few individuals at the top are guilty, and that everyone else – including often the executioners of mass violence – simply followed orders under duress.[103] Instead, they more accurately understand that these problems are the product of something deeply wrong within society, involving a lot more people. Change requires addressing deeper phenomena such as historical narratives, levels of tolerance for difference, and even internal beliefs about right and wrong that affect how relationships are managed and experienced, and how people across society feel about history, identity, their neighbors, and so on.[104] Instead of treating mass violence as being primarily a top-down phenomenon – the approach favored by Western human rights organizations and institutions such as the ICC and ad hoc criminal tribunals such as the ICTR – thick societies such as Rwanda, Uganda, and South Africa have preferred to establish institutions and processes that "treat everyday perpetrators as central, not secondary, actors, and they encourage direct communication between perpetrators and survivors."[105]

All of this indicates that transitions have multiple goals beyond justice; that these goals may contradict each other at times; and that justice needs to be placed in context so that a society can determine the most appropriate response to its needs. *Gacaca*, which seeks to address many more of these goals than an ordinary judicial regime, should not be judged through a retributive justice lens.[106]

---

[102] He also says that "Everybody talks about battling impunity, but few societies have done this with greater determination or more stubborn resistance to compromise than Rwanda." William Schabas, "Post-Genocide Justice in Rwanda: A Spectrum of Options," in Clark and Kaufman (eds.), *After Genocide: Transitional Justice, Post-Conflict Reconstruction and Reconciliation in Rwanda and Beyond* (New York, NY: Columbia University Press, 2009), 207. [Both this quote and the one in the text come from same page.]

[103] This doesn't imply that they will act on this understanding. Post World War II Japan, for instance, stands out as an example of a thick society that has preferred to bury its brutal past than address the underlying causes for it.

[104] Clark, Kaufman, and Kalypso Nicolaïdis, "Tensions in Transitional Justice," in Clark and Kaufman (eds.), *After Genocide: Transitional Justice, Post-Conflict Reconstruction and Reconciliation in Rwanda and Beyond* (New York, NY: Columbia University Press, 2009), 382–391.

[105] Clark, "All Justice is Local."

[106] Clark, Kaufman, and Nicolaïdis, "Tensions in Transitional Justice," 382–391.

This points to the importance of using the diverse and balancing elements of the Universal Declaration in a context-specific way to bridge the gaps between different societies. This is exactly the flexible universalist approach adopted by the framers of the UDHR. In the last chapter, we will look at how this approach can be practically implemented and propose a fourfold solution for furthering human rights in the new global landscape.

8

Conclusion: A Return to Basics

Jacques Maritain, in his book *Man and the State*, endorsed a flexible approach to human rights grounded in ideals very similar to liberal pluralism. He, like his fellow UDHR drafters, believed that

> What creates irreducible differences and antagonisms among men is the determination of . . . the scale of values that governs the exercise and concrete organization of these various rights. Here we are confronted with the clash between incompatible political philosophies. Because here we are no longer dealing with the simple recognition of the diverse categories of human rights, but with the principle of dynamic unification in accordance with which they are carried into effect; we are dealing with the tonality, the specific key, by virtue of which different music is placed on this same keyboard, either in harmony or in discord with human dignity.[1]

Much like Shweder the cultural psychologist asserts four decades later, Maritain argues that there are three basic frameworks for organizing a society's approach to morality. For him, these revolve around "liberal-individualistic," "communistic," and "personalist" concerns. The first of these emphasizes the autonomy of each individual to appropriate goods as he or she sees fit. The second emphasizes the role of the collective in determining the best allocation of such goods. And the third, based on Maritain's strong Catholic faith and the teaching of Thomas Aquinas, emphasized the higher spiritual, moral, and interdependent nature of human beings.[2] He continues,

---

[1]   Jacques Maritain, *Man and the State* (Chicago, IL: University of Chicago Press, 1951), 106.
[2]   William Sweet, "Jacques Maritain," in Edward Zalta (ed.), *The Stanford Encyclopedia of Philosophy* (Summer 2013 Edition), http://plato.stanford.edu/archives/sum2013/entries/maritain/.

[Each] type of society will lay down on paper similar, perhaps identical, lists of the rights of man. They will not, however, play that instrument in the same way. Everything depends upon the supreme value in accordance with which all these rights will be ordered and will mutually limit each other. It is by virtue of the hierarchy of values to which we thus subscribe that we determine the rights of man.[3]

It was with such insight – or inspiration – that the drafters of the UDHR sought to bridge great differences between cultures and unify the world behind a universal yet flexible human rights standard. Inspired by their efforts, and seeking to restore the overlapping consensus that they established, the fourfold approach outlined in this chapter should yield greater unity and clarity about rights, resulting in fewer confrontations between actors in both thick and thin societies even if the gap between them grows. This kind of approach is essential if the human rights field desires to maintain its influence in a context of growing multipolarity and declining Western influence.

THE CHANGING CONTEXT

As Maritain's observations hint – and the crafters of the UDHR experienced firsthand when debating the Universal Declaration – the human rights field will continue to be challenged as minority groups and foreign societies adhere to values hierarchies different from that of Western universalism. At home, inward migration and the secularization of parts of populations are yielding greater differences in moral matrices within Western countries. Abroad, the rising economic and political power of Asian, African, Middle Eastern, and Latin American countries is making Western-dominated international institutions and Western universalist global norms increasingly untenable. As a result, the stark difference between how thick and thin societies interpret human rights risks undermining the human rights regime's legitimacy and relevance as a multicultural, multinational project.

The rise of Eastern and Southern states that are, for the most part, wary of Western motives, uneasy with some aspect of the existing human rights agenda, and anxious to promote their different identities and cultures will likely lead to growing pressure for change in the international discourse and regime. These powers do not necessarily disagree with the goals of today's rules-based international system, but rather the "operationalization of liberal norms," and the "implicit and explicit hierarchies of international institutions"

---

[3] Maritain, *Man and the State*, 106–107.

that privilege Western countries.[4] Pushback against what is perceived to be a Western-led agenda from countries around the world is already widely evident, as we saw with the Rwandan case study in Chapter 7 and the ASEAN critique discussed in Chapters 2 and 4. Tom Carothers writes,

> After seeing its reach increase for decades, international support for democracy and human rights faces a serious challenge: more and more governments are erecting legal and logistical barriers ... publicly vilifying international aid groups and their local partners, and harassing such groups or expelling them altogether ... Pushback is global. The phenomenon no longer emanates from only a few countries and is not only directed at a narrow part of the democracy aid community.[5]

The world is becoming more multipolar, and thus less determined by Western power and Western universalist values. Whereas once thin society United States and Europe had outsized influence and could promote their norms as global values, in the future they will have to compete with alternative centers of power and influence; thick society Southern value systems, ideas, and ways of organizing society will have greater credence and sway. At the United Nations, for instance, support for European Union positions on human rights has been dropping for two decades, while the number of votes in the General Assembly in line with China's position has been increasing.[6] China, India, Indonesia, Brazil, Ethiopia, Nigeria, Russia, Turkey, Saudi Arabia, and others already have greater or at least comparable influence within their regions; combined, they can easily roll back unpopular Western initiatives.

The international Westphalian State System (or World Order) – which has significantly contributed to peace and development around the world for centuries, and which is likely to matter even more in the future – is based on the recognition that societies have a right to determine how they are organized. Ideologies that periodically appear, from the republicanism of the French Revolution to communism to Fascism to extremist Islamism, have to be quashed before they destabilize the system. Instead of imposing a totalizing

---

[4] Oliver Stuenkel, *Post-Western World* (Malden, MA: Polity Press, 2016), 184–185.
[5] Thomas Carothers and Saskia Brechenmacher, "Closing Space: Democracy and Human Rights Support under Fire," *Carnegie Endowment for International Peace*, February 2014, http://carnegieendowment.org/2014/02/20/closing-space-democracy-and-human-rights-support-under-fire/h1by.
[6] David Lewis, "The Failure of a Liberal Peace: Sri Lanka's Counter-Insurgency in Global Perspective," *Conflict, Security, and Development* 10, no. 5 (November 2010): 659. See also Richard Gowan, "Who Is Winning on Human Rights at the UN?," *European Council on Foreign Relations*, September 24, 2012, www.ecfr.eu/article/commentary_who_is_winning_on_human_rights_at_the_un.

concept – as the German princes attempted to impose their faith (whether Protestantism or Catholicism) on their neighbors during the Thirty Years War (1618–1648), and as challengers to the system have tried since – Westphalia recognized multiplicity as its starting point. The concept of "multiple societies" and domestic sovereignty remains embedded in international relations between countries in order to maintain peace and prevent a return of brutal religious violence.[7]

The changing international landscape may, perhaps counterintuitively, lead Western states to become less tolerant of cultural difference – especially at home – as economic decline, political instability, and challenges to the region's longstanding global hegemony combine to produce a backlash against religious and cultural minorities. Changing demographics – from a declining birthrate and growing immigration – and a growing divergence in value systems between increasingly assertive secular majorities and reactive religious minorities will certainly call for the opposite approach. In fact, a failure to accommodate and appreciate thick communities living within thin societies risks undermining one of the West's main advantages: its ability to tolerate difference and peacefully host minority groups. This would be a marked shift from precedent in some places, such as the United States, where courts have historically protected minority groups' ability to hold diverse beliefs and to practice according to those beliefs, without weighing whether such beliefs were right or wrong. As the Supreme Court pointed out in a 1981 decision, "religious beliefs need not be acceptable, logical, consistent, or comprehensible to others in order to merit First Amendment protection."[8]

Human rights monism threatens to yield greater social conflict domestically and declining legitimacy for human rights internationally. Issues such as circumcision and justice in postconflict settings are litmus tests for broader trends across the whole field. Moving to abolish a social custom that has been an integral part of the identity and religious faith of a large portion of the world for thousands of years risks undermining the human flourishing that governments and activists believe they are promoting.[9] Similarly, inflexibility in

---

[7] Henry Kissinger, *World Order* (New York, NY: Penguin Press, 2014).

[8] *Thomas v. Review Board of the Indiana Employment Security Division*, 450 U.S. 707 (1981). The same quote also appeared in *Church of the Lukumi Babalu Aye, Inc. and Ernesto Pichardo v. City of Hialeah*, 508 U.S. 520 (1993).

[9] "Opposing popular cultural practices because they appear to violate human rights norms may make rights rhetoric less appealing to a broader public in diverse societies and developing countries. Human rights will be a less-useful tool for promoting human dignity where it is perceived to be alien and to necessitate the complete abolition of certain ways of life." Erika George, "Virginity Testing and South Africa's HIV/AIDS Crisis: Beyond Rights Universalism

dealing with the myriad challenges of fragile states – including ethnic conflict, peacemaking, and building social cohesion – risks undermining the moral authority of human rights in the countries where it is needed most.

FORGING A CONSENSUS ACROSS THICK AND THIN SOCIETIES

A better strategy would recognize that human rights are a combination of natural and positive rights; that there is a very strong consensus on the importance of a relatively small core set of basic rights, but only a loose consensus on a broader set of rights – and this latter consensus depends on letting prioritization vary; and that the ability to maintain a global architecture robust enough to pressure violators depends very much on politics. Suzanne Last Stone writes,

> there are an increasing number of voices within the human rights tradition calling for a ratcheting down of the language of sacredness, of ethical universalism, of moral or ontological arguments, and a re-focusing on human rights as a more limited international political project: a legal regime.[10]

Jack Donnelly, among others, has urged a return to this more modest conception of human rights.[11]

Human rights, after all, are both an end in themselves and a means to an end, that of improving human lives. They are a combination of nonethno-centric cross- or supra-cultural natural rights and positive rights; while natural rights apply everywhere, positive rights may only apply in some places. Natural rights are typically broad and abstract and need to be formulated into specific conceptions and methods of implementation that can be applied in particular contexts; these often vary substantially from place to place.[12] Yet, even when they are rooted in natural rights, the promotion of human rights very much depends on political and public support: globally, only a consensus across states in an increasingly multipolar world can hold violators to account;

---

and Cultural Relativism toward Health Capabilities," *California Law Review* 96, no. 6 (2008): 1515.

[10] Suzanne Last Stone, "Religion and Human Rights: Babel or Translation, Conflict or Convergence," paper presented at *Role of Religion in Human Rights Discourse* conference, Israel Democracy Institute, May 16–17, 2012, 5–6.

[11] Stone, "Religion and Human Rights," 26; Jack Donnelly, "The Relative Universality of Human Rights," *Human Rights Quarterly* 29, no. 2 (May 2007): 281.

[12] This three-part breakdown comes from Donnelly. But my definitions and usage differ. Donnelly, "The Relative Universality of Human Rights," 299–300.

nationally, only broad support across increasingly diverse populations and throughout important institutions can ensure implementation.

Since Kant, Western intellectual thought has endowed the universal realm with transcendent status and given it priority over the specific. "But the universal was once conceived as a common or shared realm, expressing a kind of consensus gentium."[13] Returning to this previous consensual concept of the universal and retrieving the idea of human rights as a partly political and legal project without involving any particular culture-dependent philosophy of the person and society would yield greater agreement and build stronger moral authority for human rights. A return to the basics, as envisioned in the UDHR, with a strong common core and a flexible interpretation of other priorities would achieve this. It would bridge the growing differences between thick and thin societies while unifying all of humanity behind a shared agenda.

If the human rights field were dominated by a flexible universalist approach grounded in liberal pluralism it would readily prioritize four elements: (1) cross-cultural dialogue as a way to develop and support home-grown solutions, (2) institution building as a way to better implement rights, (3) empirical research that employs cultural psychology, and (4) more systematic and comprehensive assessments based only on the rights agreed to in legally binding agreements. Although they are discussed distinctly later, these four elements work together, and human rights actors should accordingly pursue a comprehensive approach that promotes a universal minimal standard while allowing local stakeholders to develop and implement context-specific strategies.

---

[13] Stone, "Religion and Human Rights," 26. Clifford Geertz believes that an effort to create a *"consensus gentium* fails: rather than moving towards the essentials of the human situation, it moves away from it." He is right that there is a constant tension in "the dualism between empirically universal aspects of culture rooted in subcultural realities and empirically variable aspects not so rooted" and that many supposed commonalities consist of "empty and near-empty categories," but too pessimistic that any congruence can only exist in a "general way" that is too "loose and indeterminate" to matter. Although it may be true that "the notion that the essence of what it means to be human is most clearly revealed in those features of human culture that are universal rather than in those that are distinctive to this people or that is a prejudice we are not necessarily obliged to share," the UDHR and other such documents clearly show that there is a common essence across all humanity – a common understanding of some basic rights and wrongs, goods and bads – and that not all things can be reduced to the particular or relative. There is a core universal shared by all of humankind. Geertz, "The Impact of the Concept of Culture on the Concept of Man," in *The Interpretation of Cultures: Selected Essays* (New York, NY: Basic Books, 1973), 37–43.

CROSS-CULTURAL DIALOGUE AND HOMEGROWN SOLUTIONS

Given the contemporary context described earlier, human rights need to be better embedded within different cultures and moral matrices around the world in order to ensure that they are promoted locally – without the need for substantial international interference. This requires, among other things, a much stronger emphasis on respectful, equal, and open dialogue between different societies and communities such that differences can be aired and appreciated even if not fully accepted. Ideally, this would involve bringing together groups who usually do not meet to discuss issues that they may deeply disagree about. Only empathy for the different histories, contexts, and world-views that shape how different groups function can make cooperation across cultures and civilizations possible. All sides will need to seriously engage different perspectives in an inclusive and humble manner if confrontations are to be reduced in frequency and scope, and disagreements turned into something constructive that everyone can at least learn from.[14]

Today, the common human rights approach declares: "Here is how you need to change to join us." Human rights actors should replace this with two questions: "What does human flourishing look like in your society, and how can we support you in encouraging it?" This shift in tone and perspective would likely reduce resistance and resentment, and result in a greater impact. But it would also require ceding power to those whom human rights actors claim to represent.[15]

Underlying many of the debates related to human rights such as the intersociety Rwandan *gacaca* and the intrasociety European circumcision cases are fundamental questions about what and whom human rights are for. Are they an end in themselves or a means to better lives and societies? Are they designed to meet the needs and build on the values and knowledge of local communities, or are they designed to meet the needs and build on the values and knowledge of major human rights organizations? How far should major human rights organizations go in respecting and enhancing local institutions rather than focusing on critiquing these (and lobbying for change)?[16]

Even though dialogue would not lead to agreement across all issues, it would yield some common areas of accord (such as those discussed later),

---

[14] Joanne Bauer and Daniel Bell, "Introduction," in Bauer and Bell (eds.), *The East Asian Challenge for Human Rights* (Cambridge: Cambridge University Press, 1999), 4.

[15] Michael Barnett and Peter Walker, "Regime Change for Humanitarian Aid: How to Make Relief More Accountable," *Foreign Affairs* 94, no. 4 (July/August 2015): 141.

[16] Phil Clark, "Dilemmas of Justice," *Prospect Magazine*, May 2007, www.prospectmagazine.co .uk/magazine/dilemmasofjustice.

some degree of mutual understanding and respect, and some blocks on which to build a better relationship. As William Twining suggests,

> Human rights discourse can provide a flexible and relatively stable framework for constructing and developing norms, processes, and institutional arrangements on a basis of a negotiated consensus that accommodates rather than represses change or irons out diversity.[17]

Different parts of the world can expand the range of instruments that promote human well-being by learning from other places. Thick societies, for instance, have much to teach thin societies about how to use social norms and institutions to address social problems and improve the overall health of society. Thin societies, on the other hand, tend to be much better at using the tools of the state to enhance well-being and protect rights. They could play a more constructive role helping improve the effectiveness of state institutions in thick societies where governments are weak.

The human rights field misses an opportunity when it dismisses various cultural elements – elements that could be used to further the overall human rights agenda if they were better understood (as the Rwandan example in Chapter 7 shows). "It is likely that in the years to come, intellectual, moral, and ideological battles over human rights issues turn, to a significant extent, on their cross-cultural intelligibility and inter-religious justifiability."[18] When Western universalists ignore the concerns of Southern and, within the West, religious actors, they undermine the credibility of the human rights field. This is especially true when those expressing concern genuinely support human rights but have specific qualms about how narrowly they are construed or whether they are considered "core" or "periphery." Figure 8.1, which is only designed to be demonstrative, outlines some of the differences between how certain rights are perceived. Although societies and intercultural dialogue will have to determine what rights go in what category, the figure illustrates how many more rights thin societies are likely to consider core than thick societies. In this example, only nonderogable or emergency-proof rights (torture, slavery, degrading punishment, and various forms of discrimination) and those with wide acceptance in both types of societies (right to life and marriage) are considered universal. Others were placed by considering common practice in a number of representative cases.

---

[17] William Twining, *General Jurisprudence: Understanding Law from a Global Perspective* (Cambridge: Cambridge University Press, 2008), 181.

[18] Tore Lindholm, "Article 1," in Guðmundur Alfreðsson and Asbjørn Eide (eds.), *The Universal Declaration of Human Rights: A Common Standard of Achievement* (The Hague: Martinus Nijhoff Publishers, 1999), 70.

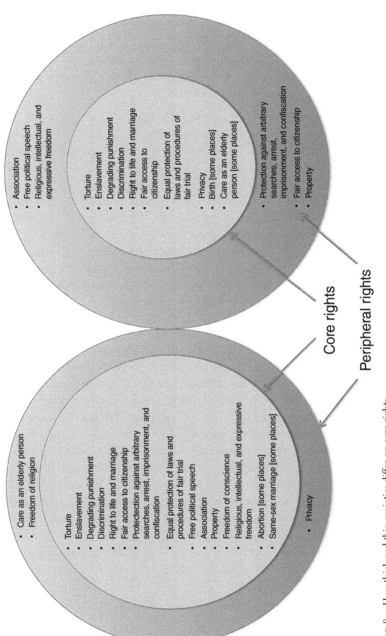

FIGURE 8.1 How thick and thin societies differ on core rights

More effort could be made to seek out aspects of local cultures ("receptors") that can be employed to promote human rights instead of just assuming that local culture is either an obstacle or an irrelevance to progress. As Tom Zwart explains,

> This can be done first by matching, i.e. identifying and making visible, domestic social arrangements supporting and protecting human rights that are already in place. Second, if these arrangements fall short of the international human rights requirements, amplification is the next step: elements must be added to the existing institutions rather than attempting to replace them with Western-centered solutions.[19]

Efforts to promote human rights and to improve human well-being are more likely to succeed when "working with the grain" of societies, rather than against it.[20] Instead of seeing culture as "simply a barrier that needs to be removed through education," human rights actors should view it as an important element of a thick society – and perhaps even an asset.[21] As Merry notes, "Practices labeled harmful and traditional are rarely viewed as part of wider systems of kinship and community, yet they are deeply embedded in patterns of family and religion."[22] Taking a society's traditions into account is much more likely to create the moral support necessary to promote and defend human rights than a confrontational approach that targets local culture and values and risks losing local support. For example, as UDHR drafter Peng-chun Chang suggested, the Confucian emphasis on interrelatedness has much to offer those constructing a human rights framework for a diverse era.[23]

---

[19] Tom Zwart, "Using Local Culture to Further the Implementation of International Human Rights: The Receptor Approach," *Human Rights Quarterly* 34, no. 2 (May 2012): 547. As Michael Walzer also notes, "The best moral and political arguments are ones that derive from or connect with the inherited culture of the people who need to be convinced." Walzer, *The Paradox of Liberation: Secular Revolutions and Religious Counterrevolutions* (New Haven, CT: Yale University Press, 2015), 117–118.

[20] Richard Crook and David Booth (eds.), "Special Issue: Working with the Grain? Rethinking African Governance," *IDS Bulletin* 42, no. 2 (March 2011): iii–iv and 1–101.

[21] Sally Engle Merry, *Human Rights and Gender Violence: Translating International Law into Local Justice* (Chicago, IL: University of Chicago Press Books, 2006), 15.

[22] Merry, *Human Rights and Gender Violence*, 11.

[23] Sumner Twiss, "Confucian Contributions to the Universal Declaration of Human Rights: A Historical and Philosophical Perspective," in Arvind Sharma (ed.), *The World's Religions: A Contemporary Reader* (Minneapolis, MN: Fortress Press, 2010), 110–114; Henry Rosemont, Jr., "Rights-Bearing Individuals and Role-Bearing Persons," in Mary I. Bockover (ed.), *Rules, Rituals, and Responsibilities: Essays Dedicated to Herbert Fingarette* (LaSalle, IL: Open Court, 1991), 71–102; Tom Zwart, "Re-Rooting International Human Rights by Revisiting the Universal Declaration of Human Rights," unpublished draft, 5–7.

As discussed in Chapters 3 and 4, culture is neither monolithic nor static. In fact, no matter how homogenous it appears, culture is always "pluralistic, interactive, and constantly evolving." Both state and nonstate actors – whether conservative or progressive – have a role to play in defining and influencing it at any given point in time.[24] As a result, governments have no monopoly on determining a country's social values, cultural norms, standards, and national objectives. Space must be provided to allow contestation of prevailing social values and priorities.[25] Distinguishing between a culture's core and contingent elements – a process that will vary across societies and may not necessarily be easy to do – can solve many disputes.[26] But flexibility – which flexible universalism provides – is crucial.

Although it may be surprising to many human rights actors, religion could be a force for promoting human rights. After all, Judaism and Christianity introduced the ideas of individual dignity and equality, laying the groundwork for democracy and human rights.[27] American NGOs with religious ties such as the American Jewish Committee and the Federal Council of Churches of Christ in America played crucial roles in ensuring that human rights were on the agenda of the United Nations in its early years. They successfully lobbied the US delegation to ensure its support for the inclusion of an explicit reference to a commission on human rights in the UN Charter (the only commission so mentioned); the US was able after much effort to get other Great Powers, which were reluctant, to agree.[28] In many parts of the world today, religious actors are on the forefront of the effort to promote human rights and provide crucial services to the poor and marginalized that are underserved or ignored by governments.

A flexible universalist approach that emphasized cross-cultural dialogue and homegrown solutions would significantly strengthen local ownership. Local ownership is the best indicator of human rights' representativeness and essential to ensuring that people everywhere attain their rights and achieve better lives. In contrast, Western universalists risk alienating many countries and communities by adopting narrow, top-down approaches to how rights are

---

[24] Abdullahi Ahmed An-Na'im, "The Cultural Mediation of Human Rights: The Al-Arqam Case in Malaysia," in Bauer and Bell (eds.), *The East Asian Challenge for Human Rights* (Cambridge: Cambridge University Press, 1999), 148.

[25] An-Na'im, "The Cultural Mediation of Human Rights," 149.

[26] Bauer and Bell, "Introduction," 17.

[27] Peter Wehner, "The Christmas Revolution," *The New York Times*, December 25, 2015.

[28] Åshild Samnøy, "The Origins of the Universal Declaration of Human Rights," in Alfreðsson and Eide (eds.), *The Universal Declaration of Human Rights: A Common Standard of Achievement* (The Hague: Martinus Nijhoff Publishers, 1999), 4–5.

interpreted and implemented. The field needs a broader exchange of ideas with less soliloquy, more adaptation to local contexts, and fewer one-size-fits-all models.

INSTITUTION BUILDING AND IMPLEMENTATION

The more each society and community feels that that their values, identities, and traditions are reflected in the human rights framework, the more likely they will make an effort to strengthen the various mechanisms – formal and informal – necessary to promote such rights.[29] Given the great – and growing – diversity in countries and the world at large, any contemporary structure of rules and norms, if it is to be relevant, cannot depend solely on treaties, laws, and the force of the state; it must be nurtured as a matter of common conviction and infuse informal institutions. Only a popular culture of human rights – fostered by the strong political backing and financial resources of indigenous middle classes, diasporas, and powerful regional actors, and encompassing religious actors and even those that sometimes object to some of the ideas related to human rights – can make this possible.[30]

Indeed, in an increasingly multipolar world, international norms and organizations that fail to take into account the context of thick societies in Asia, the Middle East, Africa, and Latin America are likely to become increasingly marginalized.[31] The weakening of Western (American) power means that, as Stephen Hopgood explains,

> In stable states with alternative social and cultural norms that enjoy legitimacy among a sizable proportion of the population, coercion and inducement are likely to be of only limited use while persuasion reaches stalemate against any authority able to effectively invoke an alternative basis for modernization like nationalism or religion. The remaining mechanism is to create local institutions that embed, promote, and legitimate rights – that build local capacity from the inside in other words.[32]

International pressure can still, however, significantly curtail the breadth of choices available to relatively weak actors such as Rwanda (as discussed in

[29] An-Na'im, *Cultural Transformation and Human Rights* in Africa (London: Zed Books, 2002).
[30] Stephen Hopgood, *The Endtimes of Human Rights* (Ithaca, NY: Cornell University Press, 2013), xv, 172, and 181.
[31] Susi Dennison and Anthony Dworkin, "Towards an EU Human Rights Strategy for a Post-Western World," European Council on Foreign Relations Policy Brief, September 21, 2011, www.ecfr.eu/page/-/towards-an-EU-human-rights-strategy-for-a-post-western-world.txt.pdf.
[32] Hopgood, *The Endtimes of Human Rights*, 117.

Chapter 7). Postconflict or less developed countries are especially vulnerable to outside pressure because of their financial and political weaknesses. In such places, government is forced to

> whittle away operational differences between national modalities and these [international] norms ... The end result is the squeezing out of local approaches that are extralegal in nature, as well as those that depart from the methods and modalities dominant internationally ... goals of retribution and general deterrence become injected into local cultures and institutions for which these goals may be neither indigenous nor innate.[33]

Similarly, as discussed in Chapter 6, Western governments and societies are narrowing the breadth of activities that religious institutions and individuals within their territories can do. Hospitals and charities may not be able to run adoption agencies if they want to offer their services only to heterosexual couples. Religious organizations may not be able to operate if they do not offer health coverage that includes abortifacient birth control options. Schools may not be able to open if they do not provide education on certain values or accept people from any background. Jews and Muslims may not be able to live in certain areas if they want to circumcise their children. When institutions are limited in their ability to support minority constituents and accommodate minority beliefs, the result is a net loss for society on many levels. Limits have an homogenizing effect, forcing states and communities to follow Western universalist norms and modalities much more than they might want to if they could formulate responses to their problems based more on local thick society histories and context.[34]

A more balanced approach, especially in less-developed countries with severe ethnic and religious cleavages, would be to prioritize inclusiveness and security over majoritarian democracy and seek incremental change based on the understanding that preserving existing institutions may be the only way to avoid instability. Indeed, at times an overemphasis on human rights can actually lead to conflict. Elections, for example, have triggered violence in many countries. As the Political Instability Task Force concluded, "by far the worst situation in terms of instability were for a political landscape that combined deeply polarized or factionalized competition with open contestation."[35] Trying to overthrow a regime can lead to civil war, as happened in Syria, Libya, Yemen, and Iraq. In these scenarios, Michael Lund suggests,

---

[33] Mark Drumbl, *Atrocity, Punishment, and International Law* (Cambridge: Cambridge University Press, 2007), 121–122.

[34] Drumbl, *Atrocity, Punishment, and International Law*, 70.

[35] Jack Goldstone, Robert Bates, Ted Gurr, and Monty Marshall, "A Global Forecasting Model of Political Instability," paper presented at the annual meeting of the American Political Science

[We must decide] whether our priority in other peoples' countries is to safeguard one of the most fundamental human rights, the right to life – security against physical threats due to social conflict – or to promote civil or other rights, which can lead to disorder and death if the social change is not managed.[36]

Liberal political and economic institutions may not be suitable in all contexts,[37] or demanded by all people, especially given the fact that order and security are the prerequisites for progress. Abraham Lincoln knew that he had to suspend some rights (such as the writ of habeas corpus) during the American Civil War in pursuit of a greater aim: preserving the unity of the state and democracy.[38] Today, liberalizing too fast may unleash communal violence. In countries with weak formal institutions and sharp ethnic, religious, or class cleavages – fragile states – elections and privatization may empower and enrich the most powerful and wealthy actors at the expense of everyone else.[39] Some nondemocratic forms of government may be highly legitimate, as evidenced by the popularity of the Chinese Community Party and other political parties who have defeated colonialism or ended a period of great instability or elite rule and have governed inclusively and effectively enough since to substantially reduce poverty and improve living standards. Singapore, Ethiopia, Rwanda, and Vietnam have similar examples.[40] Select forms of repression may reduce ethnic, religious, or ideological conflict[41] – such as in Malaysia in the 1950s, Singapore in the 1960s,[42] and some Middle Eastern countries today. Balance is essential.

Association, Washington, DC, September 1–4, 2005. See also Goldstone, Bates, et al., "A Global Model for Forecasting Political Instability," *American Journal of Political Science* 54, no. 1 (January 2010): 197.

[36] Michael Lund, "Human Rights: A Source of Conflict, State Making, and State Breaking," in Julie Mertus and Jeffrey Helsing (eds.), *Human Rights and Conflict: Exploring the Links between Rights, Law, and Peacebuilding* (Washington, DC: United States Institute of Peace, 2006), 39–50.

[37] William Galston, *The Practice of Liberal Pluralism* (Cambridge: Cambridge University Press, 2004), 197–198.

[38] Galston, *Liberal Pluralism: The Implications of Value Pluralism for Political Theory and Practice* (Cambridge: Cambridge University Press, 2002), 86–87.

[39] Seth Kaplan, *Fixing Fragile States: A New Paradigm for Development* (Westport, CT: Praeger Security International, 2008); Kaplan, *Betrayed: Politics, Power, and Prosperity* (New York, NY: Palgrave Macmillan, 2013).

[40] Yasuaki Onuma "Towards an Intercivilizational Approach to Human Rights," in Bauer and Bell (eds.), *The East Asian Challenge for Human Rights* (Cambridge: Cambridge University Press, 1999), 105–106.

[41] Galston, *The Practice of Liberal Pluralism*, 197–198.

[42] Daniel Bell, "East Asian Challenge to Human Rights: Reflections on an East West Dialogue," *Human Rights Quarterly* 18, no. 3 (August 1996): 646.

A flexible universalist approach could accordingly place more emphasis on nonstate institutions, especially in thick societies. As discussed in Chapter 4, the state in many countries is not robust enough to play a constructive role in people's lives. On the contrary, it is often a tool of the rich and powerful, used to disadvantage or even disenfranchise marginalized groups and the poor. A majority of the world's governments are unable to effectively protect even the most basic of human rights of many of their people – combined, those populations comprise roughly half or more of the world's population[43] – because of weak capacity, corruption, limited resources, and inadequate diffusion of the ideas. Even though many of these countries have ratified the most important international rights agreements, their governments are often incapable of fulfilling those commitments even if their leaders genuinely want to.

Despite this, Western universalist human rights actors place enormous emphasis on treaties and meetings, and little on building better police forces and judicial systems,[44] or on leveraging intermediate institutions (including families, social networks, social norms, community networks, and religious institutions) to advance their cause. Stronger judicial systems, more law schools, less corrupt security forces, and effective institutions to fight corruption are all essential if the billions of people across the developing world are to see their basic rights protected.[45]

International human rights actors often dismiss local or communal institutions as being inadequate or insufficient without careful study of their effectiveness. This is true even when countries and communities have institutions that can play greater roles promoting human rights. Both Uganda and the Democratic Republic of the Congo, for instance, had functional, if flawed, national courts that could have handled human rights abuses but did not.[46] The atrocities committed had little to do with the leadership of the state and its policies, so the problem of bias was relatively limited.[47] Organizing and adjudicating complex human rights cases could have improved the judicial system, increased awareness of rights within the country, and strengthened protections going forward. But as in the Rwanda case, international human rights organizations preferred to handle the cases

---

[43] Kaplan, *Betrayed: Politics, Power, and Prosperity* (New York, NY: Palgrave Macmillan, 2013), 83–100 and 143–164.
[44] There are some exceptions. See, for instance, the International Justice Mission, http://ijm.org/.
[45] Kaplan, *Betrayed*, 229–245.
[46] Owen Fiss, "Within Reach of the State: Prosecuting Atrocities in Africa," *Human Rights Quarterly* 31, no. 1 (February 2009): 59–69.
[47] Fiss, "Within Reach of the State," 59–69

through international mechanisms, part of "the overwhelming tendency toward internationalization" of African human rights cases.[48]

Similarly, there is ample opportunity to work with faith-based organizations to improve safety (as in both circumcision and female genital surgery), women's rights, healthcare access, and protections for the LGBT community that don't involve the use of punitive state action and compromising religious belief. Western human rights actors generally do very little to build or strengthen local institutions or work with faith-based organizations within the West, even though these institutions have greater influence over how well human rights are protected on a daily basis and the general quality of life than any state actions.

The human rights field would do well to reinvigorate its commitment to complementarity. Complementarity differentiates between what can and should be done locally and what requires a role for international (or national) actors and institutions. Although the principle is clearly written into international human rights agreements such as the Rome Statute, too many international organizations do not utilize the concept in the field, failing to develop the local relationships that it suggests are fundamental to the promotion of human rights.

In the ICC's case (discussed in Chapter 7), its governing statutes state that it can only prosecute crimes that national courts are unwilling or unable to. That is, the international court serves only as a backup for local courts when they are unable to handle their responsibilities.[49] For treaties such as the International Covenant on Civil and Political Rights (ICCPR) and International Covenant on Economic, Social and Cultural Rights (ICESCR), national governments are responsible for ensuring international obligations are met, and they have significant leeway in how they balance and implement their obligations.

Complementarity is a better approach to human rights than internationalization or the promotion of centralized solutions because it is more likely to ensure human rights are implemented in a way befitting local context. It is more likely to strengthen the institutions and actors that matter most to human rights protection on a daily basis. It allows local institutions and processes to play greater roles and puts the emphasis on improving their performance, a goal that undoubtedly would resonate with local people much more than some of the goals of international actors, which often seem far removed from local needs.[50] International organizations would still have an important

---

[48] Ibid.," 59–69.
[49] Clark, "Dilemmas of Justice."
[50] This has been the European experience. See, for instance, European Union, "Complementarity between EC and Member State Policies," September 9, 2007, http://eur-lex.europa.eu/legal-content/EN/TXT/?uri=URISERV:r12005.

role in a system based on complementarity as supporters and developers of local and national institutions and as a backup for when those institutions were unable or unwilling to play their roles. The key is not to force international and local institutions into a conflict-oriented relationship, but to find ways to coordinate and to sequence their activities in a more harmonious manner (something that better fits the approach of those from thick societies).[51] Developing and refining various methodologies to assess and bolster home-grown approaches to improving human rights would ensure that each society's strongest institutions – whether formal, informal, religious, traditional, village-, or clan-based social institutions – were recruited to address the important issues.

EMPIRICAL RESEARCH AND CULTURAL PSYCHOLOGY

Instead of naming and shaming rights violators, the human rights field should focus on identifying a narrower set of evils for which a broad consensus exists across societies. Empirical research can be used to clarify what these evils are, and where thick and thin societies differ.[52] As explored below, this would likely yield three categories of rights: a core set of (category one) rights that nearly all thick and thin societies can support; category two rights for which greater flexibility on prioritization and implementation is necessary and appropriate as support across societies for these is not uniformly strong; and category three rights, around which there is little consensus. By providing an opportunity to clarify minimum standards and margins of appreciation, the research could clear up many misunderstandings and produce fewer confrontations between human rights actors and countries.[53] Though it would highlight the differences that exist across cultures on some rights, it would enable the field to concentrate more thoroughly and systematically on eliminating the core set of evils.

Cultural psychology offers a unique framework and methodology to do this. As mentioned in Chapter 3, it provides an explanatory construct for studying differences in how people think, how societies organize themselves, and how cultures rank values. It can be used to organize empirical studies on human rights and then interpret the results. By helping discern what differences are legitimate and what are simply the products of authoritarian social arrangements or despotic governments, cultural psychology can help

---

[51] Some of these ideas are mentioned in Clark, "Dilemmas of Justice."

[52] Alison Dundes Renteln, *International Human Rights: Universalism versus Relativism* (Newbury Park, CA: Sage Publications, 1990), 11 and 14–15.

[53] For more on margins of appreciation, see Chapter 2.

establish stronger universal minimum standards and devise more balanced methods of evaluating differing priorities across cultures. Coupled with empirical research, it could enable the human rights field to "find a point of view which is universal and culture-independent" by learning to "separate within a culture its idiosyncratic aspects from its universal aspects" and "find 'human nature' within every particular culture" through a "culture-independent analytical framework."[54]

This research would help clarify who speaks for a people in any negotiations over or formulations of human rights to ensure that self-serving leaders and paternalistic figures do not crowd out legitimate alternative voices.[55] The goal should always be to create the strongest moral consensus across and within societies on what are the minimum standards that must be upheld at all times – including if necessary by the use of force and sanction. Such consensuses need to be built among a wide range of actors across a country or region or community and not depend too heavily on those in power – those who will, naturally, have their own interests at stake. Empirical research on "the uses, limits, and social consequences of human rights law," which are currently "relatively undeveloped," would help such efforts as well as clarify what is the appropriate role for human rights in different contexts.[56]

In all cases, it is important to differentiate between the rights that have a significant body of support within a culture (for which advocacy is legitimate) and those that have little or no support except possibly among returnees who have spent a long time exposed to Western ideas (for which advocacy ought to be avoided as much as possible).[57] In the latter case, the rights have, at least at that point in time, insufficient cultural roots to sprout. In contrast, when societies have legitimate internal disagreements on rights – a common occurrence – external advocates can play a constructive role promoting their ideas as long as they act with respect for differences and the right for local people to decide what best fits their needs.

Cultural psychology thus provides both a way for thick society Eastern and Southern countries and religious groups within the West to better articulate and defend their views, challenging and contesting the thin society assumptions of Western universalists in an academically rigorous manner, and for human rights organizations to more strongly press everyone to uphold a core

[54] Anna Wierzbicka, *Cross-Cultural Pragmatics: The Semantics of Human Interaction* (Berlin: Mouton de Gruyler, 1991), 9.
[55] Bauer and Bell, "Introduction," 17; and An-Na'im, "The Cultural Mediation of Human Rights," 148.
[56] Twining, *General Jurisprudence*, 180.
[57] Michael Walzer, interview, Princeton, NJ, January 2017.

set of values and better access the wealth of material on and influence the debates related to human rights within thick societies and groups in order to promote a wider set of rights if they wish.

Cultural psychology also signals – warns – us "how hard pluralism is to actually cultivate, how against the grain of our political and intellectual instincts it tends to cut, and thus how easy it is for a notional commitment to diversity to exclude or pressure exactly those voices that it should be protecting."[58] Indeed, it is ironic that the human rights field promotes tolerance, the acceptance of diversity, and inclusiveness in societies across the world, but "that these standards do not always apply to the discipline of international human rights law itself."[59] This is especially true when it comes to value systems and traditions that don't fit its Western universalist mold.

MORE SYSTEMATIC AND COMPREHENSIVE ASSESSMENTS

The human rights field would also enhance its credibility if it established a more scientific set of standards and procedures based on the UDHR and similar documents such that bias could be removed from its own work. The current approach depends too much on cherry-picking rights to judge, incidents to investigate, and countries to name and shame, sometimes in methodologically unsound ways, as highlighted in Chapter 7. Not only do standards grounded in liberal modernity often trump the legal requirements that countries have signed up for in treaties (or that constitutions may require in domestic cases), but they are applied very unevenly and sometimes even erroneously or unfairly across countries and communities. Context is ignored, broader goals that cannot be articulated with a rights-based approach downplayed, and local solutions undervalued; countries and communities that try to strike a balance between multiple goals in a difficult environment (e.g., conflict or postconflict) are unfairly criticized. "The West maintains control over the language of human rights, and thus over non-Western States and the standards that should be applied to them."[60]

The result is an overemphasis on noncore abuses (e.g., how governments are chosen rather than whether they are legitimate and effective); transparent countries (e.g., Israel receives far more criticism than Saudi Arabia, Syria, or

---

[58] Ross Douthat, "The Challenge of Pluralism," *The New York Times*, March 19, 2014, http://douthat.blogs.nytimes.com/2014/03/19/the-challenge-of-pluralism/.

[59] Rachel Murray, "International Human Rights: Neglect of Perspectives from African Institutions," *The International and Comparative Law Quarterly* 55, no. 1 (January 2006): 193.

[60] Murray, "International Human Rights," 195–196.

Iran); state actors (e.g., any Western country engaged in conflict with non-state actors); and secular goals (e.g., the circumcision case in Chapter 6). By misusing what limited influence and legitimacy they have, human rights institutions have weakened their ability to act against core abuses in many places.

The creation of new rights has not helped. "Unfortunately," as Jacob Mchangama and Guglielmo Verdirame write,

> much of the human rights community has not only shied away from express-ing qualms about rights proliferation, it has often led the process ... When everything can be defined as a human right, the premium on violating such rights is cheap. To raise the stock and ensure the effectiveness of human rights, their defenders need to acknowledge that less is often more.[61]

This proliferation of rights – such as the right to Internet access, a clean environment, and free education through college – allows states to self-select the rights that they support, allowing them to create a "good" human rights record even if they fail to uphold some of the core rights.[62] Research shows that few illiberal states change their behavior just because they have signed a human rights treaty, and such states continue to sign treaties to gain inter-national credibility. The Convention against Torture, for instance, has had little impact on incidents of torture in most authoritarian states.[63]

A rigorous scientific approach would mean more systematic assessments of countries but only on the agreements governments have signed up to (such as the UDHR); human rights organizations would be limited (at least internation-ally) from unilaterally expanding the number of rights they examine. Organiza-tions such as the United Nations Human Rights Council, Human Rights Watch, and Amnesty International (or similar new entities) would concentrate on documenting abuses state by state (and community by community) on a regular basis using clear standards and a demanding methodology; there would be much less ad hoc, case-by-case evaluations with no clear benchmarks, as is the case today.

This would yield a much more nuanced perspective on the role of culture and the particular needs of various communities and societies. It would

---

[61] Jacob Mchangama and Guglielmo Verdirame, "The Danger of Human Rights Proliferation: When Defending Liberty, Less Is More," *Foreign Affairs*, July 24, 2013, www.foreignaffairs.com/articles/139598/jacob-mchangama-and-guglielmo-verdirame/the-danger-of-human-rights-proliferation.

[62] Pedro Pizano, "The Human Rights That Dictators Love," *Foreign Policy*, February 26, 2014, www.foreignpolicy.com/articles/2014/02/26/the_human_rights_that_dictators_love.

[63] Mchangama and Verdirame, "The Danger of Human Rights Proliferation."

recognize that in many cases there is a wide range different practices or actions – only some of which are genuine human rights violations. Labeling them all as such invites the type of negative dynamic – and cultural defense mechanisms – described in Chapter 4.

For instance, in the female genital surgery case mentioned in Chapter 6, there is a long continuum of practices ranging from unsafe and physically damaging to harmless and physically innocent, and, arguably, if a more culture-neutral perspective was used, only those on the unsafe and physically damaging side would be considered a human rights violation. The rest would be acceptable and considered a part of some cultures. Advocates for abolishment could still work to convince groups that use female genital surgery to change their behavior, but not because the practice violated "universal" human rights and not through international sanctions and threats. Instead they could work much as those who encourage people to stop smoking or to eat more nutritiously. There would be disagreements between and within societies on where to draw the line between acceptable and unacceptable practice; negotiations supported by medical experts could forge a consensus on the minimum standard, with some countries introducing stricter rules that stopped short of outlawing the practice if they wanted to.

Many women's issues have similar continuums and complexity. For instance, whereas women's right to education, work, marriage, personal protection, and equality before the law should be universal, there are legitimate differences of opinion across cultures over both women's and men's right to choose what to wear, whom to marry, how to balance family and work, how easily they can leave a marriage, whether they can own property or not (it may be communally or family owned), and the extent of their participation in some aspects of communal leadership (e.g., religious roles). The former are necessary for a person to achieve the minimum requirements to live a life in dignity irrespective of the context. The latter, in contrast, may not be necessary in all cultures to achieve this. Individuals could, for instance, be guaranteed financial security without owning property. They could achieve leadership roles even if they were excluded from some positions. Clothes and roles could differ tremendously and not affect one's dignity and level of respect. Indeed, in some cases, a less modern outfit may enhance one's dignity more than a modern one.[64]

All of this points to the need for greater use of the margin of appreciation doctrine, especially when applied to noncore human rights in thick societies

[64] This is the case for many religious adherents.

and communities. Margins of appreciation could, for instance, be developed for each of the Universal Declaration's rights, possibly with the assistance of empirical research, such that their degree of application is clearer. As a start, an international consensus could be developed through dialogue between countries around whether to assign each a high, medium, or low margin (and what this meant in practice) based on their applicability across thick and thin societies. Table 8.1 offers one illustrative proposal; countries will of course have to make their own determination as the UDHR is open to other interpretations. The greater the margin, the greater the flexibility countries would have. Over time, these could be made more specific (or not) depending on how much consensus there was on the issues.

Such efforts would create a human rights regime that had no or very little margin of appreciation for the first group of rights (the universal core),[65] necessitating fairly uniform application everywhere (there would be scope for differences based on culture as long as they did not threaten the core principle); some margin of appreciation for the rights in the second group, yielding mixed application depending on context; and a wide margin of appreciation for the third group of rights, allowing significant regional or local differences in usage. This categorization would, among other things, help prioritize which rights should take precedence when two or more clash, a common, if not sufficiently acknowledged, occurrence. It would also make more explicit the interdependence of rights, an important legacy of the UDHR that has been mostly forgotten by those working in the field today. This interdependence necessitates making serious trade-offs at times, something the use of margins of appreciation would recognize and facilitate.

Allowances for differences – the margin of appreciation – across societies should be greater than that within a single society, where there will always be a larger need to encourage social cohesion and a common overarching identity across diverse groups. In the latter case, although it is certainly better to err on the side of flexible universalism, there will still be a greater need to promote certain rights that may not exist in minority cultures and would not be forced upon other countries (e.g., the right to own property and change religion).

A more systematic approach to developing margins of appreciation and assessing countries would fit nicely with and complement the cultural psychology-based empirical research suggested earlier. In fact, the two would go hand in hand. Both argue for a more methodologically sound approach to human rights: one in how rights are identified and categorized, the other in

---

[65] Mary Ann Glendon, *A World Made New: Eleanor Roosevelt and the Universal Declaration of Human Rights* (New York, NY: Random House, 2001), 230.

TABLE 8.1 *Proposal for margins of appreciation of the UDHR's 30 rights*

Clause	Right	Margin of Appreciation
Article 1	Right to Equality	No
Article 2	Freedom from Discrimination	No
Article 3	Right to Life, Liberty, Personal Security	No
Article 4	Freedom from Slavery	No
Article 5	Freedom from Torture and Degrading Treatment	No
Article 6	Right to Recognition as a Person before the Law	No
Article 7	Right to Equality before the Law	No
Article 8	Right to Remedy by Competent Tribunal	No
Article 9	Freedom from Arbitrary Arrest and Exile	No
Article 10	Right to Fair Public Hearing	Low
Article 11	Right to be Considered Innocent until Proven Guilty	No
Article 12	Freedom from Interference with Privacy, Family, Home, and Correspondence	Low
Article 13	Right to Free Movement in and out of the Country	Medium
Article 14	Right to Asylum in other Countries from Persecution	Medium
Article 15	Right to a Nationality and the Freedom to Change It	Low
Article 16	Right to Marriage and Family	Medium
Article 17	Right to Own Property	Medium
Article 18	Freedom of Belief and Religion	Low
Article 19	Freedom of Opinion and Information	Medium
Article 20	Right of Peaceful Assembly and Association	Medium
Article 21	Right to Participate in Government and in Free Elections	High
Article 22	Right to Social Security	High
Article 23	Right to Desirable Work and to Join Trade Unions	High
Article 24	Right to Rest and Leisure	Low
Article 25	Right to Adequate Living Standard	High
Article 26	Right to Education	Low
Article 27	Right to Participate in the Cultural Life of Community	Low
Article 28	Right to a Social Order that Articulates this Document	Low
Article 29	Community Duties Essential to Free and Full Development	Medium
Article 30	Freedom from State or Personal Interference in the above Rights	Low

how country and community performance is assessed. Together they might put the whole human rights field on a much firmer basis, with fewer flashpoints for cultural based criticism.

TOWARD A HIERARCHY OF RIGHTS

A flexible universalist human rights regime with robustly enforced core rights – and three categories of rights in all, as suggested by liberal pluralism – has the best chance to both advance the human condition and achieve a worldwide consensus, especially if decisions on which rights go into which categories are made through intercultural dialogue with the idea of a global project in mind. The first category of rights – those with no or very little margin of appreciation – would be backed by a much stronger global consensus and ideally a formal mechanism (through a treaty, as outlined later) to systematically assess and penalize countries that did not uphold them; the second category of rights would have clear minimum standards, but ample margins of appreciation, giving countries substantial discretion over their policies; the third category of rights would provide maximum flexibility for diverse approaches. The combination would create a stronger minimum universalism than exists today, and it would be less contentious than the current regime.

In order to highlight how such a system would work, the following breakdown suggests which rights might go into which categories. A hierarchy of rights that fairly represents both thick and thin societies, however, must be developed by the various stakeholders through the fourfold approach described earlier.

Although both thick and thin societies may condemn acts against what Michael Walzer, professor emeritus at the Institute for Advanced Study in Princeton, calls the "minimal and universal moral code,"[66] they may disagree over certain aspects of criminal law, family law, social and economic rights, minority rights, and legitimate political processes.[67] Gross human rights violations, such as murder, wife beating, slavery, torture, genocide, and the like are treated the same, but things like circumcision, dress codes, communal obligations, and the balance between restorative and retributive justice and economic and political rights may be treated differently.

[66] Walzer, *Interpretation and Social Criticism* (Cambridge, MA: Harvard University Press, 1987), 24.
[67] Bell, "East Asian Challenge to Human Rights," 642.

Although there is no objective standard for what makes a right fundamental, "we are structured to experience certain phenomena as great evils to be avoided at virtually all cost."[68] A consensus can be forged through empirical research[69] and negotiations that build upon existing agreements that have widespread legitimacy, such as the UDHR. After all, "diversity does not preclude the possibility that there may be convergence in the many moral systems of the world."[70]

"Despite their apparent peculiarities and diversity," human societies share many core moral principles, especially nowadays; many "fundamental interests, concerns, qualities, traits, and values ... can be identified and articulated."[71] Human sacrifice, for instance, might have been acceptable in many cultures at one point in time, but it is considered a great evil across the world today. Only extraordinary conditions – such as those facing groups living in the Arctic, stranded on a boat, lost in the desert, or in the midst of a great famine – are likely to produce exceptions to this broad consensus. Those that violate this consensus – by, for example, indiscriminately killing prisoners of war or launching suicide bombers on civilian populations – are generally condemned.

Even though the first category of rights would require the greatest commitment from countries, it ought to be the least controversial.[72] Many human rights treaties already have, in fact, a set of legally binding *notstandfeste*: nonderogable or emergency-proof rights.[73] In discussions during the drafting of several human

---

[68] Galston, *The Practice of Liberal Pluralism*, 7.

[69] Renteln calls this "empirical universalism." Renteln, *International Human Rights*, 11 and 14–15.

[70] Renteln, *International Human Rights*, 139.

[71] Abdullahi Ahmed An-Na'im, "Toward a Cross-Cultural Approach to Defining International Standards of Human Rights: The Meaning of Cruel, Inhuman, or Degrading Treatment or Punishment," in An-Na'im (ed.), *Human Rights in Cross-Cultural Perspectives: A Quest for Consensus* (Philadelphia, PA: University of Pennsylvania, 1992), 21.

[72] This is not to say that determining the list of core human rights is anything but a "thorny problem." Teraya Koji, "Emerging Hierarchy in International Human Rights and Beyond: From the Perspective of Non-derogable Rights," *European Journal of International Law* 12, no. 5 (2001): 917–941.

[73] There are great similarities across documents, but the lists of nonderogable rights are not all the same. See, as a good example, Article 4 of the International Covenant on Civil and Political Rights (ICCPR): "1. In time of public emergency which threatens the life of the nation and the existence of which is officially proclaimed, the States Parties to the present Covenant may take measures derogating from their obligations under the present Covenant to the extent strictly required by the exigencies of the situation, provided that such measures are not inconsistent with their other obligations under international law and do not involve discrimination solely on the ground of race, colour, sex, language, religion or social origin. 2. No derogation from articles 6, 7, 8 (paragraphs I and 2), 11, 15, 16 and 18 may be made under this provision." UN

rights treaties, representatives referred to these as "fundamental" and *"essential au respect de nous-mêmes."*[74] Academic works have called them "the most basic human rights," "core rights," "irreducible core," "sacrosanct rights," and *"les droits fondamentaux reserves."*[75]

The bedrock of this group would be protections against genocide; slavery; torture; cruel, inhuman, or degrading treatment or punishment; retroactive penal measures; deportation or forcible transfer of population; and discrimination based on race, color, sex, language, religion, or social origin.[76] This list could be expanded through intercultural dialogue and negotiations.[77] Of course, these rights would have to be better defined, as interpretations vary (e.g., women's rights, inhuman punishment, religious discrimination). Margins of appreciation should be zero or very limited.

Beyond this core are categories two and three. Determining which rights go into which category would surely be contentious. In addition, determining margins of appreciation for the rights in category two is likely to be difficult; there are substantial differences in opinion about their importance and implementation, especially between thick and thin societies. The former, as noted

General Assembly, *International Covenant on Civil and Political Rights*, December 16, 1966, 2200A (XXI), available at: www.ohchr.org/en/professionalinterest/pages/ccpr.aspx.

[74] See, for example, Council of Europe, *Collected Edition of the 'Travaux Préparatoires,'* Volume VI (Dordrecht; Boston; Lancaster: Martinus Nijhoff, 1985), 78–81 and 126–129.

[75] See, for example, Thomas Buergenthal, "The American and European Convention on Human Rights: Similarities and Differences," *The American University Law Review* 30 (1980–1981): 165; A. H. Robertson, "Humanitarian Law and Human Rights," in C. Swinarski (ed.), *Études et essais sur le droit international humanitaire et sur les principes de la Croix-Rouge en l'honneur de Jean Pictet / Studies and Essays on International Humanitarian Law and Red Cross Principles in Honour of Jean Pictet* (Geneva: CICR/Martinus Nijhoff, 1984), 798; Aristidis S. Calogeropoulos-Stratis, *Droit humanitaire et droits de l'homme* (Dordrecht: Springer Netherlands, 1981), 130. Koji discusses the issue at length in Koji, "Emerging Hierarchy in International Human Rights and Beyond."

[76] Ilia Siatitsa and Maia Titberidze, "Human Rights in Armed Conflict from the Perspective of the Contemporary State Practice in the United Nations: Factual Answers to Certain Hypothetical Challenges," ADH Genève Research Paper, 2011. In the UDHR, the nonderogable rights are the strict restrictions on torture, enslavement, degrading punishment, and discrimination. See Chapter 2. Fundamental rights also should include protections against atrocities such as those committed against civilians during the Sierra Leone civil war (1991–2002): "abduction, amputation, arbitrary detention, assault/beating, destruction of property, drugging, extortion, forced cannibalism, forced displacement, forced labor, forced recruitment, killing, looting, physical torture, rape, sexual abuse, and sexual slavery." The Truth and Reconciliation Commission of Sierra Leone identified these seventeen violations. Paul Williams, *War and Conflict in Africa* (Cambridge: Polity Press, 2011), 51.

[77] Some candidates for inclusion include the right to life; marriage; fair access to citizenship; protection against arbitrary searches, arrest, imprisonment, and confiscation; and equal protection of laws and procedures of fair trial.

earlier, generally prioritizes communal cohesion and economic rights over individual and political rights while the latter does the reverse.

The second category would have to be much smaller than Western universalists would want in order to achieve consensus, as Figure 8.1 portrays. It would include the right to education; travel; choice of profession; association; disposing of personal property; religious, intellectual, and expressive freedom; free political speech; marriage and family; equality before the law; freedom from arbitrary arrest; a fair public hearing; freedom from interference with privacy, family, home, and correspondence; and other rights listed in the UDHR, the International Covenant on Civil and Political Rights (ICCPR), International Covenant on Economic, Social and Cultural Rights (ICESCR), and other existing international treaties but not included in category one. More could be added over time through dialogue and negotiation. Defining what minimum standards and the relatively large margins of appreciation are would be an arduous task given the great differences between countries, but not impossible, especially given the fact that assessment and enforcement regimes would have very limited powers of intervention; the existing human rights infrastructure could be expanded to ensure countries were examined much more systematically and scientifically but pressure for change would still depend very much on moral persuasion as is the case today.

The third category would include rights for which there is no or only a limited global consensus, such as the right to privacy, same-sex marriage, own land, welfare, work, housing, birth (the right to not be aborted), euthanasia, care as an elderly person, and any other rights that don't fall into the other two categories.[78] Although differences do appear among thin societies and among thick societies (e.g., over gun rights), they are likely to be much greater between thin and thick societies. Certain social differences that are, for instance, seen as discriminatory in most thin societies may not be so in many or even most thick societies and communities, where they may be seen as essential.[79] Some rights highly prioritized in thin societies may only draw puzzlement in thick societies (e.g., same-sex marriage, the right to die) and vice versa (e.g., the right to be born, the right of the elderly to be taken care of by their children).[80] A global consensus on these rights could only be achieved

---

[78] Galston divides rights between those everyone agrees upon (my categories one and two) and those where there are disagreements (my category three) in Galston, "Between Philosophy and History: The Evolution of Rights in American Thought," in Robert Licht (ed.), *Old Rights and New* (Washington, DC: The AEI Press, 1993), 68–70.

[79] Taylor, "Conditions of an Unforced Consensus on Human Rights," 139.

[80] Licht, "Introduction," in Licht (ed.), *Old Rights and New*, 14–15; Galston, "Between Philosophy and History," 68–70.

if margins of appreciation were very large, and some states would probably prefer to have no agreement than such a limited one. As such, no strong consensus is likely to be reached on these rights, and only some countries would seek to maintain them (e.g., gay marriage, right to be born).

This hierarchy of rights would certainly not please everyone – not least Western universalists – but it would do much to forge a consensus around and promote a set of universal minimum standards and margins of appreciation – flexible universalism – for human rights across the globe. It would garner wide support across both thick and thin societies, whether they are based in the North, South, West, or East, and whether they are religious or secular. The result would be more representative and seen as a legitimate reflection of global human aspirations, and thus as a universal human project, than the existing human rights regime. It would function much better than the existing reservation system, which allows individual countries to participate in the rights regime while distancing themselves from particular issues, but provides no mechanism to ascertain how important those reservations are nor to judge the validity of their policies. Under the scheme outlined here, some reservations (mainly for the first category of rights) might be disqualified.

The four elements of flexible universalism explored earlier in this chapter would, when combined, help in developing this hierarchy of rights. The result would foster greater consensus *and* make possible the implementation of stronger controls on the core human rights. The latter could include more invasive inspections, such as those conducted in weapons control regimes, and more automatic penalties, such as the sanctions introduced by the UN or particular states from time to time.[81] Ideally it would be formalized in a global treaty, as discussed below.

A NEW GLOBAL HUMAN RIGHTS REGIME: A RETURN TO BASICS

A flexible universalist approach based on the principles originally laid out in the UDHR (and other documents that have wide legitimacy, such as the ICESCR, ICCPR, and Vienna Declaration) will bridge the growing chasm between thick and thin societies and should allow East, West, North, South,

---

[81] START I between the United States and the Soviet Union, for instance, used an "intrusive verification regime that involved on-site inspections, the regular exchange of information, including telemetry, and the use of national technical means (i.e., satellites)." Obviously a human rights regime would have to use different mechanisms but the principles would be similar. See the Arms Control Association, "U.S.-Russian Nuclear Arms Control Agreements at a Glance," April 1, 2014, www.armscontrol.org/factsheets/USRussiaNuclearAgreements March2010.

secular, and religious to cooperate on further universalizing these core human rights. It will thus restore the overlapping consensus that once existed on human rights.

Human rights advocates need to recognize that ideas and institutions inevitably change when they expand or move to new cultures, transforming some of the original characteristics in order to be accepted and effectively used.[82] Local contestation over priorities is a normal part of how societies evolve. These processes mean that only rights that have wide backing across different cultures are sustainable longer-term, at least internationally, where the writ of Western universalist actors is receding. (In intrasociety conflicts within the West, governments backed by solid majorities can, of course, always enforce laws despite strong opposition.)

There therefore ought to be a strong incentive for human rights actors to seek a political solution with Southern governments and important societal actors through negotiation and compromise with the idea of building stronger global norms. As Walzer argues, "Politics must sometimes substitute for justice, providing a neutral frame within which a common life slowly develops," and producing "negotiated" rather than "imposed" ways of living.[83] This democratization of human rights would allow for greater local interpretation and cross-cultural consensus – and make human rights much more legitimate worldwide.[84] This does not mean that there would never be interventions in the internal affairs of associations and groups at home or how governments operate abroad – as the following proposal for a stronger regime to protect category one rights would certainly allow – but that they would be done only with extreme caution and restraint, without the presumption that human rights actors know best, even when there is a divergence from their general principles.[85] Instead of a hard approach that uses trade privileges, foreign aid, access to government contracts, fines, and jail time to promote noncore human rights (from category two or three), the focus should be on a softer approach that seeks to nurture or embed the concepts behind the rights in the local culture. In some cases, this will succeed. In others, it will not.

A flexible universalist approach is more likely to foster a robust consensus for category one rights, especially the handful prioritized by the drafters of the UDHR and identified through empirical research. It would do this partly by

---

[82] Onuma, "Towards an Intercivilizational Approach to Human Rights," 112.
[83] Walzer, "'Spheres of Justice': An Exchange," *The New York Review of Books*, July 21, 1983, www.nybooks.com/articles/1983/07/21/spheres-of-justice-an-exchange/.
[84] Hopgood, *The Endtimes of Human Rights*, xv and 118.
[85] Galston, *Liberal Pluralism*, 9.

emphasizing less the newer Western universalist interpretations and additions to the original compendium of rights. This would reduce the risk of human rights inflation sapping broad political support, as discussed earlier in this chapter and in Chapter 2. By concentrating on building a strong and forceful global consensus on the need to protect a few practical norms (category one rights) and to promote in a much more flexible manner a broader set of concepts (category two rights) this return to basics approach should have relatively little difficulty gaining deep support from a wide set of people who normally are far apart in their philosophical and cultural outlook.[86] It would not end debates over rights – these are inevitable – but would bring more of them under the rubric of the rights regime, reducing attacks on and strengthening the legitimacy of it in the process.

The strong consensus on category one rights should ideally be used to forge a new global treaty that focused exclusively on a narrow set of "great evils of the human condition"[87] – equally recognized across both thick and thin societies (see Figure 8.1) – with a robust enforcement mechanism that went well beyond anything in existence today. A clear and decisive agreement across cultures on what are the most important human rights – a "minimal universalism" – would more likely prompt action when those rights are violated, enabling all humans to live with "basic decency."[88] As William Galston argues,

> A politics that does everything within reason to ward off or abolish the great evils of the human condition, while allowing as much space as possible for the enactment of diverse but genuine human goods is probably the best we can hope for, or even imagine. In any event, it would represent a significant improvement for the vast majority of the human race.[89]

---

[86] Contrast the approach introduced here with what Donnelly wrote in 1984: "Universality may take the form of a large common core with relatively few differences 'around the edges'. It may involve strong statistical regularities, in which outliers are few and are clearly overshadowed by the central tendency. There may be clusterings, or lesser but still significant overlaps, that allow us to speak of 'universality' in a very extended sense. And if we distinguish between 'major' and 'minor' rights, we might have still another sort of universality amidst substantive diversity: The definition of such categories is of course extremely controversial, but to the extent that variations in substance are concentrated among 'minor' rights, a fundamental universality would be retained." Jack Donnelly, "Cultural Relativism and Universal Human Rights," *Human Rights Quarterly* 6, no. 4 (November 1984): 405.

[87] Galston, *The Practice of Liberal Pluralism*, 7.

[88] Ibid., 3.

[89] Galston, *Liberal Pluralism*, 131–132.

This commitment to a minimal universalism would go far toward creating a supra-cultural human rights framework that transcended culture and reached into some natural essence of humanity.[90]

A new global treaty on the core rights would, however, challenge the sovereignty of countries in a way that would be politically difficult to accept, especially for countries such as the United States, China, and Russia. Even if major powers resisted, European countries could take the lead, hoping to achieve what international agreements such as the Anti-Personnel Mine Ban Convention (often referred to as the Mine Ban Treaty) did: an incomplete formal and mostly complete informal global consensus on a great evil that needed to be eliminated;[91] it has been ratified by a growing majority of countries and changed the norm by which military action is judged, though it lacks any formal means to monitor and penalize countries, and is thus only a partial solution.

None of this would prevent thin societies from expanding their sets of rights. In fact, it might encourage it by reducing the need to gain consensus with thick societies and communities. The latter would be able to opt out without affecting their overall relationship with those who opted in. This has already happened in the European Union, which allowed some countries to partially opt-out of the Charter of Fundamental Rights of the European Union in 2007, as part of the Treaty of Lisbon, in order to reach an agreement on it.[92] This example shows how even thin societies differ on some rights.

Globally, a focus on regional solutions is likely to be much more productive than a search for universal answers given the growing gap between thick and

[90] Joseph Prabhu, "Human Rights and Cross-Cultural Dialogue," *Religion and Culture Web Forum*, The Martin Marty Centre, University of Chicago Divinity School, April 2006. Federico Lenzerini emphasizes "foundational universalism," a minimum set of absolute rights that every person – with no exceptions – are entitled to. Lenzerini, *The Culturalization of Human Rights Law* (Oxford: Oxford University Press, 2014), 213–244.

[91] As of November 2014, there were 162 States Parties to the "Convention on the Prohibition of the Use, Stockpiling, Production and Transfer of Anti-Personnel Mines and on Their Destruction." Even though countries such as China, India, Pakistan, Russia, and the United States have not joined, there is consistent international pressure on any use of such mines. For more information, see the Landmine and Cluster Munition Monitor website, www.the-monitor.org/en-gb/home.aspx.

[92] Poland was concerned about social issues (e.g., gay marriage). The United Kingdom was concerned about the costs of doing business (e.g., labor laws). See, for instance, Mark Beunderman, "Poland to Join UK in EU Rights Charter Opt-out," *EUobserver*, September 7, 2009, https://euobserver.com/institutional/24723; "No EU Rights Charter for Poland," *BBC News*, November 23, 2007, http://news.bbc.co.uk/2/hi/europe/7109528.stm; British House of Commons Select Committee on European Scrutiny, "European Union Intergovernmental Conference," Thirty-Fifth Report, October 2, 2007, www.publications.parliament.uk/pa/cm200607/cmselect/cmeuleg/1014/101403.htm.

thin societies.[93] Different regions could promote rights that they deemed important (e.g., rights of the elderly, indigenous people, migrants, etc.) in a culture-specific manner, with appropriate forms of regional enforcement of minimal standards.

In the United States, individual states could be granted much more flexibility on controversial noncore issues. Some would argue that the country's federal system and ample legal protections for religious freedom already do this,[94] but courts have often applied a very Western universalist interpretation of rights,[95] preventing the populations in individual states from making their own choices.[96] In all thin societies, a similar approach could be selectively applied domestically to allow institutions, such as religious organizations, schools, communities, and closely held companies, more freedom of practice on issues such as circumcision, gay marriage, education, healthcare, etc.[97]

THE LIMITS OF RIGHTS

Although establishing a consensus on a hierarchy of rights and putting into place a stronger enforcement mechanism for a globally accepted set of core rights are essential, we must also remember that human flourishing depends on much more than an environment "structured by the concept and practice

---

[93] In fact, despite appearances to the contrary at times, "most processes of so-called 'globalisation' take place at sub-global levels." Values are more likely to be similar across countries with broadly similar backgrounds than those with extremely different pasts. Twining, *General Jurisprudence*, xviii.

[94] Chief Justice John Roberts made this very point in his Supreme Court dissent to *Obergefell v. Hodges*, the landmark case on same-sex marriage. He argued that "our Constitution does not enact any one theory of marriage. The people of a State are free to expand marriage to include same-sex couples, or to retain the historic definition." Ryan Anderson, "Symposium: Judicial Activism on Marriage Causes Harm: What Does the Future Hold?," *SCOTUSblog*, June 26, 2015, www.scotusblog.com/2015/06/symposium-ryan-anderson/.

[95] The handling of religious freedom can act as a proxy here. See the discussion and references in Chapter 6.

[96] Chief Justice Roberts argued in *Obergefell v. Hodges* that "Supporters of same-sex marriage have achieved considerable success persuading their fellow citizens – through the democratic process – to adopt their view. That ends today. Five lawyers have closed the debate and enacted their own vision of marriage as a matter of constitutional law. Stealing this issue from the people will for many cast a cloud over same-sex marriage, making a dramatic social change that much more difficult to accept." Anderson, "Symposium: Judicial Activism on Marriage Causes Harm."

[97] For an exposition on the importance of federalism and subsidiarity in a time of growing individualism and diversity, see Yuval Levin, *The Fractured Republic: Renewing America's Social Contract in the Age of Individualism* (New York, NY: Basic Books, 2016).

of rights." Such a focus limits our ability to "concern ourselves with the full range of influences on the formation of character in liberal societies."[98] This is both because "societies wholly preoccupied with claiming and exercising rights cannot provide scope for a fully rounded and worthy human existence"[99] and because the rights themselves depend on the values, attitudes, and institutions that permeate a society. Indeed, the seeming victory of secular liberalism within the West has not come without a price: by setting progress and choice as the best barometers of human flourishing, the West has reduced the role of wisdom in determining value, what it means to be human, and what human beings ought to achieve.[100]

Of the three obstacles that stand between a person and his or her goals and idea of a good life – (1) individuals standing in the way, (2) a lack of external goods (schools, legal systems, etc.), and (3) internal weaknesses of character or mind – rights are only helpful in two cases (1 and 2) and only the best protection in one case (1). Institutions and sentiments of social solidarity are at least as important as rights in providing external goods (2). Families and communities are by far the biggest influence on an individual's personal development (3).[101]

Human rights are, as Onuma Yasuaki, Professor of International Law at the University of Tokyo, has argued, a tool to realizing the spiritual and material well-being of humanity, and not a series of end goals in isolation. As such, they need to be evaluated on their merits and demerits and constantly scrutinized for how they can be more useful to achieve these aims. Otherwise, absolutism risks undermining their legitimacy and influence.[102]

Rights cannot do justice to virtues or acts that exceed or transcend their particular gamut. They do not take into account intrinsically valuable goods that are collective rather than individual; undervalue moral categories that are not based on rights exclusively; do not provide an adequate role for responsibilities, duties, and virtues; and ignore the important contribution of institutions and associations not structured by rights.[103] A rights-based

---

[98] Robert Licht, "Introduction," in Licht (ed.), *Old Rights and New* (Washington, DC: The AEI Press, 1993), 15.

[99] Galston, "Between Philosophy and History: The Evolution of Rights in American Thought," in Licht (ed.), *Old Rights and New* (Washington, DC: The AEI Press, 1993), 73.

[100] David Bentley Hart, *Atheist Delusion: The Christian Revolution and Its Fashionable Enemies* (New Haven, CT: Yale University Press, 2009), 236.

[101] Galston, "Between Philosophy and History," 73.

[102] Onuma "Towards an Intercivilizational Approach to Human Rights," 123.

[103] Joseph Raz, "Right-Based Moralities," in Jeremy Waldron (ed.), *Theories of Rights* (Oxford: Oxford University Press, 1984), 182–200; William Galston, "Between Philosophy and History:

approach to achieving the good life is, in some ways, ethnocentric, as it assumes that no other ways of living can be as good if they don't provide a role for rights. And although human rights excel at removing obstacles to the good life, by not differentiating between "liberty and license" and setting standards for individuals to aspire to, they have proven inadequate in promoting worthy acts that have a "correctness or appropriateness" to them.[104] A singular focus on rights encourages people to aggressively make claims on society while disregarding or de-emphasizing their responsibilities. It encourages self-centered behavior, promotes social conflict, and weakens the trust and social glue that holds societies together.[105] None of this means that a focus on rights is wrong, just that it is incomplete. Rather, what is called for, as Joseph Raz argues, is a "pluralistic understanding of the foundation of morality" in which rights, duties, and intrinsic values are equally important.[106]

Liberalism's future is very much tied to the promotion of some sense of responsibility, duty, and virtue, as well as the social institutions such as family, community, and religion that nurture these but are not "structured by the concept and practice of rights."[107] After all, "healthy political association requires a kind of sharing – not only agreement on common purposes, but also a network of affective ties."[108] Healthy institutions – which underpin the whole rights regime – similarly depend on the trust and common allegiance that a strong focus on individual autonomy can weaken.[109] To advance these, some individual rights may have to be curtailed, modified, or even suspended in some contexts in order to create the most effective total system to advance a community's overall goals (only some of which will involve rights) and to maximize the exercise of rights over the long term.[110] "Because individuals are partly constituted in and through relationships with others, a liberal politics dedicated to full and free human development cannot afford to ignore the

The Evolution of Rights in American Thought," in Licht (ed.), *Old Rights and New*, 65 and 73.

[104] Galston, "Between Philosophy and History," 65 and 74.

[105] Charles Taylor, "Conditions of an Unforced Consensus on Human Rights," in Bauer and Bell (eds.), *The East Asian Challenge for Human Rights* (Cambridge: Cambridge University Press, 1999), 130.

[106] Raz, "Right-Based Moralities," 182.

[107] Galston, "Between Philosophy and History," 73.

[108] Ibid., 59–60.

[109] Taylor, "Conditions of an Unforced Consensus on Human Rights," 130.

[110] Galston, "Between Philosophy and History," 64.

settings that are most conducive to the fulfillment of that ideal."[111] Indeed, a "regime of rights is incomplete without and depends upon a sense of mutual connection and shared fate among all members of the community."[112]

Liberal politics – and, as mentioned earlier, any international human rights regime – also depends on compromise and popular support, both of which are threatened by an overemphasis on rights.[113] "As the zone of individual rights expands, the space for popular determination of policy contracts."[114] Fred Siegel summarizes this argument:

> Democratic politics ideally revolves around the compromises needed to secure widespread consent for government actions. Representative government, which encourages citizen participation, leaves the losers in a political context with part of what they asked for or at least a feeling that their interests were considered. A judicialized politics, in contrast, bypasses public consent. Profoundly anti-democratic when it goes beyond vindicating the fundamental rights of citizenship, judicial politics alienates voters by placing public policy in the private hands of lawyers and litigants. And since rights are absolute, it polarizes by producing winner-take-all outcomes, in which the losers are likely to feel embittered ... [Moreover,] the assertion of rights fences off the proponents of policies from the social costs those policies impose on the public at large.[115]

IMPROVING LIVES

A flexible universalism that recognizes and addresses the practical challenges of implementing rights and improving lives on the ground, far removed from debates engaged in the media and by elites, would help more people. Rooted in liberal pluralism, it would combine the best elements of natural and positive law, reduce the scope for critics to claim it was biased, and give organizations and individuals working in communities more influence. It would consequently accommodate the needs of both thick and thin societies and make human rights more centered on the people it aims to help.

[111] Mary Ann Glendon, *Rights Talk: The Impoverishment of Political Discourse* (New York, NY: The Free Press, 1991), 137.
[112] Galston, "Between Philosophy and History," 59–60.
[113] Twining, *General Jurisprudence*, 184–185.
[114] Galston, "Between Philosophy and History," 57.
[115] Fred Siegel, "Nothing in Moderation," *The Atlantic* 265 (May 1990): 108–109.

Indeed, for most poor people around the world, it is not the absence of laws that most trouble them, but the everyday violence, discrimination, and corruption that oppress them – despite what the law says. One in five women around the world is a victim of rape or attempted rape.[116] Over 30 million people are held in slavery.[117] In both cases, the actions are illegal but few are prosecuted for their crimes. In fact, four billion people around the world – over half the global population – lack access to equitable justice systems. In many places, the greatest threats to the poor emanate not from a lack of laws but from their country's own police forces, courts, and criminal justice systems.[118] Making these systems more equitable and effective – and making societies more inclusive – would do more to help the world's poor than any new law, though the latter is also necessary in many places. The effort to put into practice human rights is "occurring in the real-life struggles of people to achieve basic dignity and human security, and is taking the forms of education, people-initiated legal and social reforms, and indigenous NGOs" around the world.[119]

Ultimately, successful human rights promotion depends on attention to thick society factors – the relationships and institutions within which individuals, families, and communities are embedded. As Eleanor Roosevelt said, documents expressing ideals "carry no weight unless the people know them, unless the people understand them, unless the people demand that they be lived."[120] And these, as she said in one of her last speeches at the UN, depend on implementation in lots and lots of "small places."

> Where, after all, do universal human rights begin? In small places, close to home – so close and so small that they cannot be seen on any map of the

---

[116] United Nations Secretary-General's Campaign – Unite to End Violence against Women, "Violence against Women," Fact Sheet, UN Department of Public Information, February 2008, www.un.org/en/women/endviolence/pdf/VAW.pdf.

[117] Walk Free Foundation, *The Global Slavery Index 2014*, Dalkeith, Australia, 2014, www.globalslaveryindex.org.

[118] Gary Haugen and Victor Boutros, *The Locust Effect: Why the End of Poverty Requires the End of Violence* (Oxford: Oxford University Press, 2014).

[119] Bauer and Bell, "Introduction," 22.

[120] Eleanor Roosevelt, "Making Human Rights Come Alive," in Allida Black (ed.), *What I Hope to Leave Behind: The Essential Essays of Eleanor Roosevelt* (Brooklyn, NY: Carlson, 1995), 559. Also see the advice Roosevelt gives on how to "know the Declaration" in an interview with Howard Langer on the record, Roosevelt, *Human Rights: A Documentary on the United Nations Declaration of Human Rights* (Folkways Records, 1958), www.folkways.si.edu/eleanor-roosevelt/a-documentary-on-the-united-nations-declaration-of-human-rights/world-history/album/smithsonian. I found these sources in Glendon, *A World Made New*, xix and footnote on 243–244.

world. Yet they are the world of the individual person; the neighborhood he lives in; the school or college he attends; the factory, farm or office where he works. Such are the places where every man, woman, and child seeks equal justice, equal opportunity, equal dignity without discrimination. Unless these rights have meaning there, they have little meaning anywhere.[121]

---

[121] Roosevelt, remarks at presentation of booklet on human rights, *In Your Hands*, to the United Nations Commission on Human Rights, United Nations, New York, March 27, 1958, United Nations typescript of statements at presentation (microfilm).

Bibliography

Adler, Hans, and Wulf Koepke, eds. *A Companion to the Works of Johann Gottfried Herder*. Rochester, NY: Camden House, 2009.

Akumu, Patience. "'African Culture' Is the Biggest Threat to the Women's Rights Movement." *African Arguments*, March 9, 2015, http://africanarguments.org/2015/03/09/african-culture-is-the-biggest-threat-to-the-womens-rights-movement-by-patience-akumu/.

Alatas, Syed Farid. *Alternative Discourses in Asian Social Science: Responses to Eurocentrism*. New Delhi: Sage, 2006.

Alfreðsson, Gudmunder, and Asbjørn Eide. "Introduction." In *The Universal Declaration of Human Rights: A Common Standard of Achievement*, ed. Gudmunder Alfreðsson and Asbjørn Eide, xxv–xxxv. The Hague: Martinus Nijhoff Publishers, 1999.

    eds. *The Universal Declaration of Human Rights: A Common Standard of Achievement*. The Hague: Martinus Nijhoff Publishers, 1999.

Alter, Karen, James Thuo Gathii, and Laurence Helfer. "Backlash against International Courts in West, East and Southern Africa: Causes and Consequences." iCourts Working Paper Series, No. 21; Duke Law School Public Law & Legal Theory Series, May 12, 2015.

American Anthropological Association Executive Board. "Statement on Human Rights." *American Anthropologist* 49, no. 4, part 1 (October–December 1947): 539–543.

Amnesty International. "Rwanda – Gacaca: A Question of Justice." AI Index AFR 47/007/2002, December 17, 2002.

Andreassen, Bård Anders. "Article 22." In *The Universal Declaration of Human Rights: A Common Standard of Achievement*, ed. Gudmunder Alfreðsson and Asbjørn Eide, 453–488. The Hague: Martinus Nijhoff Publishers, 1999.

An-Na'im, Abdullahi Ahmed. "Toward a Cross-Cultural Approach to Defining International Standards of Human Rights: The Meaning of Cruel, Inhuman, or Degrading Treatment or Punishment." In *Human Rights in Cross-Cultural Perspectives: A Quest for Consensus*, ed. Abdullahi Ahmed An-Na'im, 19–43. Philadelphia, PA: University of Pennsylvania Press, 1992.

"The Cultural Mediation of Human Rights: The Al-Arqam Case in Malaysia." In *The East Asian Challenge for Human Rights*, ed. Joanne Bauer and Daniel Bell, 147–168. Cambridge: Cambridge University Press, 1999.

ed. *Human Rights in Cross-Cultural Perspectives: A Quest for Consensus*. Philadelphia, PA: University of Pennsylvania Press, 1992.

ed. *Cultural Transformation and Human Rights in Africa*. London: Zed Books, 2002.

An-Na'im, Abdullahi Ahmed, and Francis Deng, eds. *Human Rights in Africa: Cross-Cultural Perspectives*. Washington, DC: Brookings Institution Press, 1990.

Association of Southeast Asian Nations (ASEAN). *ASEAN Human Rights Declaration*, November 18, 2012.

Atran, Scott, and Joseph Henrich. "The Evolution of Religion: How Cognitive By-Products, Adaptive Learning Heuristics, Ritual Displays, and Group Competition Generate Deep Commitments to Prosocial Religions." *Biological Theory* 5, no. 1 (2010): 18–30.

Barzilai, Gad. *Communities and Law: Politics and Cultures of Legal Identities*. Ann Arbor, MI: University of Michigan Press, 2005.

Bauer, Joanne, and Daniel Bell. "Introduction." *The East Asian Challenge for Human Rights*, ed. Joanne Bauer and Daniel Bell, 3–26. Cambridge: Cambridge University Press, 1999.

eds. *The East Asian Challenge for Human Rights*. Cambridge: Cambridge University Press, 1999.

Baumann, Gerd. *The Multicultural Riddle: Rethinking National, Ethnic, and Religious Identities*. New York, NY: Psychology Press, 1999.

Baxi, Upendra. *The Future of Human Rights*. Oxford: Oxford University Press, 2006.

Beitz, Charles. "Human Rights as a Common Concern." *American Political Science Review* 95, no. 2 (June 2001): 269–282.

Bell, Daniel. "East Asian Challenge to Human Rights: Reflections on an East West Dialogue." *Human Rights Quarterly* 18, no. 3 (August 1996): 641–667.

East Meets West: Human Rights and Democracy in East Asia. Princeton, NJ: Princeton University Press, 2000.

Bell, Lynda, Andrew Nathan, and Ilan Peleg, eds. *Negotiating Culture and Human Rights*. New York, NY: Columbia University Press, 2001.

Bennett, David, ed. *Multicultural States: Rethinking Difference and Identity*. New York, NY: Psychology Press, 1998.

Berger, Peter, ed. *The Desecularization of the World: Resurgent Religion and World Politics*. Grand Rapids, MI: Wm. B. Eerdmans Publishing Co., 1999.

Berger, Peter, Grace Davie, and Effie Fokas. *Religious America, Secular Europe? A Theme and Variation*. Burlington, VT: Ashgate Publishing, 2008.

Berlin, Isaiah. "Two Concepts of Liberty." In *Four Essays on Liberty*, 1–32. Oxford: Oxford University Press, 1969.

Vico and Herder: Two Studies in the History of Ideas. London: Hogarth Press, 1976.

"My Intellectual Path." In *The Power of Ideas*, ed. Henry Hardy, 1–23. Princeton, NJ: Princeton University Press, 2002.

Berman, Marshall. *All That Is Solid Melts into Air: The Experience of Modernity*. London: Verso, 2010.

Blankenhorn, David. *The Future of Marriage*. New York, NY: Encounter Books, 2007.

Booth, David, and Frederick Golooba-Mutebi. "Developmental Regimes and the International System." Developmental Regimes in Africa, Policy Brief 5, January 2014.

Brems, Eva. "The Margin of Appreciation Doctrine of the European Court of Human Rights: Accommodating Diversity within Europe." In *Human Rights and Diversity: Area Studies Revisited*, ed. David Forsythe and Patrice McMahon, 81–110. Lincoln, NE: University of Nebraska Press, 2003.

"Reconciling Universality and Diversity in International Human Rights: A Theoretical and Methodological Framework and Its Application in the Context of Islam." *Human Rights Review* 5, no. 3 (2004): 5–21.

"Reconciling Universality and Diversity in International Human Rights Law." In *Human Rights with Modesty: The Problem of Universalism*, ed. András Sajó, 213–230. Leiden: Martinus Nijhoff Publishers, 2004.

Buergenthal, Thomas. "The American and European Convention on Human Rights: Similarities and Differences." *The American University Law Review* 30 (1980–1981): 155–166.

Burgess, Ann Carroll, and Tom Burgess. *Guide to Western Canada*. Guilford, CT: Globe Pequot Press, 2005.

Carothers, Thomas, and Saskia Brechenmacher. "Closing Space: Democracy and Human Rights Support under Fire." Carnegie Endowment for International Peace, Brief, February 2014.

Chang, Ha-Joon. *Kicking Away the Ladder: Development Strategy in Historical Perspective*. London: Anthem Press, 2003.

Clark, Phil. "Dilemmas of Justice." *Prospect Magazine*, May 2007.

"Establishing a Conceptual Framework: Six Key Transitional Justice Themes." In *After Genocide*, ed. Phil Clark and Zachary D. Kaufman, 191–205. New York, NY: Columbia University Press, 2009.

"The Rules (and Politics) of Engagement: The Gacaca Courts and Post-Genocide Justice, Healing and Reconciliation in Rwanda." In *After Genocide*, ed. Phil Clark and Zachary D. Kaufman, 297–319. New York, NY: Columbia University Press, 2009.

The Gacaca Courts, Post-Genocide Justice and Reconciliation in Rwanda: Justice without Lawyers. Cambridge: Cambridge University Press, 2010.

How Rwanda Judged Its Genocide. London: Africa Research Institute (April 2012): 1–12.

Clark, Phil, and Zachary D. Kaufman. "Introduction and Background: After Genocide." In *After Genocide*, ed. Phil Clark and Zachary D. Kaufman, 1–19. New York, NY: Columbia University Press, 2009.

eds. *After Genocide: Transitional Justice, Post-Conflict Reconstruction and Reconciliation in Rwanda and Beyond*. New York, NY: Columbia University Press, 2009.

Clark, Phil, Zachary D. Kaufman, and Kalypso Nicolaïdis. "Tensions in Transitional Justice." In *After Genocide*, ed. Phil Clark and Zachary D. Kaufman, 381–391. New York, NY: Columbia University Press, 2009.

Connell, Raewyn. *Southern Theory: The Global Dynamics of Knowledge in Social Science*. Cambridge: Polity Press, 2007.

Cotter, Anne-Marie Mooney. *Culture Clash: An International Legal Perspective on Ethnic Discrimination*. Burlington, VT: Ashgate Publishing, 2011.

Council of Europe. *European Convention for the Protection of Human Rights and Fundamental Freedoms, as amended by Protocols Nos. 11 and 14*. November 4, 1950, ETS 5.

   Collected Edition of the 'Travaux Préparatoires.' Volume VI. Dordrecht: Martinus Nijhoff, 1985.

Council on Foreign Relations. Emerging Powers and International Institutions Meeting Series, 2009–2013, www.cfr.org/projects/world/emerging-powers-and-international-institutions-meeting-series/pr1447.

D'Andrade, Roy. *A Study of Personal and Cultural Values: American, Japanese, and Vietnamese*. New York, NY: Palgrave Macmillan, 2008.

Darwin, Charles. *The Descent of Man, and Selection in Relation to Sex*. New York, NY: D. Appleton and Company, 1882.

Delanty, Gerard. "Modernity." In *Blackwell Encyclopedia of Sociology*, ed. George Ritzer, 11 vols. Malden, MA: Blackwell Publishing, 2007.

Deng, Francis. *Identity, Diversity, and Constitutionalism in Africa*. Washington, DC: United States Institute of Peace Press, 2008.

Dennison, Susi, and Anthony Dworkin. "Towards an EU Human Rights Strategy for a Post-Western World." European Council on Foreign Relations Policy Brief (September 21, 2011). www.ecfr.eu/page/-/towards-an-EU-human-rights-strategy-for-a-post-western-world.txt.pdf.

de Tocqueville, Alexis. *Democracy in America*. New York, NY: Pratt, Woodford, & Co., 1848.

   The Old Regime and the French Revolution. Trans. Stuart Gilbert. New York, NY: Doubleday Anchor, 1955.

de Waal, Alex. *Advocacy in Conflict: Critical Perspectives on Transnational Activism*. London: Zed Books, 2015.

   "Writing Human Rights and Getting It Wrong." *Boston Review*, June 6, 2016.

Diamond, Larry. "Facing Up to the Democratic Recession." *Journal of Democracy* 26, no. 1 (January 2015): 141–155.

Donders, Yvonne. "Do Cultural Diversity and Human Rights Make a Good Match?" *International Social Science Journal* 61, no. 199 (March 2010): 15–35.

   "Human Rights: Eye for Cultural Diversity." Inaugural Lecture at University of Amsterdam, June 29, 2012.

Donnelly, Jack. "Human Rights and Human Dignity: An Analytic Critique of Non-Western Conceptions of Human Rights." *The American Political Science Review* 76, no. 2 (June 1982): 303–316.

   "Human Rights as Natural Rights." *Human Rights Quarterly* 4, no. 3 (Autumn 1982): 391–405.

   "Cultural Relativism and Universal Human Rights." *Human Rights Quarterly* 6, no. 4 (November 1984): 400–419.

   "Human Rights and Human Dignity: An Analytic Critique of Non-Western Conceptions of Human Rights." In *Third World Attitudes Toward International Law: An Introduction*, ed. Frederick Snyder and Surakiart Sathirathai, 341–357. Dordrecht, The Netherlands: Martinus Nijhoff Publishers, 1987.

Universal Human Rights in Theory and Practice. Ithaca, NY: Cornell University Press, 2003.

"The Relative Universality of Human Rights." *Human Rights Quarterly* 29, no. 2 (May 2007): 281–306.

Donoho, Douglas. "Human Rights Enforcement in the Twenty-First Century." *Georgia Journal of International & Comparative Law* 35, no. 1 (January 2006): 1–52.

Douthat, Ross. *Bad Religion: How We Became a Nation of Heretics*. New York, NY: Free Press, 2012.

"The Terms of Our Surrender." *The New York Times*, March 2, 2014, nytimes.com/2014/03/.2/opinion/sunday/the-terms-of-our-surrender.html.

Drumbl, Mark. *Atrocity, Punishment, and International Law*. Cambridge: Cambridge University Press, 2007.

Durkheim, Emile. *The Division of Labor in Society*. Trans. George Simpson. New York, NY: Free Press, 1964.

"Review of Guyau's L'irreligion de l'avenir." In *Emile Durkheim: Selected Writings*, trans. and ed. Anthony Giddens. Cambridge: Cambridge University Press, 1972.

Dworkin, Ronald. *Sovereign Virtue: The Theory and Practice of Equality*. Cambridge, MA: Harvard University Press, 2000.

Edwards, Mike. *Civil Society*, 3rd edn. Cambridge: Polity Press, 2014.

Eide, Asbjørn. "Article 28." In *The Universal Declaration of Human Rights: A Common Standard of Achievement*, ed. Gudmunder Alfreðsson and Asbjørn Eide, 597–632. The Hague: Martinus Nijhoff Publishers, 1999.

Eisenstadt, Shmuel Noah. *Comparative Civilizations and Multiple Modernities*, 2 vols. Boston, MA: Brill, 2003.

Ekeh, Peter. "Colonialism and the Two Publics in Africa: A Theoretical Statement." *Comparative Studies in Society and History* 17, no. 1 (January 1975): 91–112.

Elazar, Daniel. "How Present Conceptions of Human Rights Shape the Protection of Rights in the United States." In *Old Rights and New*, ed. Robert A. Licht, 38–50. Washington, DC: The AEI Press, 1993.

Encarnación, Omar. "Gay Rights: Why Democracy Matters." *Journal of Democracy* 25, no. 3 (July 2014): 101–102.

Engle, Karen. "From Skepticism to Embrace: Human Rights and the American Anthropological Association from 1947–1999." *Human Rights Quarterly* 23, no. 3 (August 2001): 536–559.

European Union. *Charter of Fundamental Rights of the European Union*. October 26, 2012, 2012/C 326/02.

Fagan, Patrick. "Why Religion Matters Even More: The Impact of Religious Practice on Social Stability." Heritage Foundation Backgrounder No. 1992, December 18, 2006.

Fiske, Alan Page, Shinobu Kitayama, Hazel Rose Markus, and Richard Nisbett. "The Cultural Matrix of Social Psychology." In *The Handbook of Social Psychology*, Volume 2, 4th edn, ed. Susan Fiske, Daniel Gilbert, and Gardner Lindzey, 915–981. San Francisco, CA: McGraw-Hill, 1998.

Fiss, Owen. "Within Reach of the State: Prosecuting Atrocities in Africa." *Human Rights Quarterly* 31, no. 1 (February 2009): 59–69.

Flynn, Jeffrey. "Rethinking Human Rights: Multiple Foundations and Intercultural Dialogue." Presented at the Third Berlin Roundtable on Transnationality: Reframing Human Rights, Berlin, Germany, October 3–7, 2005.

Foucault, Michel. *Discipline and Punish: The Birth of the Prison.* Translated by Alan Sheridan. New York, NY: Vintage Books, 1995.

Fukuyama, Francis. *The Origins of Political Order.* New York, NY: Farrar, Straus and Giroux, 2011.

Galston, William. "Between Philosophy and History: The Evolution of Rights in American Thought." In *Old Rights and New,* ed. Robert A. Licht, 51–74. Washington, DC: The AEI Press, 1993.

   Liberal Pluralism: The Implications of Value Pluralism for Political Theory and Practice. Cambridge: Cambridge University Press, 2002.

   The Practice of Liberal Pluralism. Cambridge, UK: Cambridge University Press, 2004.

   "Mark of Belonging: Why Circumcision Is No Crime." *Commonweal,* May 5, 2014.

Geertz, Clifford. "The Impact of the Concept of Culture on the Concept of Man." Chap. 2 in *The Interpretation of Cultures: Selected Essays.* New York, NY: Basic Books, 1973.

   "Religion as a Cultural System." Chap. 4 in *The Interpretation of Cultures: Selected Essays.* New York, NY: Basic Books, 1973.

   "Thick Description: Toward an Interpretive Theory of Culture." Chap. 1 in *The Interpretation of Cultures: Selected Essays.* New York, NY: Basic Books, 1973.

   "'From the Native's Point of View': On the Nature of Anthropological Understanding." *Bulletin of the American Academy of Arts and Sciences* 28, no. 1 (October 1974): 26–45.

Gellner, Ernest. *Plough, Sword, and Book: The Structure of Human History.* Chicago, IL: University of Chicago Press, 1988.

George, Erika. "Virginity Testing and South Africa's HIV/AIDS Crisis: Beyond Rights Universalism and Cultural Relativism toward Health Capabilities." *California Law Review* 96, no. 6 (2008): 1447–1518.

Gilley, Bruce. *The Nature of Asian Politics.* Cambridge: Cambridge University Press, 2014.

Glendon, Mary Ann. *Rights Talk: The Impoverishment of Political Discourse.* New York, NY: The Free Press, 1991.

   "Knowing the Universal Declaration of Human Rights." *Notre Dame Law Review* 73, no. 5 (1999): 1153–1190.

   A World Made New: Eleanor Roosevelt and the Universal Declaration of Human Rights. New York, NY: Random House, 2001.

   "Religious Freedom: Yesterday, Today, and Tomorrow." The 2015 Cardinal Egan Lecture, New York University Catholic Center, May 16, 2015.

Glendon, Mary Ann, and Elliott Abrams. "Reflections on the UDHR." *First Things* 82 (April 1998): 23–27.

Goodale, Mark. *Surrendering to Utopia: An Anthropology of Human Rights.* Stanford, CA: Stanford University Press, 2009, 18.

Government of Rwanda. "Establishing the Organisation, Competence and Functioning of Gacaca Courts Charged with Prosecuting and Trying the Perpetrators of the Crime of Genocide and Other Crimes against Humanity, Committed between October 1, 1990 and December 31, 1994." Organic Law N° 16/2004 of June 19, 2004. Kigali, Rwanda, 2004.

Green, Duncan. "Civil Society and the Dangers of Monoculture: Smart New Primer from Mike Edwards." *From Poverty to Power Blog,* January 15, 2015. http://oxfam blogs.org/fp2p/civil-society-and-the-dangers-of-monoculture-smart-new-primer-from-mike-edwards/.

Günzel, Angelika. "Nationalization of Religious Parental Education? The German Circumcision Case." *Oxford Journal of Law and Religion* 2, no. 1 (2013): 206–209.

Gutmann, Amy. "Introduction." In *Human Rights as Politics and Idolatry,* ed. Amy Gutmann, vii–xxviii. Princeton, NJ: Princeton University Press, 2003.

Haidt, Jonathan. *Righteous Mind: Why Good People Are Divided by Politics and Religion.* New York, NY: Pantheon Books, 2012.

Halliday, Fred. "Relativism and Universalism in Human Rights: The Case of the Islamic Middle East." *Political Studies* 43, S1 (August 1995): 152–167.

Hannum, Hurst. "The Status of the Universal Declaration of Human Rights in National and International Law." *Georgia Journal of International and Comparative Law* 25, no. 1–2 (1995/1996): 287–397.

Haugen, Gary, and Victor Boutros. *The Locust Effect: Why the End of Poverty Requires the End of Violence.* Oxford: Oxford University Press, 2014.

Hayek, Friedrich. *The Constitution of Liberty.* London: Routledge, 1976.

Henrich, Joseph, Steven Heine, and Ara Norenzayan. "The Weirdest People in the World?" *Behavioral and Brain Sciences* 33, no. 2–3 (June 2010): 61–83.

Hoebel, Edward Adamson. "Law-Ways of the Primitive Eskimos." *Journal of Criminal Law and Criminology* 31, no. 6 (Spring 1941): 672.

Hopgood, Stephen. *The Endtimes of Human Rights.* Ithaca, NY: Cornell University Press, 2013.

Human Rights Watch. "US: Revival of Guantanamo Military Commissions a Blow to Justice." May 15, 2009.

Huntington, Samuel. "The West: Unique, Not Universal." *Foreign Affairs* 75, no. 6 (November/December 1996): 28–46.

Huyse, Luc. "Introduction: Tradition-based Approaches in Peacemaking, Transitional Justice and Reconciliation Policies." In *Traditional Justice and Reconciliation after Violent Conflict: Learning from African Experiences,* ed. Luc Huyse and Mark Salter, 1–22. Stockholm: International IDEA, 2008.

Hwang, Kwang-Kuo. *Foundations of Chinese Psychology: Confucian Social Relations.* New York, NY: Springer, 2012.

Ignatieff, Michael. "Human Rights as Politics" and "Human Rights as Idolatry." In *Human Rights as Politics and Idolatry,* ed. Amy Gutmann, 3–100. Princeton, NJ: Princeton University Press, 2003.

Imani, Nikitah Okembe-Ra. "Critical Impairments to Globalizing the Western Human Rights Discourse." *Societies without Borders* 3, no. 2 (2008): 270–284.

Ingelaere, Burt. "The Gacaca Courts in Rwanda." In *Traditional Justice and Reconciliation after Violent Conflict: Learning from African Experiences,* ed. Luc Huyse and Mark Salter, 46–58. Stockholm: International IDEA, 2008.

Inglehart, Ronald, and Christian Welzel, "How Development Leads to Democracy: What We Know about Modernization." *Foreign Affairs* 88, no. 2 (March/April 2009): 33–48.

Jansen, Yolande. *Secularism, Assimilation and the Crisis of Multiculturalism*. Chicago, IL: University of Chicago Press, 2014.

Kaplan, Seth. *Fixing Fragile States: A New Paradigm for Development*. Westport, CT: Praeger Security International, 2008.

Betrayed: Politics, Power, and Prosperity. New York, NY: Palgrave Macmillan, 2013.

"Identifying Truly Fragile States." *The Washington Quarterly* 37, no. 1 (Spring 2014), 49–63.

Kersten, Mark. "Does Russia Have a 'Responsibility to Protect' Ukraine? Don't Buy It." *The Globe and Mail*, March 4, 2014, www.theglobeandmail.com/opinion/does-russia-have-a-responsibility-to-protect-ukraine-dont-buy-it/article17271450/.

Kinley, David. "Bendable Rules: The Development Implications of Human Rights Pluralism." In *Legal Pluralism and Development: Scholars and Practitioners in Dialogue*, ed. Brian Tamanaha, Caroline Sage, and Michael Woolcock, 50–65. Cambridge: Cambridge University Press, 2012.

Koji, Teraya. "Emerging Hierarchy in International Human Rights and Beyond: From the Perspective of Non-derogable Rights." *European Journal of International Law* 12, no. 5 (2001): 917–941.

Kymlicka, Will. *Multicultural Citizenship*. New York, NY: Oxford University Press, 1995.

Lebra, Takie Sugiyama. *Japanese Patterns of Behavior*. Honolulu, HI: University of Hawaii Press, 1976.

Lenzerini, Federico. *The Culturalization of Human Rights Law*. Oxford: Oxford University Press, 2014.

Lerman, Antony. "In Defence of Multiculturalism." *The Guardian*, March 22, 2010, www.theguardian.com/commentisfree/2010/mar/22/multiculturalism-blame-culture-segregation.

Lesage, Dries, and Thijs Van de Graaf, eds. *Rising Powers and Multilateral Institutions*. New York, NY: Palgrave Macmillan, 2015.

Levin, Yuval. *The Great Debate: Edmund Burke, Thomas Paine, and the Birth of Right and Left*. New York, NY: Basic Books, 2014.

The Fractured Republic: Renewing America's Social Contract in the Age of Individualism. New York, NY: Basic Books, 2016.

Licht, Robert A. "Introduction." In *Old Rights and New*, ed. Robert A. Licht, 1–37. Washington, DC: The AEI Press, 1993.

ed. *Old Rights and New*. Washington, DC: The AEI Press, 1993.

Lindholm, Tore. "Prospects for Research on the Cultural Legitimacy of Human Rights: The Cases of Liberalism and Marxism." In An-Na'im and Deng, *Human Rights in Africa*, Abdullahi Ahmed An-Na'im and Francis Deng 387–426. Washington, DC: Brookings Institution Press, 1990.

"Article 1." In *The Universal Declaration of Human Rights: A Common Standard of Achievement*, ed. Gudmunder Alfreðsson and Asbjørn Eide, 41–74. The Hague: Martinus Nijhoff Publishers, 1999.

Liu, Lydia H. "Shadows of Universalism: The Untold Story of Human Rights around 1948." *Critical Inquiry* 40 (2014): 385–417.

Locke, John. "A Letter Concerning Toleration." In *The Works of John Locke Esq: In Three Volumes*, Volume 2. London: Printed for John Churchill at the Black Swan, 1714.

"Second Treatise on Government." In *Two Treaties of Government*. Cambridge: Cambridge University Press, 1963.

Lund, Michael. "Human Rights: A Source of Conflict, State Making, and State Breaking." In *Human Rights and Conflict: Exploring the Links between Rights, Law, and Peacebuilding*, ed. Julie Mertus and Jeffrey Helsing, 39–61. Washington, DC: United States Institute of Peace, 2006.

Maimon, Dov. "European Jewry – Signals and Noise." The Jewish People Policy Institute, Jerusalem, Israel, 2013.

Maimon, Dov, and Nadia Ellis. "The Circumcision Crisis: Challenges for European and World Jewry." The Jewish People Policy Institute, Jerusalem, Israel, 2012.

Mamdani, Mahmood. "Reconciliation without Justice." *Southern African Review of Books* 46 (November/December 1996): 3–5.

Maritain, Jacques. "Introduction." In *Human Rights: Comments and Interpretations, A Symposium*, ed. UNESCO, 9–17. New York, NY: Columbia University Press, 1949.

  Man and the State. Chicago, IL: University of Chicago Press, 1951.

Markus, Hazel Rose, and Alana Conner. *Clash! 8 Cultural Conflicts That Make Us Who We Are*. New York, NY: Hudson Street Press, 2013.

Markus, Hazel Rose, and Shinobu Kitayama. "Culture and the Self: Implications for Cognition, Emotion, and Motivation." *Psychological Review* 98, no. 2 (1991): 224–253.

Marsella, Anthony, and Wade Pickren. "Foreword." In *Foundations of Chinese Psychology: Confucian Social Relations*, by Kwang-Kuo Hwang, vii–x. New York, NY: Springer, 2012.

McConnell, Michael. "The Origins and Historical Understanding of Free Exercise of Religion." *Harvard Law Review* 103, no. 7 (1990): 1409–1517.

Mchangama, Jacob, and Guglielmo Verdirame. "The Danger of Human Rights Proliferation: When Defending Liberty, Less Is More." *Foreign Affairs*, July 24, 2013.

Merry, Sally Engle. *Human Rights and Gender Violence: Translating International Law into Local Justice*. Chicago, IL: University of Chicago Press Books, 2006.

  "Transnational Human Rights and Local Activism: Mapping the Middle." *American Anthropologist* 108, no. 1 (March 2006): 38–51.

Mill, John Stuart. *On Liberty and Other Writings*. Cambridge: Cambridge University Press, 2003.

Mitchell, Joshua. "Religion Is Not a Preference." *The Journal of Politics* 69, no. 2 (May 2007): 351–362.

Morsink, Johannes. *The Universal Declaration of Human Rights: Origins, Drafting, and Intent*. Philadelphia, PA: University of Pennsylvania Press, 1999.

Murray, Charles. *Coming Apart: The State of White America, 1960–2010*. New York, NY: Crown Forum/Random House, 2012.

Murray, Rachel. "International Human Rights: Neglect of Perspectives from African Institutions." *The International and Comparative Law Quarterly* 55, no. 1 (January 2006): 193–204.

Mutua, Makau. "The Ideology of Human Rights." *Virginia Journal of International Law* 36 (1996): 592–593.

"Savages, Victims, and Saviors: The Metaphor of Human Rights." *Harvard International Law Journal* 42, no. 1 (Winter 2001): 201–245.

Human Rights: A Political and Cultural Critique. Philadelphia, PA: University of Pennsylvania Press, 2002.

Nagle, John. *Multiculturalism's Double Bind: Creating Inclusivity, Cosmopolitanism, and Difference*. Burlington, VT: Ashgate Publishing, 2009, 129.

Nathan, Andrew. "Universalism: A Particularistic Account." In *Negotiating Culture and Human Rights*, ed. Lynda Bell, Andrew Nathan, and Ilan Peleg, 349–368. New York, NY: Columbia University Press, 2001.

Nelson, Eric. *The Hebrew Republic: Jewish Sources and the Transformation of European Political Thought*. Cambridge, MA: Harvard University Press, 2011.

Ngoga, Martin. "The Institutionalisation of Impunity: A Judicial Perspective of the Rwandan Genocide." In *After Genocide*, ed. Phil Clark and Zachary D. Kaufman, 321–332. New York, NY: Columbia University Press, 2009.

Nisbet, Robert. *The Quest for Community: A Study in the Ethics of Order and Freedom*. Wilmington, DE: ISI Books, 2010.

Nisbett, Richard. *The Geography of Thought: How Asians and Westerners Think Differently…and Why*. New York, NY: The Free Press, 2003.

Nisbett, Richard, and Takahiko Masuda. "Culture and Point of View." *Proceedings of the National Academy of Sciences* 100, no. 19 (September 16, 2003): 11163–11170.

Nisbett, Richard, Kaiping Peng, Incheol Choi, and Ara Norenzayan, "Culture and Systems of Thought: Holistic vs. Analytic Cognition." *Psychological Review* 108, no. 2 (April 2001): 291–310.

North, Douglass C. *Institutions, Institutional Change and Economic Performance*. Cambridge: Cambridge University Press, 1990.

"Institutions." *The Journal of Economic Perspectives* 5, no. 1 (Winter 1991): 97–112.

"Economic Performance through Time." *American Economic Review* 84, no. 3 (June 1994): 359–368.

Onuma, Yasuaki. "Towards an Intercivilizational Approach to Human Rights." In *The East Asian Challenge for Human Rights*, ed. Joanne Bauer and Daniel Bell, 103–123. Cambridge: Cambridge University Press, 1999.

Opsahl, Torkel, and Vojin Dimitrijevic. "Article 29 and 30." In *The Universal Declaration of Human Rights: A Common Standard of Achievement*, ed. Gudmunder Alfreðsson and Asbjørn Eide, 633–652. The Hague: Martinus Nijhoff Publishers, 1999.

Organization of African Unity (OAU). *African Charter on Human and Peoples' Rights* ("Banjul Charter"). June 27, 1981, CAB/LEG/67/3 rev. 5, 21 I.L.M. 58 (1982).

Organization of American States (OAS). *American Convention on Human Rights*, "Pact of San Jose, Costa Rica." November 22, 1969.

Panikkar, R., and R. Panikkar, "Is the Notion of Human Rights a Western Concept?" *Diogenes* 30, no. 120 (1982): 75–102.

Parekh, Bhikhu. *Rethinking Multiculturalism: Cultural Diversity and Political Theory*. Cambridge, MA: Harvard University Press, 2002.

Parsons, Talcott. *The Social System*. New York: Free Press, 1951, 39–40.

Perry, Michael. "Are Human Rights Universal? The Relativist Challenge and Related Matters." *Human Rights Quarterly* 19, no. 3 (August 1997): 461–509.

The Idea of Human Rights: Four Inquiries. Oxford: Oxford University Press, 1998, 11.

Pinker, Stephen. *The Better Angels of Our Nature: Why Violence Has Declined.* New York: Viking, 2011.

Popenoe, David. *Sociology.* Englewood Cliffs, NJ: Prentice Hall, 1995, 83.

Popper, Karl. *The Poverty of Historicism.* New York, NY: Routledge, 2002.

Public Policy Advisory Network on Female Genital Surgeries in Africa. "Seven Things to Know about Female Genital Surgeries in Africa." *Hastings Center Report* 42, no. 6 (November/December 2012): 19–27.

Putnam, Robert. *Bowling Alone: The Collapse and Revival of American Community.* New York, NY: Simon & Schuster, 2000.

Our Kids: The American Dream in Crisis. New York, NY: Simon & Schuster, 2015.

Putnam, Robert, and David Campbell. *American Grace: How Religion Divides and Unites Us.* New York, NY: Simon & Schuster, 2010.

Rao, Vijayendra, and Michael Walton, "Culture and Public Action: Relationality, Equality of Agency, and Development." In *Culture and Public Action*, ed. Vijayendra Rao and Michael Walton. Stanford, CA: Stanford University Press, 2004, 3–36.

Rawls, John. "The Idea of an Overlapping Consensus." *Oxford Journal of Legal Studies* 7, no. 1 (Spring 1987): 1–25.

Political Liberalism. New York, NY: Columbia University Press, 2005.

Raz, Joseph. "Right-based Moralities." In *Theories of Rights*, ed. Jeremy Waldron, 182–200. Oxford: Oxford University Press, 1984.

Reno, R. R. "Against Human Rights." *First Things* (May 2016), www.firstthings.com/article/2016/05/against-human-rights.

Renteln, Alison Dundes. "Relativism and the Search for Human Rights." *American Anthropologist* 90, no. 1 (March 1988): 56–72.

International Human Rights: Universalism versus Relativism. Newbury Park, CA: Sage Publications, 1990.

"Report Attacks Multiculturalism." *BBC News*, September 30, 2005, http://news.bbc.co.uk/2/hi/uk_news/4295318.stm.

Roth, Kenneth, Alison DesForges, and Helena Cobban. "Justice or Therapy?" *Boston Review*, June 1, 2002.

Rupprecht, Marlene. "Children's Right to Physical Integrity." Parliamentary Assembly of the Council of Europe, September 6, 2013.

Sailer, Steve. "Fragmented Future." *American Conservative*, January 15, 2007, www.theamericanconservative.com/articles/fragmented-future/.

Salter, Frank. *On Genetic Interests: Family, Ethnicity, and Humanity in an Age of Mass Migration.* Piscataway, NJ: Transaction Publishers, 2006, 146.

Samnøy, Åshild. "The Origins of the Universal Declaration of Human Rights." In *The Universal Declaration of Human Rights: A Common Standard of Achievement*, ed. Gudmunder Alfreðsson and Asbjørn Eide, 3–22. The Hague: Martinus Nijhoff Publishers, 1999.

Schabas, William A., ed. *The Universal Declaration of Human Rights, The Travaux Prépataratoires.* Cambridge: Cambridge University Press, 2013.

Sen, Amartya. "Elements of a Theory of Human Rights." *Philosophy and Public Affairs* 32, no. 4 (Autumn 2004): 315–356.

Shestack, Jerome. "The Philosophic Foundations of Human Rights." *Human Rights Quarterly* 20, no. 2 (May 1998): 201–34.

Shi, Tianjian. *The Cultural Logic of Politics in Mainland China and Taiwan.* Cambridge: Cambridge University Press, 2014.

Shweder, Richard. "Cultural Psychology – What Is It?" In *Cultural Psychology: Essays on Comparative Human Development*, ed. James Stigler, Richard Schweder, and Gilbert Herdt, 1–43. Cambridge: Cambridge University Press, 1990.

   "In Defense of Moral Realism: Reply to Gabennesch." *Child Development* 61, no. 6 (December 1990): 2060–2067.

   "Moral Maps, 'First World' Conceits, and the New Evangelists." In *Culture Matters: How Values Shape Human Progress*, ed. Lawrence Harrison and Samuel Huntington, 158–176. New York, NY: Basic Books, 2000.

   "'What about Female Genital Mutilation?' And Why Understanding Culture Matters in the First Place." In *Engaging Cultural Differences: The Multicultural Challenge in Liberal Democracies*, ed. Richard Shweder, Martha Minow, and Hazel Rose Markus 216–251. New York, NY: Russell Sage Foundation, 2002.

   "Shouting at the Hebrews: Imperial Liberalism v Liberal Pluralism and the Practice of Male Circumcision." *Law, Culture and the Humanities* 5, no. 2 (June 2009): 247–265.

   "Relativism and Universalism." In *A Companion to Moral Anthropology*, ed. Didier Fassin, 85–102. Malden, MA: Wiley-Blackwell, 2012.

   "The Goose and the Gander: The Genital Wars." *Global Discourse: An Interdisciplinary Journal of Current Affairs and Applied Contemporary Thought* 3, no. 2 (2013): 348–366.

Shweder, Richard, Martha Minow, and Hazel Rose Markus. "Engaging Cultural Differences." In *Engaging Cultural Differences: The Multicultural Challenge in Liberal Democracies*, ed. Richard Shweder, Martha Minow, and Hazel Rose Markus 1–16. New York, NY: Russell Sage Foundation, 2002.

   eds. *Engaging Cultural Differences: The Multicultural Challenge in Liberal Democracies.* New York, NY: Russell Sage Foundation, 2002.

Shweder, Richard, and Nancy Much. "Determinations of Meaning: Discourse and Moral Socialization." In *Thinking through Cultures: Expeditions in Cultural Psychology*, ed. Richard Shweder, 186–240. Cambridge, MA: Harvard University Press, 1991.

Shweder, Richard, Nancy Much, Manamohan Mahapatra, and Lawrence Park. "The 'Big Three' of Morality (Autonomy, Community, and Divinity) and the 'Big Three' Explanations of Suffering." In *Morality and Health*, ed. Allan Brandt and Paul Rozin, 119–169. New York, NY: Routledge, 1997.

Spiro, Melfred. "Is the Western Conception of the Self 'Peculiar' within the Context of the World Cultures?" *Ethos* 21, no. 2 (June 1993): 107–153.

Stone, Suzanne Last. "Religion and Human Rights: Babel or Translation, Conflict or Convergence." Paper presented at Role of Religion in Human Rights Discourse conference, Israel Democracy Institute, Jerusalem, May 16–17, 2012.

Svoboda, J. Steven. "Circumcision of Male Infants as a Human Rights Violation." *Journal of Medical Ethics* 39, no. 7 (July 2013): 469–474.

Talhelm, Thomas, Xuemin Zhang, Shigehiro Oishi, C. Shimin, Dechao Duan, Xiaoli Lan and Shinobu Kitayama. "Large-Scale Psychological Differences within China Explained by Rice versus Wheat Agriculture." *Science* 344, no. 6184 (May 9, 2014): 603–608.

Taylor, Charles. "Conditions of an Unforced Consensus on Human Rights." In *The East Asian Challenge for Human Rights*, ed. Joanne Bauer and Daniel Bell, 124–144. Cambridge: Cambridge University Press, 1999.

A Secular Age. Cambridge, MA: Harvard University Press, 2007.

Taylor, Charles, and Amy Gutmann, eds. *Multiculturalism*. Princeton, NJ: Princeton University Press, 1994.

The Editors. "Contending Modernities." *The Immanent Frame*, 2010. http://blogs.ssrc.org/tif/2010/11/17/multiple-modernities/.

Tönnies, Ferdinand. *Gemeinschaft und Gesellschaft*. Leipzig: Fues's Verlag, 1912.

Trigg, Roger. *Equality, Freedom, and Religion*. Oxford: Oxford University Press, 2012.

"Threats to Religious Freedom in Europe." *Public Discourse*, June 28, 2013.

Turner, Jonathan. *The Institutional Order: Economy, Kinship, Religion, Polity, Law, and Education in Evolutionary and Comparative Perspective*. New York, NY: Longman Publishing, 1997.

Tutu, Desmond. *No Future without Forgiveness*. New York, NY: Doubleday.

Twining, William. *General Jurisprudence: Understanding Law from a Global Perspective*. Cambridge: Cambridge University Press, 2008.

Twiss, Sumner. "Confucian Contributions to the Universal Declaration of Human Rights: A Historical and Philosophical Perspective." In *The World's Religions: A Contemporary Reader*, ed. Arvind Sharma, 102–114. Minneapolis, MN: Fortress Press, 2010.

United Nations. *Vienna Convention on the Law of Treaties*. May 23, 1969. United Nations, Treaty Series, vol. 1155.

UN General Assembly. *Universal Declaration of Human Rights*. December 10, 1948. 217 A (III).

International Covenant on Civil and Political Rights. December 16, 1966. United Nations, Treaty Series, vol. 999.

International Covenant on Economic, Social and Cultural Rights. December 16, 1966. United Nations, Treaty Series, vol. 993.

Declaration on the Elimination of All Forms of Intolerance and of Discrimination Based on Religion or Belief. November 25, 1981. A/RES/36/55.

Convention on the Rights of the Child. November 20, 1989. United Nations, Treaty Series, vol. 1577.

Declaration on the Right and Responsibility of Individuals, Groups and Organs of Society to Promote and Protect Universally Recognized Human Rights and Fundamental Freedoms. August 3, 1999. A/RES/53/144.

Summary Records, 182nd Plenary Session.

UN General Assembly Third Social and Humanitarian Committee. "Draft International Declaration of Human Rights (E/800) (continued)." October 6, 1948. 95th meeting, summary records, Official Records of the Third Session of the General Assembly.

United Nations Office of the High Commissioner for Human Rights (OHCHR). "Report on the Situation of Human Rights in Rwanda." February 8, 1999. UN Doc. E/CN.4/1999/33.

Wade, Robert. "Japan, the World Bank, and the Art of Paradigm Maintenance: The East Asian Miracle in Perspective." *New Left Review* 217 (May/June 1996): 3–36.

Walzer, Michael. *Spheres of Justice: A Defense of Pluralism and Equality*. New York, NY: Basic Books, 1983.

Interpretation and Social Criticism. Cambridge, MA: Harvard University Press, 1987.

Thick and Thin: Moral Argument at Home and Abroad. South Bend, IN: University of Notre Dame Press, 1994.

"Justice, Justice Shalt Thou Pursue." In *Radical Responsibility: Celebrating the Thought of Chief Rabbi Lord Jonathan Sacks*, ed. Michael Harris, Daniel Rynhold, and Tamra Wright, 79–94. Jerusalem: Maggid Books, 2013.

The Paradox of Liberation: Secular Revolutions and Religious Counterrevolutions. New Haven, CT: Yale University Press, 2015.

Watters, Ethan. "We Aren't the World." *Pacific Standard*, March/April 2013, 46–53.

Weiss, Thomas. "Principles, Politics, and Humanitarian Action." *Ethics and International Affairs* 13, no. 1 (1999): 1–22.

Wierzbicka, Anna. *Cross-Cultural Pragmatics: The Semantics of Human Interaction*. Berlin: Mouton de Gruyler, 1991.

Wilson, David Sloan. *Darwin's Cathedral: Evolution, Religion, and the Nature of Society*. Chicago, IL: University of Chicago Press, 2002.

Wilson, Edmund. *Sociobiology: The New Synthesis*. Cambridge, MA: Harvard University Press, 1975.

Winter, Joseph. "Zimbabwe's Robert Mugabe." *BBC*, August 16, 2013, www.bbc.com/news/world-africa-23431534.

Wiredu, Kwasi. "The Moral Foundation of an African Culture." In *Philosophy from Africa: A Text with Readings*, ed. Pieter Hendrik Coetzee and A. P. J. Roux, 306–316. Oxford: Oxford University Press, 2002.

World Health Organization. *Male Circumcision: Global Trends and Determinants of Prevalence, Safety and Acceptability*. Geneva: WHO, 2007.

Neonatal and Child Male Circumcision: A Global Review. Geneva: WHO, 2010.

World Trade Organization. *United States – Standards for Reformulated and Conventional Gasoline*. WTO Appellate Body Report WT/DS2/AB/R, adopted 20 May 1996, DSR 1996:I.

Zartman, William. *Preventing Deadly Conflict*. Malden, MA: Polity Press, 2015.

Zaum, Dominik. "Balancing Justice and Order: State-Building and the Prosecution of War Crimes in Rwanda and Kosovo." In *After Genocide*, ed. Phil Clark and Zachary D. Kaufman, 363–379. New York, NY: Columbia University Press, 2009.

Zechenter, Elizabeth. "In the Name of Culture: Cultural Relativism and the Abuse of the Individual." *Journal of Anthropological Research* 53, no. 3 (Autumn 1997): 319–347.

Zwart, Tom. "Using Local Culture to Further the Implementation of International Human Rights: The Receptor Approach." *Human Rights Quarterly* 34, no. 2 (May 2012): 546–569.

"Balancing Yin and Yang in the International Human Rights Debate." *Collected Papers of the Sixth Beijing Forum on Human Rights*, China Society for Human Rights Studies, Beijing, 2013, 410–421.

"Safeguarding the Universal Acceptance of Human Rights through the Receptor Approach." *Human Rights Quarterly* 36, no. 4 (November 2014): 898–904.

"Re-Rooting International Human Rights by Revisiting the Universal Declaration of Human Rights." Unpublished draft.

Index

For EU product safety concerns, contact us at Calle de José Abascal, 56–1º, 28003 Madrid, Spain or eugpsr@cambridge.org.

www.ingramcontent.com/pod-product-compliance
Ingram Content Group UK Ltd.
Pitfield, Milton Keynes, MK11 3LW, UK
UKHW020355140625
459647UK00020B/2477